Dublin Irish Race Convention

Proceedings of the Irish Race Convention which met in Dublin the first three days of Sept., 1896;

The most Rev. Dr. O'Donnell, Bishop of Raphoe in the chair, with list of delegates, proceedings that led up to the Convention

Dublin Irish Race Convention

Proceedings of the Irish Race Convention which met in Dublin the first three days of Sept., 1896;
The most Rev. Dr. O'Donnell, Bishop of Raphoe in the chair, with list of delegates, proceedings that led up to the Convention

ISBN/EAN: 9783337723606

Printed in Europe, USA, Canada, Australia, Japan

Cover: Foto ©ninafisch / pixelio.de

More available books at **www.hansebooks.com**

Irish Race Convention.

Dublin.

September, 1896.

PROCEEDINGS

OF THE

IRISH RACE CONVENTION

WHICH MET IN DUBLIN THE FIRST THREE
DAYS OF SEPTEMBER, 1896,

THE

Most Rev. Dr. O'Donnell, Bishop of Raphoe

IN THE CHAIR;

WITH

LIST OF DELEGATES,
PROCEEDINGS THAT LED UP TO THE CONVENTION,
AND
DECLARATION OF DELEGATES FROM ABROAD
ON CONCLUSION OF SAME.

———◆———

By Permission from the Freeman's Journal Selected and Arranged.

———◆———

𝔇ublin:
PRINTED FOR THE IRISH NATIONAL FEDERATION,
RUTLAND SQUARE,
BY SEALY, BRYERS & WALKER.

———

1896.

It has been thought well that some permanent record should be preserved of the proceedings of such a memorable gathering as the IRISH RACE CONVENTION. I have been honoured with the task of arranging the materials at hand, and seeing them through the press.

Almost all is taken, by permission, from the admirable reports which have from time to time appeared in the columns of *The Freeman's Journal*.

Such alterations as appeared desirable have been made in order and form. Interruptions on the part of the audience have been omitted, except such as affected the course of the speeches. The work, to be of use, had to be published without delay. It was therefore impossible to submit proofs of the debates to the speakers, or of the list of delegates to the branches they represented. The best, under the circumstances, has been done to procure accuracy.

The cover is an adaptation of Miss M'Grane's beautiful design for the Delegate's certificates.

No one but myself is responsible for the selection of material, for general shortcomings, and errors of inclusion and exclusion.

ALFRED WEBB.

DUBLIN, *October*, 1896.

Contents.

	PAGE
CONVENTION SUGGESTED BY ARCHBISHOP OF TORONTO ...	1
ACCEPTANCE OF SUGGESTION BY IRISH PARTY	4
CONSTITUTION OF THE CONVENTION	5
ALL IRISH NATIONALIST MEMBERS INVITED	7
RESOLUTIONS AND MOTIONS	7
LIST OF DELEGATES:	
IRISH RACE ABROAD	8
MEMBERS OF PARLIAMENT	9
CLERGY	9
COUNTY AND CIVIC	12
GREAT BRITAIN	12
CENTRAL BODY, IRISH NATIONAL FEDERATION ...	15
IRELAND	16
LETTER FROM UNITED STATES AND CANADIAN DELEGATES...	30
STEWARDS	30
LEINSTER HALL	31
FIRST DAY'S PROCEEDINGS	33
SECOND DAY'S PROCEEDINGS	72
THIRD DAY'S PROCEEDINGS	120
RESOLUTIONS OF THE CONVENTION	166
DROPPED RESOLUTIONS	169
JUSTIN M'CARTHY, M.P., ON THE CONVENTION	174
IMPRESSIONS OF THE CONVENTION, BY A "SPECTATOR" ...	177
ADDRESS OF DELEGATES FROM ABROAD TO THE IRISH PEOPLE AT HOME AND ABROAD	179
VERY REV. DR. RYAN, OF TORONTO, AT CLONMEL ...	181

Index to Speakers.

	PAGE
CHAIRMAN, MOST REV. DR. O'DONNELL, Bishop of Raphoe,	
Opening Address	36
Closing Address	163

[Also on procedure, pp. 33, 34, 40, 46, 60, 63, 72, 76, 79, 87, 93, 96, 97, 106, 120, 121, 126, 128, 129, 133, 134, 135, 139, 143, 149, 150, 159, 160.]

AMBROSE, DR., M.P.	33
BLAKE, HON. EDWARD, M.P.	97, 143, 165
BROMBY, MR. CHARLES H., Tasmania	53
CLANCY, VERY REV. M. A., Newfoundland	62
CLANCY, REV. M. J., Tipperary	135
CORNWALL, MR. MOSES, Kimberley	52
COSTIGAN, HON. JOHN, Ottawa	130
DAVITT, MR. MICHAEL, M.P.	146
DEVLIN, MR. J. B., Wilkesbarre, Pennsylvania	156
DEVLIN, MR. JOSEPH, Belfast	129
DILLON, MR. JOHN, M.P.	107, 160, 162
DORAN, MR. DAVID, Kenmare	153
DUFFY, MR. THOMAS, P.L.G., Longford	153
DUNLEVY, MR. PATRICK, Philadelphia	57
FERGUSON, MR. JOHN, Glasgow	64
FITZGERALD, MR., Bermondsey	133
FLANNERY, REV. DR., St. Thomas', Canada	155
FLYNN, REV. P. F., P.P., Waterford	73, 76, 95
FOLEY, REV. DR., Nova Scotia	58
HARRIS, VERY REV. DEAN, Ottawa	54, 121, 162
HENEY, CHEVALIER, Ottawa	123
HERRON, MR. CHARLES, South Derry	156
HUNT, MR. THOMAS, Melbourne	47
KENNEDY, REV. M. B., Blarney	93
KENNEDY, MR., Wellington, New Zealand	60
KILBRIDE, MR. DENIS, M.P.	151
LOUGHLIN, MR. THOMAS, Bradford	127
LUNDON, MR. WILLIAM, Limerick	147
LYNCH, REV. P., Manchester	56
LYNSKEY, VERY REV. CANON, Clifden	33
LYNSKEY, MR. G. J., Liverpool	154
LYTTLE, REV. MR., Moneyrea	152
M'CARTHY, JUSTIN, M.P.	33, 46
M'CARTAN, VERY REV. CANON, Donaghmore ...	123, 128
M'FADDEN, REV. JAMES, P.P.	33
M'KEOWN, MR. JOHN, Q.C., St. Catherine's, Canada ...	157

INDEX TO SPEAKERS.

	PAGE
MARSHALL, REV. GEORGE F., New Hampshire	60
MEAGHER, REV. WILLIAM, C.C., Clonmel	83
MURNANE, REV. E., Bermondsey	79, 92
MURPHY, MR. HUGH, Glasgow	126
O'BRIEN, MR. WILLIAM	137
O'CALLAGHAN, REV. D., Boston	50
O'CONNOR, MR. T. P., M.P.	75, 161
O'DONNELL, REV. P. J., Montreal	128
O'HARA, VERY REV. D., P.P., Kiltimagh	148
O'HIGGINS, MR. JOHN B., Boston, U.S.A.	104
O'LEARY, REV. P., P.P., Castlelyons	87
O'LEARY, VERY REV. JOHN, P.P., Clonakilty	82
O'MARA, MR. M., Dundalk	95
O'MEARA, DR. W. P., Southampton	86
PHILLIPS, REV. E. S., Pennsylvania	62, 149
QUINN, MR. ALPHONSUS, Arboe	155
RYAN, REV. DR., Toronto, Reads Letter	35, 44
RYAN, MR. JOSEPH P., New York	139
SCANLON, REV. J., P.P., Cloughjordan	162
SHEEHY, MR. DAVID, M.P.	35
SHINKWIN, VERY REV. CANON, Bandon	33
SMITH, ALDERMAN W. J., Mayor of Waterford	73
SULLIVAN, MR. WILLIAM, Bradford	84
TIMMONS, DR., Boston	158
WEBB, MR. ALFRED, Dublin	41

Index to Letters, Messages, and Telegrams.

	PAGE
HIS HOLINESS, POPE LEO XIII. ...	34
ARCHBISHOP OF PHILADELPHIA ...	66
ARCHBISHOP OF TORONTO ...	1, 35
BYRNE, HON. THOMAS J., Attorney-General, Queensland ...	121
CONATY, REV. T. J., Plattsburgh, New York ...	68
CRONIN, REV. PATRICK, Buffalo, New York ...	69
DELEGATES FROM ABROAD ...	179
,, ,, UNITED STATES AND CANADA ...	30
EMMET, THOMAS ADDIS, M.D., New York ...	35
FREEHILL, MR. FRANK B., Sydney ...	117
HOWLEY, MOST REV. M. F., Bishop of St. John's, Newfoundland	115
HENEY, CHEVALIER, Telegrams regarding false insinuations ...	122
HENRY, REV. MICHAEL J., New York ...	120
IRISH NATIONAL FEDERATION, Auckland, N.Z. ...	68
,, ,, ,, Darwen Branch ...	71
,, ,, ,, Great Britain ...	60
,, ,, ,, Islington ...	71
,, ,, ,, South Australia ...	67
IRISH PROFESSORS AND SEMINARISTS, Cher, France ...	69
IRISHMEN in Brisbane, Queensland ...	120
,, Farnworth ...	157
,, Hunslet, Leeds ...	120
,, Leith ...	70
,, Newfoundland, per Bishop of St. John's	115
,, West Coast of New Zealand ...	116
,, Pretoria, South Africa ...	119
,, Quebec ...	60
,, Queensland ...	67
,, North Queensland ...	117
,, Rockhampton, Queensland ...	118
,, Pan-Celtic Convention, Sydney ...	69
,, South Tasmania ...	118
JAMESON, MAJOR J. EUSTACE, M.P. ...	70
O'CONNOR, MR. JAMES, M.P. ...	71
O'LOGHLIN, MR. J. V., Adelaide, South Australia ...	69
ST. PATRICK'S SOCIETY, Cornwall, Ontario ...	118

Irish Race Convention, 1896.

A Convention Suggested by His Grace the Archbishop of Toronto.

St. Michael's Palace, Toronto, 8th October, 1895.

To Hon. EDWARD BLAKE, Q.C., M.P., Humewood, Toronto.

My Dear Mr. Blake—I regret exceedingly to learn that you are very much run down in health, and that, in consequence of nervous prostration, brought on by excessive work, you have felt obliged to decline the public reception with which the citizens of Toronto intended to greet your return and to give you a hearty welcome home. I regret that this reception had to be abandoned for this reason also, that the leading citizens of Toronto wished to give public endorsement to the course you have pursued in advocating the cause of Home Rule for Ireland, and because they wished to repel with righteous indignation the malignant attacks made upon you, not so much by political antagonists as by false brethren and treacherous co-labourers. The sacrifices you have made in the cause of Home Rule ought to have been more than sufficient to shield you from mean insinuations and vindictive calumnies, and should also have proved to the most suspicious and incredulous your absolute devotion to the Irish cause.

If I mention, in passing, the enormous sacrifices you have made, it is not on your account, but for the sake of good and true men at home who might be led astray in your regard by false statements and misrepresentations. Here in Canada, where you were bred, born and reared, and where you are well known both as to your private and public life, you need no certificate of character from any individual or from any body of citizens, for you possess in an eminent degree the esteem, admiration, and confidence of your countrymen. In saying this much I am sure that I voice the public opinion of Canada.

I think, too, sir, that we in this country have a right and a duty to raise our voice in protest against the destructive dissensions that rend the ranks of the Irish Parliamentary representatives, that do so much to discredit their cause and ruin their effectiveness. Canada has contributed generously towards the Home Rule Parliamentary Fund. Not much more than a year ago we here in Toronto, in the midst of great financial depression, subscribed the handsome sum of something more than seven thousand dollars. In other cities and districts of the Dominion sums proportionately as large were freely given for the purpose. In view of these large monetary contributions, in view of the material and moral aid which by words and acts, and even by resolutions unanimously passed in the Dominion Parliament, we have given towards the Irish cause, we Canadians have a right to deplore and deprecate the fatal dissensions that have weakened and paralysed the Irish Parliamentary representation, and that have thwarted and baffled the Home Rule cause. This is not the place to discuss the cause of these dissensions; it must suffice here to raise our voice in protest against them, and to declare that those responsible for them have brought shame and dishonour on their country, and are guilty of high treason against the Irish race at home and abroad.

For those fatal dissensions it is our solemn conviction that neither you nor those with whom you are working are in any wise responsible. You have but been their victims. In order to try to keep peace and harmony in your ranks you have borne quietly with misrepresentations and calumnies until patience ceased to be a virtue, and your silence was construed by some into an admission of guilt. Will Irishmen never give heed to the warning of our national poet, which is also the teaching of our sad history?—

> "Erin, thy silent tear never shall cease,
> Erin, thy languid smile ne'er shall increase,
> Till like the rainbow's light
> Thy various tints unite
> And form in Heaven's sight
> One arch of peace."

How is this necessary union to be effected? How are the Irish National forces to be focussed into a great centre of strength and power? It seems to me that to the solution of this problem Irish patriotism and Irish statesmanship should now devote themselves. Surely Ireland must still have the power and vitality to shake off from her the fatal dissensions that have of late preyed upon her and threatened the extinction of her national life; surely she must not allow herself, like a derelict ship at sea, to drift about aimlessly and hopelessly, a prey to the waves and storms of angry passions and internecine feuds.

This is not a time for despondency or despair, it is rather a time for courageous resolve and earnest action. The Home Rule cause has cost the Irish race too many sacrifices, it has been pushed too far towards realisation to be now abandoned because of the difficulties that beset it. These difficulties are for the most part the direct result of personal jealousies, animosities and ambitions indulged in by certain of the Irish representatives, and doubtless they can be pushed out of the way by the united and determined action of the Irish people.

As an Irishman interested in the destinies of my native land, I trust I may, without presumption, venture to make a suggestion, which if acted on, would, in my opinion, be instrumental in securing that unity of counsel and of action amongst the Nationalists of Ireland so necessary for the success of the cause they have at heart. My suggestion is this: Let a great National Convention be held in Dublin, composed of chosen representatives of the clergy and people of Ireland and of an advisory representation of the Irish race abroad. In that Convention let Ireland speak out her mind, let not her voice be like a broken musical instrument emitting discordant notes and jarring sounds, but let it on the contrary be clear, loud, and emphatic, insisting on unity and condemning faction. Let her point out and uphold the Parliamentary representatives whose methods and conduct she approves, and let her mark out and condemn those whose intolerance of control, personal jealousies and animosities have done so much to break the unity and waste the strength of the National Party. Dissensions and feuds have, in the past, been the ruin and curse of Ireland. Let her stamp them out and cast them from her as things more noxious than the serpents St. Patrick banished from her shores. In that Convention let the voice of Ireland's sons abroad be heard and advice considered. They live under free institutions and are accustomed to the workings of deliberative assemblies and representative governments, and hence the advice and experience of their chosen delegates in the present condition of Irish affairs would be of the utmost value and importance. Surely representative Irishmen in convention assembled, free from prejudices and passions, having at heart not the triumph of party or faction, but the welfare and honour of their race and the triumph of their country's cause, will be able to concert and adopt such measures as will enforce proper discipline and due subordination in the ranks of the nation's representatives, and, in this way, will be able to secure amongst them that unity of purpose and action so absolutely vital to their success.

A great National Convention, such as I venture to suggest, speaking with the authority of the nation, and voicing its fixed and unalterable purpose to labour for and to win the right of self-government, would give new hope and heart and energy to Irishmen at home and abroad, and it would be able to restore unity amongst the ranks of the Irish Nationalist representatives, to make of them once more a compact body and an irresistible power in the Imperial Parliament. When Ireland speaks to Englishmen through such a body her just demands cannot be long refused her.

Wishing you a safe and prosperous voyage to the sunny lands of the Southern Cross, and with sentiments of sincere esteem,

Believe me to be, my dear Mr. Blake,

Yours very faithfully,

✠ JOHN WALSH,

Archbishop of Toronto.

Acceptance of Suggestion by Irish Party.

IN pursuance of notice, a meeting of the Irish Parliamentary Party was held in Dublin, 14th November, 1895. The following present :—

W. Abraham, North-East Cork
Dr. R. Ambrose, West Mayo
M. Austin, West Limerick
E. Barry, South Cork
P. G. Garvill, Newry
Bernard Collery, North Sligo
T. J. Condon, East Tipperary
T. Curran, South Sligo
T. B. Curran, North Donegal
E. Crean, Ossory, Queen's Co.
Daniel Crilly, North Mayo
John Dillon, East Mayo
C. J. Engledow, North Kildare
James P. Farrell, West Cavan
Thomas J. Farrell, South Kerry
P. Ffrench, South Wexford
J. Finucane, East Limerick
J. C. Flynn, North Cork
Dr. J. F. Fox, Tullamore
James Gibney, North Meath
James Gilhooly, West Cork
John Hammond, Carlow
T. M. Healy, North Louth
M. Healy, Cork
T. J. Healy, North Wexford
J. F. Hogan, Mid-Tipperary
J. Jordan, South Fermanagh
D. Kilbride, North Galway
E. F. V. Knox, Derry City
D. MacAleese, North Monaghan
P. M'Dermott, North Kilkenny
Dr. M. A. MacDonnell, Leix
J. G. S. MacNeill, South Donegal
F. Mandeville, South Tipperary
M. J. Minch, South Kildare
B. C. Molloy, Birr, King's Co.
S. Morris, South Kilkenny
M. M'Cartan, South Down
Justin M'Carthy, North Longford
E. L. M'Hugh, South Armagh
P. A. M'Hugh, North Leitrim
J. F. X. O'Brien, Cork City
P. J. O'Brien, North Tipperary
A. O'Connor, East Donegal
James O'Connor, West Wicklow
T. P. O'Connor, Scotland Ward, Liverpool
F. E. O'Keeffe, Limerick City
W. O'Malley, Connemara
P. J. Power, East Waterford
John Roche, East Galway
J. J. Shee, West Waterford
D. Sheehy, South Galway
Donald Sullivan, Sth. Westmeath
T. D. Sullivan, West Donegal
Dr. C. K. D. Tanner, Mid-Cork
James Tuite, North Westmeath
S. Young, East Cavan

Mr. JOHN DILLON moved, and Mr. J. C. FLYNN seconded :—" That this party approves of the suggestion made by the Archbishop of Toronto in favour of a National Convention representative of the Irish race throughout the world, and that with the view of carrying this decision into effect the Chairman and Committee of the Irish Party are hereby authorised to communicate with the Executive of the National Federation and jointly with them to make arrangements for the holding of such a Convention."

Mr. T. M. HEALY moved, and Dr. Fox seconded, the following amendment :—" That a Convention of the people of Ireland be called forthwith, and that the Council of the Federation be asked to appoint a committee to arrange the basis of representation and invitations of the delegates and clergy according to established precedents in times past; that invitations to prominent and representative Irishmen or organisations should be issued by the Chairman of the Irish Party."

The amendment was negatived without a division, and Mr. Dillon's motion was carried without a division.

Constitution of the Irish Race Convention.

At a meeting of the Irish Parliamentary Party, held on 20th May, 1896, Mr. JOHN DILLON in the chair, the Chairman reported that in pursuance of the following resolution passed at the meeting of the Irish Parliamentary Party, held in Dublin on Thursday, November 14th, 1895—" That this party approves of the suggestion made by the Archbishop of Toronto in favour of a National Convention representative of the Irish race throughout the world, and that with a view of carrying this decision into effect the Chairman and Committee of the Irish Party are hereby authorised to communicate with the Executive of the National Federation and jointly with them to make arrangements for the holding of such a Convention "—the Executive of the National Federation and the Chairman had prepared the following scheme :—

A National Convention of representatives of the Irish race throughout the world, supporters of the Irish Home Rule movement, is summoned to meet in Dublin, on 1st September, 1896.

The delegates shall be as follows :—

I.—IRELAND.

(1) Three delegates from each branch of the Irish National Federation, and if there are more than 300 members in the branch, one additional delegate for each 100 members in excess of 300.

The delegates are to be elected at a meeting of the branch to be held after not less than one week's notice on some day, not later than 16th August, and a certificate of election, signed by the Chairman and Secretary of the meetings, is to be forwarded to the Secretary of the Irish National Federation, 24 Rutland Square, Dublin, so as to be received not later than 18th August.

(2) One delegate from each parish in which there is no branch of the Federation. The delegate is to be elected at parish meeting to be called by local Nationalists, and the foregoing provisions are to apply.

(3) Clergymen of all denominations.

(4) Nationalist members of local public bodies.

(5) All members of the Central Body of the Irish National Federation. (This included all members of the Irish Parliamentary Party.)

(6) Three delegates from each Gaelic Athletic Club, Young Ireland Society, National Literary Society, Labour Organisation, and Irish National Foresters, having not less than 50 members, and if there are more than 300 members in the branch, one additional delegate for each 100 members in excess of 300. The delegates from the abovementioned organisations shall be elected at meetings to be called by the officers of the organisation, and all the foregoing provisions are to apply.

II.—GREAT BRITAIN.

One delegate from each branch of the Irish National League of Great Britain, having not less than 50 members, and one additional delegate for each 100 members in excess of 50.

The foregoing provisions are to apply, subject, however, to such further provision as may be made by the Executive of the Irish National League of Great Britain, which is now charged with the administration of the matter.

GENERAL PROVISION FOR DELEGATES FROM ABROAD.—As distance and expense preclude the possibility of the attendance of any large number of delegates from abroad, and local knowledge is required intelligently to adjust the distribution of representation, no express limitation of numbers is proposed. Certificates of election are in all cases to be forwarded, so as to reach the Secretary of the Irish National Federation, Dublin, no later than 15th August.

III.—NORTH AMERICA.

(a) UNITED STATES OF AMERICA.

Delegates to be chosen.—(1) By the Irish National Federation of America; (2) by the Ancient Order of Hibernians; (3) by the Ancient Order of Hibernians (Board of Erin).

The delegates are to be chosen by each organisation according to the rules to be made by the Executive of the organisation concerned.

(b) CANADA.

Delegates to be chosen for their own cities and the country at large by the Irish National organisations in each of the following cities:— Ottawa; Montreal; Toronto; Quebec; St. John; Halifax.

The delegates are to be elected at a meeting of the organisation, or if there be more than one organisation at a joint meeting of the organisations of the city, to be called by concerted action of the executive in the city.

IV.—AUSTRALASIA.

Delegates for the city and district and the country at large to be chosen by the local branch of the Irish National Federation, or where there is no such branch by the concerted action of the local Nationalists— AUSTRALIA :—Sydney; Melbourne; Adelaide; Brisbane; Perth. NEW ZEALAND :—Auckland; Wellington; Dunedin; Westland District. TASMANIA :—Hobart; Launcestown.

GENERAL PROVISIONS.—Further provisions as to the supply to and delivery by delegates of credentials, and other necessary preliminaries for the organisation of the Convention will be prepared and issued in due time.

On the motion of Mr. DENIS KILBRIDE, seconded by Mr. P. C. DOOGAN, the following resolution was unanimously adopted :—" That having considered the scheme drawn up by the Executive of the Irish National Federation and the Chairman of the Irish Parliamentary Party for holding a National Convention in Dublin in September next, which has been submitted to us, we approve of the constitution and mode of election proposed herein."

All Irish Nationalist Members of Parliament Invited.

AT the foregoing meeting of the Irish Parliamentary Party held in Dublin on the 20th May, 1896, it was moved by Mr. JOHN DILLON, seconded by Dr. M. A. MACDONNELL, and adopted with one dissentient:—Resolved—"That we, the members of the Irish Parliamentary Party, in meeting assembled, feel it our duty to record our conviction of the supreme importance to the National cause of a restoration of unity amongst the supporters of the Home Rule movement, and in our earnest desire to accomplish that result we are prepared to meet on fair and equal terms those from whom we are unhappily now divided, and to join in the reconstitution of a united Home Rule party, in which every supporter of the movement shall be cordially received and justly considered, regardless of all past differences, and having regard only to his capacity to render service to the common cause. We cordially invite Mr. John Redmond and his friends to co-operate with us in a common earnest endeavour to make the coming Convention an effective means of satisfying the widespread yearning of the Irish race for a thorough re-union. While it is obviously impossible for us, without the concurrence of those concerned, to include them in the arrangements for the National Convention, we ask them to join us in making such arrangements as will secure to them a full representation in the Convention on the basis hereinbefore indicated."

Resolutions and Motions.

UPON 20th August, 1896, the Organising Committee of the Convention gave public notice that resolutions and notices of motion received up to the 29th would be placed upon the Agenda Paper.

List of Delegates.

The Irish Race Abroad.

UNITED STATES OF AMERICA.—T. C. Boland, Scanton, Pennsylvania; Hon. William L. Brown, New York; John Cashman, Manchester, New Hampshire; M. J. Cooney, Montana; Patrick Cox, Rochester, New York; John B. Devlin, Wilkesbarre, Pennsylvania; James Duggan, Norwich, Connecticut; Patrick Dunleavy, Philadelphia Council, N.F.; Rev. D. W. Fitzgerald, Manchester, New Hampshire; Martin Fitzgerald, Manchester, New Hampshire; P. Gallagher, New York; John Guiney, Wilkesbarre, Pennsylvania; Anthony Kelly, Minneapolis, Minnesota; Edward Mackin, Wilkesbarre, Pennsylvania; Hon. Martin M'Mahon, New York; Rev. George F. Marshall, Milford, New Hampshire; Patrick Martin, Baltimore, Maryland; Michael Murphy, representing Irish National Federation of America, New York; Rev. Denis O'Callaghan, Boston; Hon. Edmond O'Connor, Binghampton, New York; Denis O'Reilly, Boston; Hon. C. T. O'Sullivan, New York; Rev. Edward S. Phillips, Pennsylvania; Michael J. Rooney, representing Irish National Federation of America, New York; Joseph P. Ryan, New York; M. J. Ryan, Philadelphia; James Sullivan, M.D., Manchester, New Hampshire; Edward Treacy, Boston; P. W. Wren, Bridgeport, Connecticut.

CANADA.—Hon. John Costigan, M.P., P.C.; Very Rev. M. A. Clancy, Placentia, Newfoundland; P. F. Cronin, Toronto; Rev. Dr. Flannery, St. Thomas, Ontario, representing Ancient Order of Hibernians in Canada; Very Rev. Dr. Foley, Halifax, Nova Scotia; James J. Foy, Q.C., Toronto; Edward Halley, First Vice-president Young Irishmen's Literary and Benefit Association, Montreal; Very Rev. Dean Harris, St. Catherines; Chevalier John Heney, Ottawa; John M. Keown, Q.C., St. Catherine's; Lieut.-Colonel MacShane, Nova Scotia; James J. O'Brien, Halifax, Nova Scotia; Rev. P. F. O'Donnell, Montreal; Rev. F. O'Reilly, Hamilton; Rev. Frank Ryan (representing Archbishop of Toronto), Toronto; Hugh Ryan (Constructor Sault Ste. Marie Canal and portion Canadian Pacific Railway), Toronto; James D. Ryan, President of the Benevolent Irish Society, St. John's, Newfoundland; Gerald B. Tiernan, Halifax.

AUSTRALASIA.—Charles Hamilton Bromly, Ex-Attorney-Genéral, Northern Tasmania; Michael Davitt, M.P., Delegated for Dunedin, New Zealand; Thomas Hunt, Victoria; Mr. Kennedy, Wellington, New Zealand; Rev. Father O'Callaghan, C.C., Mallow, delegated to represent Southern Tasmania.

SOUTH AFRICA.—Moses Cornwall, J.P., Kimberley, representing Irishmen of Griqualand, West; H. J. Haskins, Johannesburg.

Members of Parliament.

William Abraham ; Dr. R. Ambrose ; Michael Austin ; Hon. E. Blake ; Bernard Collery ; T. J. Condon ; Eugene Crean ; Daniel Crilly ; Thomas Curran ; Michael Davitt ; John Dillon ; Captain Donelan ; P. C. Doogan ; C. J. Engledow ; Sir Thomas G. Esmond, Bart. ; Thomas J. Farrell ; J. Finnucane ; M. J. Flavin ; J. C. Flynn ; James Gilhooly ; J. F. Hogan ; Jeremiah Jordan ; Denis Kilbride ; Michael M'Cartan ; Justin M'Carthy ; Patrick M'Dermott ; Dr. M. A. M'Donnell ; Richard M'Ghee ; P. A. M'Hugh ; J. G. S. MacNeill ; F. Mandeville ; M. J. Minch ; George Murnaghan ; J. F. X. O'Brien ; P. J. O'Brien ; T. P. O'Connor ; F. A O'Keeffe ; William O'Malley ; J. Pinkerton ; P. J. Power ; John Roche ; J. J. Shee ; David Sheehy ; Dr. Tanner ; J. Tully ; Samuel Young.

Clergy.

FROM this list are omitted the names of many clergymen who appear as delegates under other categories. As under the constitution of the Convention clergymen were admitted without credentials, it has been impossible to distinguish between those who attended as delegates and as visitors ; and many may have been omitted who did not give in their names, or whose names were not correctly taken down at the doors.

Most Rev. Dr. O'Donnell, Lord Bishop of Raphoe ; Rev. R. Barrett, St. Patrick's, Cork ; Rev. Michael Bonfield, Chicago, U.S.A. ; Rev. T. Boylan, Drumshambo ; Very Rev. P. Bermingham, P.P., Carrickmacross ; Rev. Father Berney, Scotland ; Rev. James Brady, Ballymahon ; Very Rev. John Brady, Gowel, Carrick-on-Shannon ; Rev. John Brady, C.C., Uxbridge, Middlesex ; Rev. J. Brennan, C.C., Slieverue ; Rev. E. Brennan, C.C., Cullohill ; Rev. P. F. Brennan ; Rev. Thomas Brennan, C.C., Castlecomer ; Rev. M. Buckley, St. Mary's, Haslingden ; Rev. John Burke, P.P. ; Rev. J. E. Burke, Bolton, Lancashire ; Rev. Michael Burke, C.C., Kilgobnet ; Rev. B. Butler, Bath, England ; Very Rev. Dr. Butler, Dublin ; Rev. Arthur Byrne, C.C. Monasterboice ; Rev. Father Byrne, Jarrow-on-Tyne ; Rev. Father Byrne, Strokestown.

Rev. H. B. Callachor, O.S.B., B.A., Sydney, New South Wales ; Rev. P. Callan, Errigal, Truagh ; Rev. J. Campbell, Whitehaven, Cumberland ; Rev. J. Campbell, C.C., Inniskeen, Dundalk ; Rev. P. P. Campbell, P.P., Loughbrickland ; Rev. N. C. Cantwell ; Rev. W. Conway, P.P., Glenamaddy ; Rev. A. Clancy, P.P., Killimer ; Rev. J. Clancy, C.C., Rathcabbin, Birr ; Rev. M. A. Clancy, Placentia, Newfoundland ; Rev. M. J. Clancy, Templemore ; Rev. P. Clarke, P.P., Kilmore ; Rev. P. Clough, P.P. Ballina ; Rev. P. Coffey, P.P., Tramore ; Rev. M. Colleran, C.C., Miltown, Tuam ; Very Rev. Canon Columb, P.P., Ballinakown, Athlone ; Rev. Terence Conlan, P.P., Donaghmoyne ; Rev. James Connolly, C.C., Liverpool ; Rev. Richard Connolly ; Rev. M. D. Conroy, Rosscahill ; Rev. M. Considine, C.C., Kilmihill ; Rev. P. Cooney, C.C., Innishannon ; Rev. D. E. Coyle, C.C., Convoy, Co. Donegal ; Rev. P. J. Crimmins, C.C. ; Rev. J. R. Crowe, P.P., Cappawhite ; Rev. Joseph Cullinan, Newbliss ; Rev. J. Cunningham, Sheffield ; Rev. James Curran, P.P., Kilconey ; Rev. John Curry, St. Mary's, Drogheda ; Rev. M. B. Curry, P.P., Bournea.

Rev. D. Daly, P.P., Templeglantine; Rev. P. J. Daly, Boston, U.S.A.; Rev. J. Dempsey, C.C., Celbridge; Rev. M. J. Dillon ; Rev. Timothy Doheny, C.C., Cloughjordan; Rev. J. Doherty, New York ; Rev. John Doherty, P.P.; Rev. P. J. Donoghue, St. Mary's, Boston, England ; Rev. P. Dooley, P.P., Galway ; Dr. Anthony F. Dougherty, Luzerne, Co. Pa, U.S.A. ; Rev. M. Doyle, C.C., Tubbercurry; Rev. B. Duffy, Fintona ; Rev. W. Duggan, C.C., Athy; Rev. L Duncan, P.P., Magheraclone, Carrickmacross ; Rev. Father Dunleavy, Edinburgh ; Rev. William Dunphy, P.P., The Naul; Rev. W. J. Dunphy, P.P., Arklow.

Rev. P. Egan, P.P., Duniry ; Rev. Denis English, Cappamore.

Rev. Peter Farnan, C.C., Derrygonnelly ; Rev. John J. Fennelly ; Rev. D. Fitzgerald ; Rev. P. Fitzgerald, Kilconnell ; Rev. T. Flanagan, Roscommon ; Rev. A. Forrest, P.P., Innishannon ; Rev. John Francis, Rahoon, Galway ; Rev. P. M. Furlong, P.P., Taghmon.

Right Rev. James Gallagher, P.P., Carrigart, County Donegal ; Rev. James Gallagher, P.P., Rathmullan ; Rev. P. Gilchreest, P.P., Drumreilly; Rev. T. Gillic, C.C., Dunshaughlin ; Rev. L. Gilligan, Kilmurry; Rev. Father Glevin ; Rev. P. Glynn, P.P., Ogonnelloe ; Rev. Patrick Godfrey, Moyne ; Rev. L. W. Goughran, P.P. Arney, Enniskillen ; Very Rev. Canon Grealy, P.P., V.F., Newport, Mayo ; Rev. Denis Greany, C.C., Headford, Co. Galway ; Rev. J. Greany, Athlone ; Rev. J. Grace, C.C., Ballyuskill, Athenagh ; Rev. B. G. Greeley Behan, Ballyhaunis ; Rev. Thomas F. Gregg, New York.

Rev. J. Hally, Kingstown ; Rev. James C. Harte, S.J., Clongowes Wood College ; Rev. M. Harte, Collaney; Rev. John M. Harty, Maynooth ; Rev. Father Healy, Acton, Hamilton, Canada ; Rev. W. Healy, P.P., Johnstown ; Rev. Thomas Heany, Ballyhaunis; Rev. T. Hearne, P.P., Portlaw; Rev. J. Halloran, Birr ; Rev. Martin Holohan, C.C., Kilkenny; Rev. Thomas Hunt, C.C.; Rev. F. Jones, Athlone.

Rev. R. Kavanagh, Monamolin ; Rev. Thomas Kearney, Adm., Skibbereen ; Rev. J. Keely, C.C., Gort ; Rev. M. Keveney, P.P., Charlestown ; Very Rev. B. Kelly, P.P., Ballyshannon ; Rev. J. Kelly, Birmingham ; Right Rev. Mons. Kelly, P.P., V.G., St. Peter's, Athlone ; N. Kennedy, C.C. ; Rev. M. B. Kennedy, C.C., Blarney ; Rev. M. Kennelly, C.C., Achill ; Rev. Patrick Kenny, P.P., Oulart ; Rev. P. Kenny, P.P., Raphoe ; Rev. W. J. Kinane, Castleiny, Templemore.

Rev. E. Lalor, P.P., Allen, Kilmeague ; Rev. T. J. Larkin, P.P., Moneymore ; Rev. Richard Little, Moneyrea ; Very Rev. Canon Loftus ; Rev. J. Loftus, C.C.; Rev. Denis Lundon ; Very Rev. Dr. Loughran, C.C., Dromintee, Newry ; Very Rev. Canon Lowry, Gurteen ; Rev. A. Lowry, Mayobridge ; Very Rev. Canon Lynskey, Clifden.

Rev. P. M'Caffery, Adm., Inver ; Rev. J. McAteer, C.C. ; Rev. A. Macauley, P.P., Aghagallon, Lurgan ; Rev. J. J. McCabe, SS. Joseph and Cuthbert, Loftus, Saltburn-on-Sea ; Rev. B. McAndrew, P.P., Ballinakill ; Rev. F. McCormac, C.C.; Very Rev. Canon McCartan, P.P., Donaghmore; Rev. T. McCarthy, P.P., Barryroe ; Rev. D. F. McCrea, M.R.I.A., Maghera ; Rev. J. McDermott, Strokestown ; Rev. J. McIlroy, P.P., Currin ; Rev. Father McEvilly, C.C. ; Rev. J. McEvoy, Banbridge ; Right Rev. Mons. McGlynn, P.P., V.G., Stranorlar : Rev. P. McGinity, P.P., Kilskeery ; Rev. Father McGowran, P.P., Ballinagleragh ; Rev. M. McGrath, P.P., Drangan, Fethard ; Right Rev. Mon-

LIST OF DELEGATES.

signor McFadden, Gweedore; Rev. P. McGirr, C.C., Westport; Rev. John Mackey, P.P., Knockbridge; Rev. A. Maguire, C.C., Enniskillen; Rev. M. J. M'Hugh, Adm., 'Tuam; Rev. Father McKenna; Rev. E. Mackey, C.C., Rathfarnham; Rev. M. Mackle, C.C., Meigh, Newry; Rev. P. McLoughlin; Rev. John McNamara, P.P., Bodyke; Rev. M. McPolin, Adm., Newry; Rev. J. McSwiney, P.P., Newmarket; Rev. S. McTernan, P.P., M.R.I.A.; Rev. J. Maher, P.P., Kilglass; Rev. John Maher, C.C., Luggacurran; Rev.William Meagher, C.C., Clonmel; Rev. J. Meegary, Monaghan; Rev. Father Meelin, C.C., Clogher, Co. Tyrone; Rev. Joseph A. Moloney, P.P., Roundstone; Rev. James Monaghan, C.C., Cloughjordan; Rev. F. Murphy, C.C., Drimcong; Rev. B. Mulholland, P.P. Coleraine; Rev. P. Mulligan, P.P., Curry, Co. Sligo; Rev. Michael Munnelly, Belmullet; Rev. A. Murphy, C.C., Carlowgraigue; Rev. F. P. Murtagh, C.C. Ardee; Rev. L. Murphy, Donoughmore; Rev. Thomas Murphy, P.P., Kilmore and Drumsnat.

Rev. M. Nevin; Rev. Patrick Nicholson, C.C., Dunmore, Co. Galway; Rev. J. Nolan, C.C., Allen, Kilmeague.

Rev. William O'Brien, Chicago, U.S.A.; Rev. John O'Brien, P.P., Holycross, Thurles; Very Rev. John O'Brien, P.P., V.F., Banbridge; Rev. C. M. O'Callaghan, C.C., Mallow; Rev. D. O'Callaghan, Boston, Mass., U.S.A.; Rev. J. O'Callaghan, C.C.; Rev. Michael O'Callaghan, Clonakilty; Very Rev. Canon O'Connor, P.P., Newtownbutler; Rev. J. O'Connor, Ballaghadereen; Rev. John O'Donnell, C.C., Kill; Rev. J. J. O'Donnell, Killybegs; Rev. P. O'Donnell, P.P., Doon; Rev. P. O'Donnell, Adm., Monaghan; Rev. P. O'Donnell, C.C.; Rev. William O'Donnell, C.C., Waterford; Rev. Patrick O'Donovan, C.C., Drinagh, Dunmanway; Rev. P. S. O'Grady, C.C., Collooney; Rev. T. O'Grady, C.C., Bohola; Rev. William O'Halloran, Cork; Rev. J. O'Haire, C.C., Derrymacash, Lurgan; Rev. P. O'Halloran, P.P., Muckalee; Rev. D. O'Hara, P.P., Kiltimagh; Rev. John O'Hea, P.P., Ardfield, Clonakilty; Rev. Peter O'Leary, P.P., Castlelyons; Very Rev. John O'Leary, P.P., V.F., Clonakilty; Very Rev. Canon O'Neill, P.P., Clones; Rev. H. O'Neill, C.C., Bundoran; Rev. John M. O'Reilly, C.C., Sydney, N.S.W.; Rev. W. O'Reilly, Liverpool; Rev. F. O'Reilly; Rev. John O'Shea, C.C., Kilkenny; Rev. Jeremiah O'Toole, C.C., Westport.

Very Rev. W. L. Penny, V.F.; Rev. Father Phelan, Boofield, U.S.A.; Rev. W. J. Phelan, P.P., Ardfinane, Cahir; Rev. E. S. Phillips, Plains, Luzerne Co., Pennsylvania; Very Rev. Canon Pope, Donoughmore, Co. Cork; Rev. John Power, P.P., Kilteely; Rev. Michael Power, P.P., New Inn, Cahir; Rev. M. Power, P.P., Ballyduff; Rev. J. S. Prendergast, Ballylooby.

Rev. James Queally, C.C., Kilrossinty; Rev. B. Quinn, Thurles; Rev. C. Quinn, C.C., Camlough; Rev. C. S. Quinn; P.P., V.F., Duneane; Rev. Bernard Quinn, C.C., Bangor-Erris; Rev. Father Quinn, C.C., Cavan; Rev. M. J. Quinn, C.C., Camlough.

Very Rev. Dean Regan, V.G., P.P., Mitchelstown; Rev. J. Rochford, Aghaboe; Rev. James Rockett, Rathdowney; Rev. Daniel Ryan, P.P., Clonoulty, Co. Tipperary; Rev. Gabriel Ryan, C.C., Middlesboro', England; Rev. W. Ryan, C.C., Boherlahan; Rev. Harold Rylett.

Rev. J. J. Savage, C.C., Hilltown; Rev. J. Scanlan, P.P., Cloughjordan; Rev. J. Sheridan Donegal; Rev. M. Shinnors, London; Very

IRISH RACE CONVENTION.

Rev. Canon Shinkwin, Bantry; Very Rev. Canon Shortall, P.P., Durrow; Very Rev. P. Canon Smyth, P.P., Ballybay; Rev. P. Spait, P.P., Cappoquinn; Rev. T. Stafford, Dublin; Rev. James Stephens, P.P., Crossboyne; Rev. J. Sullivan, Templebredin, Pallasgreen; Rev. Daniel Sweeney, C.C., Kincoslagh, Donegal; Very Rev. J. Sweeney, P.P., Killybegs.
Rev. P. Tracey, C.C., Galmoy; Rev. Joseph Tully, Achill; Rev. J. Twomey, C.C., Glountane, Mallow; Rev. Timothy Twomey, C.C., Middlesboro.
Right Rev. Mons. Walker, Letterkenny; Rev. T. Whelahan, St. Patrick's, Plumstead, S.E.; Rev. C. Woods, C.C., Warrenpoint; Rev. Nicholas Woods, C.C., Mullingar; Rev. John Woods, C.C., Drogheda.

County and Civic.

Messrs. Thomas Barry, Cork; Jerome Boyce, Donegal; Thomas Byrne, Galway; Daniel Corry, Meath; Joseph Devlin, Belfast; John Dolan, Leitrim; Rev. P. F. Flynn, P.P., Waterford City; Simon F. Hanratty, Newry Borough; Laurence T. Kelly, Queen's County; William Lundon, Limerick; Rev. J. Meegan, Monaghan; James Neary, Roscommon; John O'Dowd, Sligo; Rev. D. O'Hara, P.P., Mayo; Bernard O'Neill, Armagh; Thomas Robertson, Kildare; Rev. John Rock, P.P., Tyrone; N. K. Shee, Tipperary; John Ward, Sligo Borough; John F. Wray, Fermanagh.

From Great Britain.

(Under Localities and Societies from which delegated.)

ACCRINGTON—Samuel Bridges, Edward Burke.
ALEXANDRIA, SCOTLAND—Patrick Cassidy.
BARNSLEY, WILLIAM O'BRIEN—Dr. Haiton, J.P.; D. Payne, P. Neary.
BARROW-IN-FURNESS, No. 1—Thomas M'Mullen. I. N. CLUB—Neil M'Creesh.
BARRY, WALES, MANDEVILLE—John M'Donnell, Owen M'Cann, Dr. P. J. M'Donnell.
BATLEY CARR, EMMET—Thomas Cox.
BIRKENHEAD, WILFRED BLUNT—Dr. J. T. Martin, Thomas Mohen, Thomas Cusack.
BIRMINGHAM—James Doherty.
BIRSTALL, O'CONNELL—Mrs. J. Gorman.
BLACKBURN, SARSFIELD—Peter Doolan, Austin Moran, Bernard Fury.
BLANTYRE, SCOTLAND, O'CONNELL—Joseph Kennedy.
BOLTON, No. 1—Richard Kelly, Rev. D. O'Brien, William O'Malley, Rev. Joseph A. Burke, T.C.D.; W. Kearns, T.C.; M. Coghlan. HOME RULE CLUB—W. Devlin, Charles Connolly.
BRADFORD, CENTRAL—W. Sullivan, Councillor M. O'Flynn, M. J. Barry, J.P.; W. Sullivan, John Daly, John Cawley. DWYER—Patrick Kane, Michael Conboy, John Kane, Michael Kearns. GRATTAN—Fenton Kenny, Richard Cullen, William Narey, William H. Fitzgerald, James Kelly, Owen Connolly. DILLON-O'BRIEN—T. Browne, William Conroy, John Walling, J. Tane, William

LIST OF DELEGATES.

Rowan. LADIES' CENTRAL—Miss M. Bennett, Mrs. C. E. Cawley, Mrs. K. O. Flynn, Miss M. Keeffe. LADIES' DILLON-O'BRIEN—Mrs. Pendergast. WOLFE TONE—James Gorman, James Kenehan, William Gorman, Thomas Nailon, Terence White, Thomas Loughlin,
BRISTOL—John Valentine, John Downey, M. Hanrahan.
BROXBURN, SCOTLAND—William Mahon, John Mulhern, Hugh Molloy, Thomas Dobie.
BURNLEY—John Tighe.
BURNBANK, SCOTLAND, O'CONNELL—John Cassidy.
BURY, DAVITT—E. Timlin.
BUSBY, SCOTLAND, GRATTAN—John Fitzpatrick.
CARDIFF, WALES, EMMET—Jeremiah M'Carthy, William O'Neill, James Courtney, James Neagle, John Hack, Frank A. Fox, Alderman P. W. Carey, J.P.; Dr. James Mullin, M.A., J.P.; James J. Buish, M.B., C.C.
COATBRIDGE, SCOTLAND, DAVITT—John Graven, Michael Hughes, Dr. O'Neill, John M'Evoy.
CONSETT—Thomas Barry.
DEWSBURY, GRATTAN—Edward Rourke, Thomas Walsh, John M'Cann, John O'Hara.
DUMBARTON, HEART OF ERIN—Joseph M'Elhaw, Edward M'Allister.
DUNDEE, SCOTLAND, ST. ANDREW'S—Joseph Birmingham, John Hogan. A. M. SULLIVAN—Mathew M'Kenna, Daniel Daily.
EARLSTOWN—Thomas Galligan, Dominic Caffrey.
EDINBURGH, SCOTLAND, DILLON—Daniel Donworth, John M'Manus. GLADSTONE—Francis M'Aweeney.
FARNWORTH—James Kelly, Hugh Gallagher.
GATESHEAD, EMMET—Edward M'Keown, Councillor F. J. Finn, J.P. DAVITT—James O'Donnell.
GLASGOW, BRIDGETON — Henry Aylmer, Peter Campbell, Michael M'Ginty, Henry Logan. HOME GOVERNMENT — Bailie Joseph Shaughnessy, John Ferguson, T.C.; M. J. O'Connell, B.A.; Michael Dunbar, Denis Brogan, Dr. Joseph Scanlan, Hugh Murphy, Thomas Colgan, William M'Killop, Arthur Murphy, John Carnin, James Kelly, C. J. M'Elhawe, Thomas C. Nelson, J.P. INDEPENDENCE— Dr. M'Loughlin. WILLIAM O'BRIEN—James Stafford. ARCHBISHOP WALSH—D. J. Sheahan. DILLON—Richard St. John, James Burns. FATHER MAGUIRE—John M'Quin. DAVIS—William Coyle, J. F. M'Groary. CELTIC FOOTBALL AND ATHLETIC CLUB—John Glass, President; James M'Kay, Treasurer; and William Maley, Secretary. FATHER M'GINN—John M'Guire, Vice-President.
GORTON, T. P. O'CONNOR—Councillor E. Scully, J.P.; Councillor M. Bushell.
GOVAN, SHEEHY—Martin Hester, James Grant, Patrick M'Loughlin.
GREENOCK, SCOTLAND, DILLON—Neal Haughey.
HALIFAX—Mrs. Mary M'Hugh, Michael M'Hugh, Owen Canning, Martin Delaney.
HAMILTON, SCOTLAND, DAVITT—Bailie M'Hale, J.P.
HANLEY, ALLEN, LARKIN AND O'BRIEN—Stephen D'Arcy, Dr. W. Dowling Prendergast.
HARTLEPOOL, WEST, DAVIS—Francis Jones, P.L.G.

IRISH RACE CONVENTION.

HASLINGDEN, DAVITT—Michael Welsh, Patrick Glynn.
HUDDERSFIELD—Patrick Hopkins.
HULL, CENTRAL—T. W. Morrissey, J. B. O'Neill. EAST—James Grayson, John Cunningham, Austin Boyle.
KEIGHLEY, No. 1—James Walsh, T.C.; Michael Howley, T.C. HOME RULE—Michael O'Hara, J. T. Carroll.
KIDDERMINSTER, WILLIAM O'BRIEN—John Boyle.
KILBIRNIE, GLADSTONE—Edward M'Intyre, John M'Grath, C. J. M'Elhaw.
LANARK, SCOTLAND, OWEN ROE O'NEILL—Peter Martin.
LEICESTER, DILLON—T. Irwin.
LONGTON, O'CONNELL—Patrick Howley.
LEEDS, DILLON—Martin Silk. GRATTAN—Patrick Coyle. HUNSLETT—Peter Walsh, Rev. M. Dillon. I. N. CLUB—William Riley, M. O'Donnell, Miss R. O'Neill, Terence O'Neill, S. M'Farlane, O. Kiernan, Miss M. Durnan, Miss B. Durnan. O'BRIEN-DAVITT—Felix Byrne, Michael Hogan, Miss M. A. Durnan. EMMET—Michael Collins.
LIVERPOOL, DAVITT—Joseph Hawkshaw, Thomas Flynn, Edward Clarke, John Clancy. DILLON—Michael T. Bolger. MANDEVILLE—Edward Purcell, C.C.; James Bolger, C.C., P.L.G.; James Shortell. NORTH—Martin Coyne, T. E. Brady, P.L.G. ST. PAUL'S—Bernard M'Bennett, Joseph Hughes, Peter Murphy, J. G. Taggart, C.C. W. TOXTETH—John Quinn, George J. Lynskey, C.C. CENTRAL—A. Mullen, T. J. Flynn, C.C. EAST—Dr. J. G. M'Cann. O'CONNELL—Patrick G. O'Neill, Patrick J. Deery, C.C.
LONDON, BATTERSEA—John Enright BERMONDSEY—Rev. E. Murnane, J. Moloney, E. Reilly. CLERKENWELL—John Ball. DEPTFORD—James Herlihy. EAST FINSBURY—George Whitehead, James Nolan. FOREST GATE AND UPTON—T. P. O'Halloran. SOUTH ISLINGTON—William Finn, James Madden. KENSINGTON, SARSFIELD—Patrick Morris, Michael Walsh, James C. Ahern. MARYLEBONE WEST—M. C. Walsh, Michael O'Rorke. METROPOLITAN—J. M'Cormack, Frank Porter, R. J. Geraghty, J. Vincent Taaffe, Martin Hoban, Maurice Ahern.
MERTHYR TYDFIL, WALES, GLADSTONE—William J. Jones, John Morley.
MOTHERWELL, SCOTLAND, A. M. SULLIVAN—Thomas Monaghan.
MANCHESTER, DAVITT—Councillor D. M'Cabe, J.P.; Thomas Q. Ruddin, P.L.G.; John Kelly, Patrick Jeffers, F. J. Farley, James Reilly, Luke Hoy, Rev. T. Cusack. ESMONDE—Councillor D. Boyle, Michael Smith. O'CONNELL—Peter Burke, J. M'Kinnon, James Merry. POLAND STREET—Joseph Carney, Patrick Cosgrove. FATHER SHEEHY—W. H. Gaffney, Martin Ryan, James Rooney. ARCHBISHOP WALSH—Rev. Patrick Lynch, M.R.
NEWPORT, MONMOUTHSHIRE, DAVITT—James De Lacy, Michael M'Eniry.
NORMANTON, WILLIAM O'BRIEN—Thomas M'Dermott, Thomas Rush.
NEWCASTLE-ON-TYNE, No. 1—Edward Timlin, P.L.G. BYKER—Thomas Maley. SEXTON—John Collins (Newcastle School Board).
OLDHAM, CENTRAL—James Byrne, Patrick May.

LIST OF DELEGATES.

PAISLEY, JUSTIN M'CARTHY—John M'Carthy.
PARTICK, EMMET—Thaddeus M'Goverin.
PERTH, DILLON—Michael Kerrigan, P.C.
PLYMOUTH, THREE TOWNS—P. J. Clarke.
PORTSMOUTH—H. D. Rice.
PORT GLASGOW, SARSFIELD—James Fitzpatrick, James M'Loughlin, J.P., Joseph Dunne. GRATTAN—Thomas Flannery, Felix M'Cluskey.
RAMSBOTTOM, T. P. O'CONNOR—John Keenaghan, T.C.
ROCHDALE, T. P. O'CONNOR—W. H. Capstick.
SOUTHAMPTON, GRATTAN—Florence O'Sullivan, Dr. W. P. O'Meara.
SHIELDS, NORTH—Michael Lydon.
SPRINGBURN—Patrick Corr.
STALYBRIDGE—Peter Hickey.
SWANSEA, DAVITT—J. T. O'Hara.
SHEFFIELD, I. N. L. CLUB—Thomas Walsh, Thomas Crosby. DAVIS RYAN—M. J. Flynn.
TALL CROSS, SCOTLAND, EXILE—D. J. M. Quin.
WARRINGTON—John C. Dalton.
WIDNES, T. P. O'CONNOR.—Hugh O'Donnell.
WINGATE, DAVITT—John Mazel.
WORKINGHAM, P. J. POWER—Michael M'Carthy.
WREXHAM—Edward M'Hale.
A.O.H., ENGLAND—Thomas Larkin.
A.O.H., SCOTLAND—Michael Fitzpatrick, Patrick Doherty, John Gribbin, Michael M'Inally, Peter Mallon, Bernard Coyle, Richard Stapleton, Samuel Kilpatrick, Daniel Harkins, Thomas Brown, Thomas Flannery, James Gallagher, F. Kierney, James Connor.

Central Body J. A. Federation.

Messrs. Thomas Caicy; Charles Conlan; Major J. J. Crooks; Bernard Dempsey, Glasgow; Nicholas H. Devine, Tubbercurry; Andrew Donnelly, Lurgan; James Dwyer, Roscrea; Joseph Dwyer, Roscrea; Francis Fitzgerald, Glin; Wm Fitzgerald, Cappoquin; John Fogarty; Charles Gallen, J.P.; E. Gallagher; Frederick Gilroy; Laurence Ginnell, B.L., Dublin; John Harrington, J.P.; Michael Hayden, Castlerea; James Hayes, Tipperary; Michael Hearne, William Hodnett, Solicitor; Arthur Houston, Q.C.; Dr. Keary, Woodford; M. J. Kelly, Belfast; P. J. Kelly, Chairman Westport Board of Guardians; Valentine Kilbride, Solicitor; Wm. Lynch, Solicitor; Murtagh McCann, Lurgan; John McDonnell, P.L.G.; John McGinn; Edward McGrane, Dundrum; James H. McGrane; William McGrath; C. S. M'Guinness; Surgeon Murray MacKenzie, R.N.; P. M'Manus, Cavan; Thomas P. M'Quaid; J. C. M'Walter, L.P.S.I.; John J. Meldon, Solicitor; James Molony; Thomas Monahan; Martin Morris; David Murphy; M. M. Murphy, Solicitor, Kilkenny; Patrick O'Brien; Charles O'Connell, B.L.; John O'Neill; Timothy O'Sullivan; S. P. Preston; William E. Reigh; John C. Rooney; William Taaffe, Ardee; George J. Wake, Lurgan; Peter Ward; Alfred Webb, Dublin; William Whiteside.

Delegations and Members of Public Boards, Delegates from the Branches of the Federation, Parishes, and Societies in Ireland.

ANTRIM.

BOARDS OF GUARDIANS: BALLYMENA—Gerald S. M'Camphill, J.P.; James Neeson. BALLYCASTLE—John M'Canghlan, J.P., vice-chairman; E. F. M'Cambridge, J.P.; J. P. O'Kane. BALLYMONEY—John Boyd, J.P.
BRANCHES I.N.F.: BELFAST—John J. Donovan, William Downey, John Rooney, James Boyle. BALLYMONEY—James O'Kane, sen., George M'Fall, Daniel Dempsey.
BELFAST YOUNG IRELAND SOCIETY—Patrick Flanagan, Francis Blair, T. J. Hanna.
LIBERAL AND NATIONAL UNION OF ULSTER—Joseph M'Cauley, J.P., solicitor; Rev. Richard Lyttle, Dr. Logan.
A.O.H.B. OF ERIN—John Crilly.

ARMAGH.

TOWN COMMISSIONERS, KEADY—Michael Smith, chairman; John Nugent, P. Reynolds.
BOARD OF GUARDIANS, ARMAGH—Michael Kelly.
BRANCHES I.N.F.: BLACKWATERTOWN—Henry Lennon, Felix Fox, James Garvey. ARMAGH—Jas. Donnelly, James M'Mahon, Michael Garvey. CAMLOUGH—Very Rev. C. Quinn, P.P., V.F.; Rev. C. M'Donnell, C.C.; James O'Hare, J.P., P.L.G.; James Aikyn, J.P.; L. Donnelly, P.L.G.; Rev. Michael J. Quinn, C.C. COLLEGELAND—Henry Toal, Huge M'Cluskey, Felix O'Leary. JONESBORO' AND DROMINTEE—Michael P. Rice, Michael O'Hare, Thomas O'Rourke. LURGAN, ARTHUR DONNELLY—Andrew Donnelly, James M'Mullan, Henry, M'Larnon. DERRYMACASH—John C. O'Reilly, James Blayney, Henry M'Geown. LOUGHGILLY—John J. M'Parland, John M'Parland, James Kenny. KEADY—James M'Kennedy, James Mone, Thomas Kelly.

CARLOW.

TOWN COMMISSIONERS, CARLOW—Michael Molloy.
BOARD OF GUARDIANS, CARLOW—Laurence M'Loughlin, Charles F. M'Nally, J.P.
BRANCH I.N.F., CARLOW—Michael Molloy, T.C.; Patrick J. Conlon, J. Kelly.

CAVAN.

TOWN COMMISSIONERS: CAVAN—Francis O'Reilly, Bernard Brady, James Galligan, Daniel Reilly, Patrick Ganney, John M'Carran, James Gallagher. COOTEHILL—Andrew Smith. BELTURBET—F. Boland, chairman; P. Farley, P. Fitzpatrick, E. Gleeson, and W. Gillick.
BOARDS OF GUARDIANS: CAVAN—J. Jones, Bernard O'Connor, F. Maguire, James Gilchreest, Luke Lee. COOTEHILL—John O'Reilly. BAWNBOY—Bernard Kean, Hugh Reynolds, Thomas M'Govern, J. Phillips.
BRANCHES I.N.F.: DRUNG—Patrick Reilly, Francis Reilly. VIRGINIA—John Tierney, J.P.; Thomas M'Cabe, John M'Evoy. MULLAHOVAN AND LOUGHDUFF—Felix M'Manus, Edward O'Reilly.

LIST OF DELEGATES.

CLARE.

TOWN COMMISSIONERS: ENNIS—M. S. Horan, Michael A. Scanlon. KILRUSH—Joseph Finnucane, James Clancy.
BOARDS OF GUARDIANS: KILDYSART—N. Studdart Gibson, vice-chairman. KILRUSH—John Mulqueen. ENNISTYMON—Michael Leydon, Patrick Vaughan.
BRANCHES I.N.F.: ENNISTYMON—John Cassidy, Mathew Curran, Michael O'Brien. KILRUSH—James Kelly, John Egan. OGONNELLOE—Dominick Stuart, hon. secretary; Michael Slattery, vice-president; John Corbett, P.L.G. FEAKLE—Patrick M'Mahon, Michael Hogan, Thady Kelly. MILTOWNMALBAY—Denis O'Loughlin. BODYKE AND TOMGREANY—Michael Brady, J.P.; Thomas Scanlon, Denis Tuohy. KILLIMER AND KNOCKERRA—John Hassett, J.P.; Michael Behan, P.L.G.; Thomas Talty. KILLALOE—Corney Hayes, Patrick Sheehan, Michael M'Keogh, Michael Scanlan.
PARISHES: KILBALLYOWEN—Cornelius Haugh. KILDIMO—John Cahill. KILLOKENNEDY—John Gunning.—BRADFORD—P. Vaughan.

CORK.

CORPORATION, CITY OF CORK—Alderman Fitzgerald, Alderman Martin Flavin, J.P.; William Kinmonth, Jeremiah Ahern, John T. O'Donnell.
TOWN COMMISSIONERS: BANDON—Thomas Scanlan, chairman; J. Burke. MIDLETON—Richard Fitzgerald, chairman; J. O'Brien. MALLOW—Michael Nunan, chairman; Cornelius Buckley, J. Cronin, Stephen O'Dwyer, J.P.; John Golden. YOUGHAL—Richard Carey, J.P., chairman; John Condon, T.C.; James Lynch, T.C.; William Hodnett, solicitor. CLONAKILTY—Daniel O'Leary, chairman. FERMOY—Edward Byrne, J.P. QUEENSTOWN—William Meehan, Timothy Murray, J. H. Campbell. SKIBBEREEN—John Murphy.
BALTIMORE AND SKIBBEREEN HARBOUR BOARDS—Patrick Sheehy.
BOARDS OF GUARDIANS: BANDON—Edward Graigner, John Harris, Edward M'Carthy, John Kelly. MILLSTREET—J. J. Corkerry, chairman; Bryan MacSwyney, J.P.; Patrick O'Callagan. CORK—P. J. Scannell, Thomas Fuller, Patrick O'Connor, J. M'Carthy Barry, J. J. Humphreys, P. O'Neill, Michael Murphy. MIDLETON—Martin Reardon, chairman; T. J. Burke, Michael Buckley, J.P. MALLOW—James Byrne, deputy vice-chairman; Cornelius O'Callaghan, D. J. O'Callaghan, Patrick Vaughan, Thomas Barry. MACROOM—Michael Healy, J.P.; Daniel M'Carthy, John Moynihan. MITCHELSTOWN—P. Rayleigh, J.P., chairman; Thomas Drake, J.P. YOUGHAL—Thomas V. Farrell, J.P., chairman; Peter Keefe, R. R. Russell, Patrick Linehan. DUNMANWAY—Michael Connolly, deputy vice-chairman; T. M. Kearney, Jerome Mahoney, Cornelius Reardon. William Cotter, Daniel M'Carthy, C. O'Driscoll. SCHULL—Edward Roycroft, J.P., chairman; T. Coghlan, deputy vice-chairman; John Kelly. KANTURK—Buckley Daly, chairman; John Linehan, deputy vice-chairman; Charles C. Daly, Patrick Lane. FERMOY—D. Verling, J. Maye, A. Heskin, G. Baylor, J. P. Collins. KINSALE—Jeremiah Bowen. SKIBBEREEN—Daniel M'Carthy, deputy vice-chairman; D. Burke.

BRANCHES I.N.F.: BALLYVOURNEY—Daniel Lynch, M.D., J.P.; Cornelius Lynch, Timothy Twomey. BANDON—Thomas Dinneen, P. J. M'Carthy, solicitor; Thomas Cummins. DUNMANWAY—James H. Purcell, solicitor; Florence Cronley, James M'Carthy. CORK CITY—Thomas Crosbie, proprietor *Cork Examiner*; Michael Murphy, solicitor; Daniel Horgan, John O'Connor, Michael Ryan, Cornelius Millard, Edmund Russell, William Desmond. KILBRIN—Timothy Dennehy, P.L.G.; John Riordan. BALLINDANGAN—Patrick Hanly, James O'Riordan, John O'Keeffe. DONERAILE—John O'Connor. KANTURK—Francis J. Burton, D. D. Mahony, Thomas Lenehan. MIDLETON—William Cogan, J.P.; Michael Lynch, T.C.; William Moore. MALLOW—P. R. Fitzgibbon, solicitor; Patrick Donovan, Denis Lynch, T.C. CASTLELYONS—Garrett Verling, E. P. Kent, Cornelius Ronan. DRUMTARIFFE—Bryan M'Sweeney, J.P.; Charles Daly, P.L.G.; J. J. Hanlon, M. J. Casey. KILLAVULLEN—William Stackpoole. MITCHELSTOWN—Very Reverend Dean O'Regan, P.P., V.G.; Thomas O'Brien, Michael Cusack. CLONAKILTY—Daniel O'Leary, J.P., chairman, Town Commissioners; Dr. O'Cleary, Stephen O'Brien, solicitor. AGHADA—Edmond Rohan, William Hegarty. DUNGOURNEY AND MOGEELY—J. J. Beechinor, P.L.G. FREEMOUNT—Rev. T. Twomey, Simon J. Barry, V.C.; John Foley. SKIBBEREEN—Rev. T. Kearney, Adm.; Joseph J. Healy, solicitor. BANTRY—William Cotter, P.L.G.; Daniel Donovan, P.L.G.
PARISHES: CAHERAGH—Rev. Thomas Palmer, P.P.; Jeremiah Sweeney, Patrick Hayes, Patrick M'Carthy. NEWCESTON—James Daly, J.P. ENNISKEEN—Patrick Foley. BALLINASCARTHY—Daniel Nyhan, T. White. LEAP—Dr. M. O'Driscoll, J.P.; B. Cullinane, J.P. WHITECHURCH—Denis Hegarty, J.P. INNISHANNON—William Curtin. DOUGLAS—John Collins. BALLYCLOUGH—W. Fitzgerald. BLARNEY—John (Dan) Coleman; Mr. Cornelius Coakley attended from Agheena parish, Cork. LISGOOLD—Edmond Stack. BALLYHOOLY—J. W. Walsh. CASTLEMARTYR AND DUNGOWNEY—J. J. Beechinor, P.L.G. BALLINHASSIG—Peter O'Neill, P.L.G.; James P. Murphy. KILWORTH—John Hanlon.
CORK NATIONAL SOCIETY—Thomas Lynch, George Crosbie, B.L.; P. D. O'Brien, J.P.; Thomas Dooley, Thomas Goggin.

DONEGAL.

BALLYSHANNON TOWN COMMISSIONERS—James Moohan.
BOARDS OF GUARDIANS: MILFORD—Robert A. Whyte, J. A. Diamond STRANORLAR—Francis Callaghan, deputy vice-chairman; Tague M'Gee, J.P.; Patrick M'Dermott, J.P. DONEGAL—Hugh M'Ginty, William M'Devitt, Michael Dunnion. GLENTIES—John O'Donnell, J.P.; John Sweeney, John Kilbride. BALLYSHANNON—P. J. Fergas, chairman; Michael Cassidy, J.P., vice-chairman; James M'Gurran, deputy vice-chairman. INNISHOWEN—Michael White, vice-chairman; Bernard Hannigan, J.P.
BRANCHES, I.N.F.: BALLYSHANNON (BERNARD KELLY)—Bernard Reynolds, John M'Cartney, Myles Sweeney. PETTIGO—Francis Britton, J.P.; John M'Caffrey, James Britton. DONEGAL (RED HUGH O'DONNELL)—Rev. C. Cassidy, C.C.; Hugh Gallagher, J.P.;

LIST OF DELEGATES.

Patrick Gallagher. BALLYBOFEY AND STRANORLAR—James Boyle, James Connolly, Owen Sheil. BALLYSHANNON (HUGH TUTHILL)—James Gavigan, James Burns, T. J. M'Fadden. INVER—William M'Devitt, P.L.G.; Robert Meehan, Rev. P. M'Caffrey, Adm.

DOWN.

TOWN COMMISSIONERS: NEWRY—Patrick Connolly, M. J. M'Cartan, Mathew J. Dowdall, James Rice. BANBRIDGE—Bernard M'Givern.
BOARDS OF GUARDIANS: NEWRY—John O'Hare, vice-chairman; John Lowry, William Ronan, J.P.; Edward Lowry, J.P.; Samuel M'Court, Daniel Maginn, Laurence M'Court, Michael M'Cartan, J.P. (Governor Co. Down Asylum); John Campbell. BANBRIDGE—James Rooney, James Maguire, J.P. NEWTOWNARDS—R. B. Caughey.
BRANCHES I.N.F.: BALLYHOLLAND AND GRINAN—Hugh M'Nally, John Ryan, Terence M'Laughlin. BANBRIDGE—John S. Farrell, solicitor; John Flanigan, Peter M'Givern. BARNMEEN—H. Mallon. BURRAN—James Byrne, James Woods. John M'Grath. HILLTOWN—Joseph M'Polin, Andrew Murphy, James M'Aleavey, J. T. M'Laughlin, J.P.; Edward Lowry, J.P. KILCOO—John Magee, Peter Fitzpatrick, Peter M'Polin. MAYOBRIDGE—James Loughran, John O'Hare, Bernard Kelly, John Downey. WARRENPOINT—William J. M'Cornish, Michael Higgins. TULLYLISH AND GILFORD—Henry M'Inerney, Hugh Molloy. DOWNPATRICK—D. M'Cartan, solicitor; Philip M'Cartan. NEWRY—James Rice, T.C.
PARISHES: ANNACLONE—Dr. Fegan. DONAGHMORE—Rev. F. M'Loughlin, P.P.; John M'Avoy.
A. O. H., BOARD OF ERIN—P. M'Gennis.

DUBLIN.

DUBLIN CORPORATION—Alderman R. Toole.
BOARDS OF GUARDIANS: NORTH DUBLIN—John M'Donnell, J.P. BALROTHERY—P. M'Cabe, James Clinton.
BRANCHES I.N.F.: BLACKROCK—T. M'Grath, Mathew A. Lazenby, John Nugent, hon. sec. CLONDALKIN—Michael Coghlan, Christopher Hanlon, Bernard Dowd. DRUMCONDRA—Michael F. Mooney, Oliver J. O'Connor, Patrick M'Ardle. RATHMINES AND HAROLD'S CROSS—Arthur Hanlon, Patrick Cumming, John M'Donnell. BALBRIGGAN—James Tolan, John Knox, Richard M'Cabe. SAGGART, RATHCOOL AND NEWCASTLE—John M'Cann, Joseph Coonan, Peter Daly. ARRAN QUAY WARD—Denis Moran, Francis Gibney, John J. Richmond. ST. PATRICK'S—William O'Brien, — Byrne, E. Brennan.
EDMUND BURKE LITERARY AND DEBATING SOCIETY—H. J. M'Cann, president; Frederick Ryan, auditor.
FAWCETT ASSOCIATION, DUBLIN BRANCH—John T. Kelly.

FERMANAGH.

ENNISKILLEN TOWN COMMISSIONERS—Hugh R. Lindsay, chairman; J. M'Govern, Patrick Crumley, J.P.
BOARDS OF GUARDIANS: ENNISKILLEN—Francis Maguire, — M'Quaid, Arthur Duggan, J.P. LISNASKEA—James Mulligan, J.P.; Thomas Mortimer. IRVINESTOWN—James Mulhern, — Teague.

BRANCHES I.N.F.: ARNEY—Philip M'Gloney, James Curran, Francis Keenan. ENNISKILLEN—Edward Meagher, Joseph Cox, Bernard Coyle. AUGHALURCHER—Edward Morris Flanagan, Peter Crudden. NEWTOWNBUTLER—Michael Harte, James M'Kiernan, A. Maguire. IRVINESTOWN AND WHITEHALL—John Lee, Patrick O'Reilly, John Woods.

A. O. H., BOARD OF ERIN—James M'Kiernan, Charles Curry, Luke Drum, James Malone.

GALWAY.

TOWN COMMISSIONERS: GALWAY—Francis Lydon. BALLINASLOE—John Cogavin. TUAM—Patrick Culkin, chairman; John M'Philphin, John G. Glynn, John Patterson, Patrick Glynn.

BOARDS OF GUARDIANS: LOUGHREA—Michael Clasby, Ulick Bourke, Stephen Ruane. GORT—John Burke. GLENAMADDY—J. Keavney, A. Keenan, Martin Freeney. WOODFORD—J. Blake. PORTUMNA—J. P. Page. TUAM—Patrick Glynn, Francis Tanman. BALLINASLOE—Timothy O'Connell, William Rorke. GALWAY—Martin Cunningham, A. G. Scott. OUGHTERARD—Patrick Conroy. CLIFDEN—Patrick O'Hara. MOUNTBELLEW—James Naughton, Thomas Graigner.

BRANCHES I.N.F.: TUAM—Thomas Flately, T.C.; P. Lyons, P.L.G.; Francis Maher. BALLINASLOE—W. J. Coselloe, John Egan, John Donovan, James Kilmartin. TIERNASCRA—James Gibbons, William Hogan, John Nevin. GALWAY—Very Rev. P. Dooley, P.P.; Rev. Father Whelan, J. C. M'Donnell. ATHENRY—P. P. Broderick, John Henehan, John Connolly, T. G. Finnerty, J. Sweeny. LOUGHREA—John Sweeny, T.C.; Patrick Connolly, T.C.; Thomas Mulkern, W. J. Duffy, Edward O'Dea. WOODFORD—Dr. Keary, F. Roche, J. Roche, M.P.

PARISHES: DUNMORE—Thomas Fahy. GLENAMADY—Martin B. Collins. HEADFORD—William Kyne.

KERRY.

TRALEE TOWN COMMISSIONERS—M. J. Kelleher, J.P.; Jeremiah O'Keeffe, John O'Donnell, Thomas Slattery, John O'Connor.

BOARDS OF GUARDIANS: KENMARE—David Doran, vice-chairman; John Gain, deputy vice-chairman; P. J. O'Sullivan. LISTOWEL—M. J. Nolan, J.P.; William Fitzgerald, E. J. Stack, J.P.; F. Fitzgerald, J.P. TRALEE—Jeremiah Roche, chairman; Thomas Kearney, J. K. O'Connor, Eugene O'Connor, John O'Donnell, M. M'Mahon, J.P.; F. O'Sullivan, J.P.; J. Leonard, J.P.; T. Galvin, J.P.; George Rice.

BRANCHES I.N.F.: TRALEE—St. J. H. Donovan, J.P., T.C.; Thomas O'Regan, T.C.; T. J. Healy. GLENFLESK AND BARRADUFF—Daniel Lynch, Denis Lynch, Michael Doherty. BALLYLONGFORD—James Brassil, Patrick Ahern, Patrick Stack. DINGLE—Timothy M. O'Flaherty, Michael T. Moriarty. KENMARE—Daniel J. O'Sullivan, Laurence Egan, Timothy J. O'Sullivan. KILLARNEY—Daniel O'Shea, James O'Leary, Daniel J. O'Connor.

PARISHES: LISTOWEL—Jeremiah Kennelly. ASDEE—Nicholas Mulvihill. FOSSA—Daniel D. Sheehan.

BALLYLONGFORD YOUNG IRELAND SOCIETY—Joseph N. O'Sullivan, John Farrell.
LISTOWEL YOUNG IRELAND SOCIETY—M. J. Flavin, M.P.; J. F. Cronin.

KILDARE.

TOWN COMMISSIONERS: ATHY—P. J. Murphy, Thomas Hickey. NAAS —Edward Byrne.
BOARDS OF GUARDIANS: NAAS—Edward Fenlon, chairman; Patrick Driver, Bartle Kelly, Peter Healy, J. P. Moore, J.P.; Denis Nolan, Patrick Dunne, Thomas Walshe. ATHY—Michael Treacy, Hugh Nolan, James Julian, Michael Hickey, John M'Loughlin, W. Hughes.
BRANCHES I.N.F.: ALLEN—John Cribbin, Daniel Healy, J. Morrin. CASTLEDERMOTT—Thomas Byrne, John Delany, Michael J. Aylmer. NARRAGHMORE—Jeremiah Kenna, Peter Cullen, Andrew Costello. NEWBRIDGE—Patrick Flood, Thomas Pringle, M. O'Shaughnessy. SUNCROFT—James Kelly, J.P.; James Morrin, Nicholas Cullen. NURNEY—Thomas O'Beirne. ATHY—Patrick Knowles, David Walsh, Stephen O'Brien. NAAS—William Staples, Patrick Cunningham, John Grehan, James Hyland, P. J. Doyle. CARAGH AND PROSPEROUS —Edward Ennis, Edward Fitzharris, William Tierney. TWOMILE- BORRIS—Joseph O'Connor, James Brennan, Henry Dillon.
MILTOWN PARISH—John Tiernan.

KILKENNY.

CORPORATION, CITY OF KILKENNY—Major P. O'Leary, Mayor; Alder- man Thomas Cantwell, Alderman Murphy, M. Ring.
CALLAN TOWN COMMISSIONERS—James Pollard.
BOARDS OF GUARDIANS: CALLAN—James Power, chairman; W. F. Mullally, J.P.; M. Gleeson, Patrick Fennelly, V.C.; James Cahill, J.P.; Philip Lynch. URLINGFORD—William De Courcey, chairman; Arthur Cavanagh, R. Rafter, Maurice Kelly. CASTLECOMER—Michael Brennan, John Rowe, Jeffrey Brennan. THOMASTOWN—Michael Doyle, jun., chairman; Michael Hogan, vice-chairman.
BRANCHES I.N.F.: WINDGAP—John Comerford, James Landy, Edward Cornan. JOHNSTOWN AND CROSSPATRICK—Joseph Delany, Martin Brennan, John Broderick, Robert Rafter, P.L.G.; J. Phelan, P.L.G. THOMASTOWN—Michael Hogan, Peter Carron, Thomas Whelan. SLIEVERUE—Michael Rock, Patrick Grant. MUCKALEE—Charles Copley, Michael Moran, Henry Sherman, Samuel Copley. ST. JOHN'S, KILKENNY—D. Guilfoyle, John Barrett, P.L.G.; J. Morrissey, P.L.G.
GALMOY PARISH—Arthur Kavanagh, P.L.G.; Richard Gannon.

KING'S COUNTY.

TOWN COMMISSIONERS: BIRR—J. C. Moran. TULLAMORE—Joseph Ryan, Henry Egan.
BOARDS OF GUARDIANS: PARSONSTOWN—Michael Dooley, deputy vice- chairman; John Powell. TULLAMORE—Richard Kelly.
EDENDERRY BRANCH I.N.F.—Thomas Groome, James Byrne.
PARISHES: BALLINAHOWN—Robert Dalton, P.L.G. MILLANE—Peter Seahill, P.L.G.

LEITRIM.

BOARDS OF GUARDIANS: CARRICK-ON-SHANNON—John Fox, deputy vice-chairman; Peter Caslin, James Pakenham, J.P.; Thomas Beirne, Thomas Duignam, J.P. MOHILL—Robert P. Wallace, Michael Murphy. MANORHAMILTON—John Dolan, chairman; Thomas Fallon, deputy vice-chairman; M. Devaney, Myles Woods, John M'Guinness, John Meehan, Patrick Clancy.

BRANCHES I.N.F.: BORNACOOLA—Patrick M'Gushin, Michael Canning. DRUMSHAMBO—Francis Conway, James Cooney. DRUMSNA—Thomas W. Daly, Patrick M'Nabola, Francis Daly. LOWER DRUMREILLY—Thomas M'Govern, Laurence Dolan, Patrick Prior. BALLINAGLERAGH—Rev. Thomas M'Gauran, P.P.; James J. Flynn. KILTUBRID—Thomas Beirne, Michael Judge. MOHILL—John M. Mulligan, James Reilly. GLENFARNE—John Keany, president. DRUMKEERIN—T. Ward, P.L.G.; P. Keaveney. ROSSINVER—Myles M'Keown. MANORHAMILTON—James Synott, jun. DRUMLEASE—John J. Rorke. KILLINUMERY—John Kelly, Patrick Kaveney. KILLASNET—Patrick Lea, Patrick Fox (Frank), M. Devaney, P.L.G. FENAGH—Rev. D. Gray, P.P.; Bernard Hetherton.

LIMERICK.

CORPORATION, CITY OF LIMERICK—Alderman Stephen O'Mara, P. E. Bourke, J.P.; Patrick O'Neill, Michael Spain, Patrick Tracey.

RATHKEALE TOWN COMMISSIONERS—John Fremen, John Ambrose.

BOARDS OF GUARDIANS: LIMERICK—Thomas B. Mitchell, vice-chairman; T. Lane, Edmund M. Kirby, R. T. O'Kennedy, J.P.; Patrick Connolly. RATHKEALE—Daniel O'Brien, James O'Connor, P. Fitzsimons. KILMALLOCK—J. Ryan, J.P.; James Lyons, E. Barry. CROOM—Michael O'Brien. NEWCASTLE WEST—D. O'Leary Hannigan, J.P.

BRANCHES I.N.F.: ABBEYFEALE—Rev. W. Casey, P.P.; M. Moloney, P.L.G.; George Barry, William O'Sullivan, John H. Banaher. ATHEA—John M. White, Patrick Griffin, T. D. Danaher. GRANGE—D. S. O'Connell, N. J. Hayes. KILTEALY—David O'Meara, David Barry, John O'Mahony. RATHKEALE—John Burke, Patrick Barrett, Timothy Cusack, T.C.; J. H. Danaher. LIMERICK CITY—J. H. Roche, J. J. Ryan, E. J. Long. FEDAMORE—W. J. Clancy, Michael Fielly, Henry Casey. KILFINANE—James Galligan, John Doherty, David J. Condon. STONEHALL—Timothy Foley, Michael Madigan. HERBERTSTOWN—Michael B. Moroney, John Condon, Thomas J. Moroney. BALLYHAHILL—Daniel M'Coy, P.L.G.; P. Danagher, R. Fitzgerald. MURROE AND BOHER—Very Rev. Michael Ryan, P.P., V.F.; William Fitzgerald, P.L.G.; Bryan Kennedy, John J. Ryan, Daniel Ryan, John O'Meara, John Ryan, John Humphreys, CAPPAMORE—Patrick Duggan, P.L.G.; Martin Ryan, T. Corboy, D. M. English. PALLASGREEN—Michael Cunningham, PL.G.; Patrick Ryan, John M'Grith. PATRICKSWELL AND BALLYBROWN—Michael Mulqueen, James Dundon, John Costello. OOLA—Daniel Ryan, P.L.G.; Timothy Hayes, Morgan Hayes. ANGLESBORO'—Rev. T. Canty, C.C.; John English, jun.; Jeremiah O'Donnell. HOSPITAL—Very Rev. Canon Scully, P.P.; Rev. Hugh Mockler,

LIST OF DELEGATES.

Michael O'Donnell, James Hannon. GLIN—Francis Fitzgerald, J.P.; David Riddle, P.L.G. ROCKHILL AND BRUREE—Thomas Potter, Patrick Horgan, Jeremiah Donworth. ASKEATON—Michael Feheny, John Lynch, Thomas Ryan. SHANAGOLDEN—David O'Brien, Patrick Madigan, Maurice Fitzgibbon DOON—John Ryan, Patrick Kilbride, James Ryan. KNOCKANY—John Casey, Edmond Byrnes, John O'Kane.
TEMPLEGLANTINE PARISH—Michael Wren.

LONDONDERRY.

MAGHERAFELT BOARD OF GUARDIANS—Felix Ferran, J.P.; Charles Rogers, J.P.; James Shivers.
BRANCHES I.N.F.: BELLAGHY—Charles Agnew, Joseph Davison, John Kearney. LISSAN—T. Crilly, J.P.; John Hagan, Felix M'Cracken. MAGHERA—Daniel Lagan, J. M'Kenna, M. M'Closker. MAGHERAFELT—Roger Convery, Thomas Larkin, John Kane. MONEYMORE (THOMAS SEXTON)—Henry Devlin, J.P.; F. Hughes, Patrick Devlin. BALLINASCREEN—Michael O'Kane, Joseph D. Kelly, Bernard Rogers. SWATERAGH—Michael Doherty, J. M'Keefry. DERRY (M'CARTHY)—Daniel M'Bride, James M'Gowan, Daniel Gallivan.

LONGFORD.

TOWN COMMISSIONERS: LONGFORD—Matthew Farrell, John Mathews, Joseph Maguire. GRANARD—Francis Reilly, Chairman.
BOARDS OF GUARDIANS: LONGFORD—Michael Kiernan, Thomas Duffy, William Farrell. GRANARD—John Kenny, Thomas Reilly, George Walker. BALLYMAHON—Joseph Flood.
BRANCHES I.N.F.: CLONBRONEY—James O'Neill, John Connolly, P. Duffy. DRUMLISH AND BALLINAMUCK—Patrick Dervine, J. Reynolds, Patrick Masterson. LONGFORD—Joseph Wilson, Robert Noud, Owen Victory. GRANARD—Thomas Dawson, Owen Carney, P.L.G.; Richard Harte. CLONGUISH—William Prunty, Michael Drake.
PARISHES: DROMARD—P. Duignan, Matthew Gray. CLOUGH—Mr. Gerety.
RATHCLINE GAELIC CLUB.—John Rhatigan.

LOUTH.

CORPORATION, CITY OF DROGHEDA—Peter Lynch, Mayor; Alderman Simon Jordan, T. Tallon, John Slevin, Thomas Callan, J. Drew, John Dolan, William T. Skeffington.
HIGH SHERIFF OF DROGHEDA—Francis Gogarty, T.C.
DROGHEDA HARBOUR BOARD.—Joseph Connolly, R.N.; R. Nulty, James P. Kelly.
BOARDS OF GUARDIANS: DROGHEDA—John Feehan, Patrick Reddy, L. Moore, F. Smith. DUNDALK—M. O'Meara, P. Hughes. ARDEE—Joseph Dolan.
BRANCHES I.N.F.: COLLON—John Drumgoole, Matthew Downey, Bernard Cook. DROGHEDA—M. A. Casey, T. H. Clancy, Patrick M'Quail. MONASTERBOICE—James Dolan, James M'Donnell, John Mullen. INNISKEEN—James Gartlan, James Callan. SANDPIT—Laurence M'Keown, Patrick Devin, L. Finn. REAGHSTOWN AND TALLANSTOWN—Thomas Ward, James M'Keever.

PARISHES: KNOCKBRIDGE—N. B. King, P.L.G. MORNINGTON AND BETTYSTOWN—David Aherne. KILLANY—James Green.
IRISH NATIONAL FORESTERS (BRANCH T. P. GILL, No. 159).—James Gray, C.R.; Patrick Waters, secretary; John Blake.

MAYO.

TOWN COMMISSIONERS: WESTPORT—Michael Browne, William Scott, Patrick Toole. CASTLEBAR—James Gill.
BOARDS OF GUARDIANS: SWINFORD—M. C. Henry, chairman; J. Irwin, vice-chairman; Francis Kean, J.P.; John Davitt, Mark Waldron, Francis Davitt, W. J. Waldron, Thomas Roughneen. WESTPORT—John Flannery, John Curran, John Walsh, A. O'Malley, Thomas Joyce, William Joyce. FOXFORD—T. E. Gallagher. CASTLEBAR—Patrick Vahey, Chairman; William O'Malley. CLAREMORRIS—M. M. Waldron, vice-chairman.
BRANCHES I.N.F.: ACHILL—Rev. J. P. Connolly, P.P.; Anthony Mullery, Joseph Tully, Rev. M. Hennelly, C.C. BALLYHAUNIS—Rev. J. R. Canning, P.P.; Michael Delaney, P.L.G.; James Grealy. KILTIMAGH—M. O'Donnell, J.P.; Thomas Roughan, P.L.G.; Charles Burke, Thomas Gallagher, Miss Amy Mander. KNOCK—James Connell, Martin M'Loughlin, Francis Burke. MIDFIELD—John Davitt. KILLASSER—Rev. J. M'Keon, C.C.; Patrick Gallagher, P.L.G.; Patrick M'Henry. NEWPORT—William Chambers, John M'Govern. BEKAN—Rev. B. G. Freely, P.P.; Martin Healy, Thomas Connell. CLOGHER—Dr. Ambrose, M.P.; William Doris, John O'Donnell. SWINFORD—P. M. Henry. AUGHAMORE—William J. Waldron. Darby Glavy, Martin Henry. KILMEENA AND KILMACLASSER—Rev. Father Healy, Adm.; Austin Gibbons, John O'Donnell, Wm. Rice. BALLAGHADEREEN—Thomas Spelman, John Casey, B. M'Dermott, J. P. Jordan, James Cawley. TIERNAUR—John Curran, P.L.G.; Hugh Moran. BALLA—Thomas Reilly, Malachy Henegan. CASTLEBAR—P. Gillespie, Dr. Jordan, James Daly. KILMOVEE—Very Rev. Canon O'Hara, John Irwin, P.L.G.; B. Flannery, Patrick Cox, John Reid.
LOUISBURGH PARISH—Thomas Lyons, P.L.G.

MEATH.

TOWN COMMISSIONERS: NAVAN—Patrick Sheridan. KELLS—John S. Kelly.
BOARDS OF GUARDIANS: NAVAN—Francis Sheridan, chairman; Lawrence Rowan, vice-chairman; Joseph Keappock. KELLS—Patrick Farrelly, T. P. M'Kenna. TRIM—Joseph Quirke. OLDCASTLE—James Tuite, John Gilsenan, Patrick Gaynor.
BRANCHES I.N.F.: KILCLOONE—John Leonard, William Moore, Thomas Dillon. COOLE—Michael Connolly, Patrick Kerrigan, John Jiles. SLANE—Joseph Maken, J.P.; John M'Donough, Thomas Wall. STAMULLEN AND JULIANSTOWN—Richard Drew, James Bagnal, Edward F. Malone. DUNSHAUGHLIN—L. T. Canning, A. Mahon, John M'Entee.

MONAGHAN.

TOWN COMMISSIONERS: CARRICKMACROSS—James Daly, M.P., chairman; Thomas Phelan, J.P.; J. J. Downs, J.P.; Anthony Clinton, Patrick M'Nally, James Keenan, Owen J. Smith, Peter Dwyer, Owen Sherry. BALLYBAY—Bernard M'Kenna, chairman; S. P. Smyth, Patrick Connolly, James Hanratty.

BOARDS OF GUARDIANS: MONAGHAN—Edward Maguire, F. Hughes. CLONES—Edward P. Murray, Jason Graham. CASTLEBLAYNEY—Francis Connolly, J.P.; James Ward, James Duffy, John Duffy. CARRICKMACROSS—Thomas Phelan, J.P., chairman; Peter Dwyer, James Daly, J.P.

BRANCHES I.N.F.: CORDUFF—Peter Kelaghan, James Hand, James O'Connor, Francis O'Connor. CLONES—Edward Brady, Edward Moore, Hugh M'Donald, William M'Phillip, jun.; James M'Govern. MONAGHAN—D. C. Rushe, solicitor; James Moreton, William Ward. AGHABOY—Edward M'Phillips, Joseph Duffy, James Brady. CARRICKMACROSS—John D. M'Veigh, Richard Boyle, John Shankey. CLONTIBRET—James Mohan, Henry M'Adam, Patrick Brennan, Patrick M'Kernan, James Coleman, Patrick Walsh, Patrick Lavelle. CORCAGHAN AND THREEMILEHOUSE—Bernard Clerkin, J.P.; John M'Conville, Owen Kerans. TULLYCORBET—John Boylan, Thomas M'Carney, James Boylan. KILLEEVAN—Charles Toal, James Quigley. ERRIGAL TRUAGH—Peter M'Kenna, Owen M'Kenna, Arthur Ireland.

PARISHES: CURRIN—John Fitzpatrick. TYHOLLAND—James Hughes. MAGHERACLOONE—Patrick M'Gurke, P.L.G.; Owen Lamb. DONAGHMOYNE—John Daly.

CARRICKMACROSS TRADE AND LABOUR LEAGUE—John Martin, Patrick Coyle.

QUEEN'S COUNTY.

BOARDS OF GUARDIANS: MOUNTMELLICK—Michael Kinsella, P.L.G.; John Carroll. ABBEYLEIX—James M'Mahon, J.P., deputy vice-chairman; James M'Evoy.

BRANCHES I.N.F.: KILLASMEESTIA, KNOCKAROO, AND BORRIS-IN-OSSORY—Thomas Lowery, J.P.; Patrick Kavanagh, Richard M'Evoy. BALLYADAMS AND WOLFHILL—Thomas Breen, John Healy, Edward Whelan. KYLE—Richard Moloney, Denis Egan, Thomas Delany. KNOCK—Michael Brennan, Thomas Kealey. CAMROSS—Patrick Kelly, Thos. Costigan, Thomas Delaney. AGHABOE AND BALLACOLLA—John Carroll, P.L.G.; Laurence Commins, Joseph Hart. BALLYROAN—Patrick Campion, Denis Delaney, Michael Kehoe. DURROW AND CULLOHILL—John Clancy, P.L.G.; Daniel Bergin, P.L.G.; Michael Molloy, Very Rev. Canon Shortall, P.P., V.F.; Rev. E. Brennan, C.C. RAHEEN—William Parkinson, Patrick Parkinson, John Maher.

KILLESHIN PARISH—P. Brennan.

ROSCOMMON.

BOARDS OF GUARDIANS: STROKESTOWN—James Neary, J.P.; M. J. Hanly, J.P.; H. Owens. ROSCOMMON—William J. Hanly.

BRANCHES I.N.F.: DRUMLION—Michael Keegan. KILMORE—P J. Connellan, Patrick Beirne, Michael Doherty. TULSK—Bernard M'Gann, James Dufficy. TARMONBARRY—Michael Fallon, Thomas Geraghty, Patrick Igoe. BALLYOUGHTER AND KILMARGEL—Joseph Feely. CASTLEREA—James M'Loughlin, P. G. M'Conville, E. J. M'Dermott. CROSSNA—Patrick Regan, Edward Doyle, Patrick Connolly. KILTULLAGH—Patrick M'Cormack, Thomas Donelan, Michael Higgins, Michael Murphy, Michael Loftus. CARRIGEENROE—Michael M'Dermott, James J. Nangle.

SLIGO.

CORPORATION, CITY OF SLIGO—P. A. M'Hugh, M.P., Mayor; Owen Dolan, Thomas Hannery, John J. Keenan, J.P.; F. N. White, J.P.

BOARDS OF GUARDIANS: SLIGO—W. A. Mitchell, Patrick Kelly, James D. O'Brien, Patrick Flynn, Patrick Beirne. DROMORE WEST—Peter S. Kilgallen. TUBBERCURRY—P. J. O'Dowd, James N. Durkan.

BRANCHES I.N.F.: BALLYMOTE—James Hannon, J.P.; James Walsh, treasurer; John Gilmartin, assistant secretary; John J. M'Getrick. BUNNINADDEN—John O'Dowd, President; Thomas Hunt, P.L.G.; Michael Gormley. CLOONLOO—Patrick M'Manamy. MULLINABREENA—Denis Gallagher, Peter Foye, Neill O'Donnell. RIVERSTOWN—John H. Judge, Michael Brennan, Thomas M'Donagh. SLIGO—Martin Mulligan, Thomas Flanigan, Charles Sweeney. SOOEY—Patrick Clerkin, William Flanagan, John M'Loughlin. DRUMCLIFFE—Matthew Scanlan, Patrick Devine. MOYLOUGH—Patrick J. O'Dowd, P.L.G.; Michael J. O'Connor, John Davitt. BALLINTOGHER—E. A. Brennan, Thomas Mulrooney, James Gilmartin. KEASH—J. M. Cryan, Michael Gray, P.L.G. GEEVAGH—T. J. Nangle, James M'Donagh, James Waters, Michael Harte. HIGHWOOD—Peter Conlon, Michael M'Donagh. BALLYRUSH—John Walsh, James Lyons. COLLOONEY—P. D. Harte, D. P. Bree, Dominick Benson.

TIPPERARY.

CLONMEL CORPORATION—Alderman Nugent, Mayor; John F. O'Brien, Town Clerk; James White, John Magner, John F. Slattery.

TOWN COMMISSIONERS: NENAGH—James Hogan, Dr. H. F. Powell, J.P.; John J. Tumpane, J.P.; M. M'Mahon, Dr. W. Courtney, J.P.; P. J. O'Brien, F. R. Moloney, Town Clerk. FETHARD—M. Coffey, John Wall, Richard Maher. THURLES—Thomas Ryan. CARRICK-ON-SUIR—Edmund Burke. TEMPLEMORE—John Connolly, John Walsh, Thomas Morkan.

BOARDS OF GUARDIANS: CASHEL—James Walsh, chairman; Richard O'Connell, Timothy Fahy, William Maher, T. Cahill, Paul Cusack, Patrick Moclair. TIPPERARY—Patrick Duggan, Robert Gubbins, J.P.; John Kelly, D. Ryan. BORRISOKANE—James Cahalane, John Costello, J.P.; Michael Tuohy. THURLES—Thomas Collier, chairman; Patrick Finn, vice-chairman; Patrick Maher, T. Harney. CLOGHEEN—E. Riordan, chairman; P. O'Donnell, J.P.; P. Keating, Michael Ahern. ROSCREA—Michael Loughnan. M. Farrell, James Fitzpatrick, Patrick Egan. CARRICK-ON-SUIR—John Shea, William Britton, J.P.; William Hearn, J.P. NENAGH—Thomas Burke, Vice-chairman; Thomas O'Brien, deputy vice-chairman; Thomas M'Soley, Laurence Butler, William Carroll, Stephen Seymour, Patrick Kennedy, Thomas Ryan, J.P.

BRANCHES I.N.F.: ARDCRONEY—James Costello, J.P.; Denis Hogan, Thomas Doheny. BORRISOKANE—Michael Costello, Michael M'Kenna. CLERIHAN—John Moclair, Denis Hunt, William Slattery. CLOONEEN—Thomas O'Halloran, Robert H. O'Shea Wm. Tobin. CLOUGHJORDAN—Stephen Maher, William Moylan, Patrick M'Carthy. DUHILL—Patrick J. Walsh, Thomas Prendergast, Jeremiah Hanrahan. EGLISH—Patrick Ryan, Denis Meara, P.L.G.; Thomas Moylan. GRANGEMOCKLER—John P. Fox, James Cahill, Pierce Walsh. HOLYCROSS—Philip Dwyer, James Heffernan, John Ryan. KILRUANE—Michael Flannery, P.L.G.; George O'Leary, Cornelius Cleary. NEW INN AND KNOCKGRAFFIN—Andrew Hennessey, P.L.G.; John Smyth, John Smyth, Michael Purcell. MALLYCAHILL—Michael Dwyer, James Bannon, John Maher. SOLOGHEAD—James English, John M'Carthy, John Ryan, P.L.G. GRANGE—Thomas Keating, David Hickey, John Sullivan. TEMPLEDERRY—Thomas Burke, P.L.G.; James Harrington, Michael Donohoe. LORRA AND DORRHA—Thomas Haugh, J.P.; Michael O'Donohoe, J.P.; Michael Hogan, P.L.G. ARDFINAN AND BALLYBACON—John J. Lonergan. CAHIR—William O'Loghnan, P.L.G.; Patrick Hennessy, P.L.G.; Thomas Ryar. CASHEL—Michael Devitt, Philip Hickey, James Hanly. KILFEACLE—John Fogarty, James Butler, Thomas Cleary. MULLINAHONE—Thomas O'Brien, Patrick Egan, John Gorman. THURLES—Patrick Finn, Patrick Darmody, James K. Moloney. BALLYLOOBY—Patrick Keating, P.L.G. CLONMOULTY AND ROSSMORE—John Byrne, P.L.G.; Cornelius O'Dwyer, Daniel Byrne, John Murphy. MOYNE—James Maher, Richard Quinn, Michael Fogarty. KNOCKNAVELLA AND DONNASKEIGH—John M'Grath, Denis Kelly, William Ryan. KILSHEELAN—Michael O'Shea. KILCASH—Patrick S. Manning, John Quinlan, Patrick O'Shea. BOHERLAHAN—Michael Ryan, P.L.G; Richard Hennessy, P.L.G.; William O'Brien. FETHARD—James Smith, Thomas Frehy, Redmond Burke. KILLUSTY—Thomas Keane, Jerome Duggan, John Walsh. CARRICK-ON-SUIR—Thomas A. Lynch, solicitor; Richard Walsh (president Young Ireland Society), John Quirke. CASTLEINY—Michael O'Connell, John Sheppard. NEWCASTLE—David Hennessy. SHINRONE—Edward Enright. DROMBANE—Rev. M.O'Sullivan, C.C.; James O'Brien, Thomas Britt. GOLDEN—Rev. M. M'Donnell, P.P.; Patrick Merrick, J.P.; William Dalton. BANSHA AND KILMOYLER—Daniel Heffernan, William Googan, John Cullinan. TERRYGLASS—James Cahalan, P.L.G.; Michael Flannery. GOLDEN—Rev. M. M'Donnell, P.P.; Patrick Merrick, J.P.; William D'Alton. UPPERCHURCH—James Kennedy, J.P.; Timothy Ryan. KILLEA—Edward Fogarty, P. A. Ryan, Richard Ryan. CLONMEL—Jeremiah Condon, Thomas Fennessy, John Pike. TEMPLEMORE—F. J. Searson, Thomas Comerford, T.C.; Michael Harney. MOYCARKEY—John Molumby, William Fogarty, T. Maher, P. T. Hogan.

PARISHES: NEWTOWN—Patrick Toole. DROM—James Hoare. KILBARRON—Patrick Cleary. TERRYGLASS—Michael Flannery. TWOMILE BORRIS—Daniel Hayes, Thomas Fanning.

TIPPERARY AND LIMERICK FARMERS' SOCIETY—John Conway, Denis Quinlan, P.L.G.; J. R. M'Cormack.
KNOCKAVILLA FOOTBALL CLUB—Denis Tierney, James Madden, William Ryan.
BALLINGARRY GAELIC ATHLETIC ASSOCIATION—T. J. Power.
IRISH NATIONAL FORESTERS (CLONMEL)—John Cunningham, C.R.; Philip Bulhert, secretary.

TYRONE.

TOWN COMMISSIONERS: COOKSTOWN—Patrick Corr. STRABANE—John M'Crossan, John Torish.
BOARDS OF GUARDIANS: COOKSTOWN—Bernard Quin, J.P., deputy vice-chairman; M. M'Guirk, B. M'Guirk, Thomas Eccles. OMAGH—Charles Clarke. STRABANE—Patrick Boyle, M. M'Aleer. DUNGANNON—William Edwards, Joseph C. Falls, J.P.; P. M'Kean, J.P.; James Quinn. CLOGHER—Michael M'Elmeel.
BRANCHES I.N.F.: CLONOE—John Connolly, Patrick Corr, Joseph M'Guinness. FINTONA—Patrick Meehan, J.P.; James M'Quade, Daniel M'Nulty. CARRICKMORE—T. O'Neill. GREENCASTLE—James Donnelly, Hugh Keenan, Patrick Conway. KILLETER—Rev. J. O'Kane, P.P. LOWER BADONEY—Charles Clark, Hugh M'Cullough, Peter M'Cullough. ARBOE—Felix Taggart, Felix Laverty, Alphonsus Quin. OMAGH AND CAPPAGH—Hugh Campbell, Michael Mullen, Edward Phillips. POMEROY—John M'Guirk, Hugh Hagan, Francis M'Gurk. COALISLAND—John M'Cudden, James Toner. DONAGHMORE—John Campbell, David Loughnan, Henry O'Neill. DUNGANNON—John A. Quinn, James Rodgers, Joseph Madden. KILDRESS—Bernard Quin, J.P.; M. M'Gurk, B. M'Gurk. CLOGHER—Rev. J. Rapmond, C.C. CALEDON—James Wilson, Francis J. Cullen. COOKSTOWN—Michael Quinn, W. J. Harbinson, Patrick M'Larnon, T. J. Harbinson. STRABANE—John M'Crossan, T.C.; J. E. Maguire, B.A.
PARISHES: DROMORE—Patrick Muldoon. EGLISH—T. M'Connell.
KILSKEERY (CO. TYRONE)—Mr. Thomas Charleton, Michael Keenan, Jas. M'Quaid, P.L.G.; Edward Teague, P.L.G.
IRISH NATIONAL FORESTERS (BRANCH WILLIAM ORR, 189)—James Mayne, C.R.
A.O.H., BOARD OF ERIN—Michael Keenan, James Devlin.

WATERFORD.

CORPORATION, CITY OF WATERFORD.—Alderman W. J. Smith, Mayor; Alderman Richard Power, J.P.; John Curran, David M'Donald, Richard Hearn, J.P.; A. S. Furlong.
BOARDS OF GUARDIANS: WATERFORD—J. Dunphy. DUNGARVAN—James Queally, John V. Kiely, J.P.; Thomas Power, Thomas Flynn, John Walsh. LISMORE—A. Heskin, P.L.G.
BRANCHES I.N.F.: KILROSSINTY AND FEWS—Richard Costin, secretary. ABBEYSIDE—John Green. CARRICKBEG—Patrick Walsh, Edmond Walsh, Thomas Healy. DUNGARVAN—Captain John Veale, Patrick O'Brien, T.C.; John M'Carthy, P.L.G., deputy vice-chairman.

LIST OF DELEGATES.

WATERFORD CITY—Alderman Richard Power, J.P.; John Curran, T.C. BALLYGUNNER—John Delahunty, P.L.G.; Patrick Phelan. SCART—Michael Walsh, P.L.G.; Patrick Sheehan, P.L.G. PARISHES: KILGOBNET—John White. NEWTOWN—Patrick Nugent. OLD—Thomas O'Connor. TRAMORE—M. C. Murphy. DRUMRUSH—James Hearn.
WATERFORD NATIONAL AND COMMERCIAL CLUB.—John Hayes, William Queally, J. E. O'Mahony.

WESTMEATH.

ATHLONE TOWN COMMISSIONERS.—D. O'Donnell, William Hannon.
MULLINGAR BOARD OF GUARDIANS.—James King.
ROCHFORDBRIDGE BRANCH I.N.F.—Lawrence Galvin, Martin Quinn, jun.
IRISH NATIONAL FORESTERS BRANCH, MULLINGAR (No. 262)—John O'Sullivan, C.R.
MULLINGAR NATIONAL WORKINGMEN'S CLUB.—George Byrne, Michael Murtagh.

WEXFORD.

CORPORATION, CITY OF WEXFORD—Michael O'Connor.
ENNISCORTHY TOWN COMMISSIONERS—John Bolger, chairman; Mathew Ryan, G. Dempsey.
GOREY BOARD OF GUARDIANS—John M'Dermott, J.P.; P. Sullivan.
BRANCHES I.N.F.: CRAANFORD AND MONASEED—Daniel Kennedy, P.L.G.; Michael Lyons. CUSHIONSTOWN—James Furlong, William Kehoe, Michael Cloney, John Cloney, James Kehoe. OYLEGATE—John Bolger, John Cullin, James Crowley. OULART—Laurence Lacy, James Crowe, William Doran. TAGOAT AND KILRANE.—Michael Doyle, Nicholas Murphy, James Browne. MONAMOLIN—Thomas Mulligan, Arthur Gahan, Valentine Crowe. GOREY—James Redmond, Patrick Kinsella, James Dunne. CROSSADEG—John Lambert, John Baggan.

WICKLOW.

BRAY TOWN COMMISSIONERS—Philip Condron.
WICKLOW HARBOUR BOARD—John V. Gahan.
BOARDS OF GUARDIANS: RATHDRUM—Michael Byrne. BALTINGLASS—E. P. O'Kelly, J.P., chairman; William M'Loughlin.
BRANCHES I.N.F.: BALTINGLASS—Rev. T. O'Neill, P.P.; Thomas B. Doyle, J.P.; Nicholas O'Brien, Matthers Byrne, Anthony O'Dwyer. KILLAVENEY AND ANNACURRA—J. O'Toole, J. Doyle, P. Doyle, Richard Kavanagh. DUNLAVIN—James Kealy, John Burke, James Lawler.
BRAY PARISH—James Coffey, Mathew O'Byrne.

Letter from United States and Canadian Delegates.

Dublin, 31st August, 1896.

To the Editor of the Freeman's Journal.

Dear Sir—Will you permit us through your columns to remove the impression which a portion of the Dublin Press has endeavoured to create—that the delegates from abroad who are now here are committed to any section of the Irish Parliamentary representation. As secretaries of the American and Canadian delegations respectively, we are empowered to state that they come here thoroughly unpledged and uncommitted to any expression of opinion touching the relative merits of any section of the Irish representation in Parliament. From conversation with individual members of the American, Australian, Canadian, and African delegations, we can assure you that they are wholly unbiassed. May we add that they have a right to expect courteous treatment, if not a cordial welcome, from every Irish newspaper that professes to advocate Home Rule for this country. The members of the delegations from abroad have come to Ireland at their own expense, and at a considerable sacrifice of time and personal convenience, and are entitled to fair treatment from the Irish Press,

Yours respectfully,

Jos. P. Ryan,
Secretary Irish National Federation of America.

P. F. Cronin,
Secretary Canadian Delegation.

Stewards.

The following gentlemen kindly acted as stewards :—

Chief Stewards—John Denver; D. Boyle; Owen Kiernan; J. O'Connell; and M. Sheehan.

Under Mr. Boyle—F. J. Farley; J. Shortell; J. Reilly; G. Holt; T. Casey; and J. Walsh.

Under Mr. O'Connell—Michael O'Rourke, London, North; Patrick Lyons, do.; Maurice Ahern, do.; John Ball, do.; Geraghty, do.; and J. Herilghley, do.

Under Mr. Sheehan—John Glass, Glasgow; James Stafford, do.; John Hughes, Coatbridge; John Craven, do.; J. Kennedy, Blantyre; and J. Cassidy, Hamilton, N.B.

Under Mr. Kiernan—Stephen M'Farlane; William Reilly; Terence O'Neill; Michael O'Donnell, Leeds Irish National Club Francis Jones; John Macgee, West Hartlepool.

The Leinster Hall.

This Hall, in which meetings of the Convention were held, is said to hold from 2,500 to 3,000. Both at opening and conclusion of each day's sitting it appeared full with numbers standing at back of seats and in the passages.

The Convention sat, without break, on the first day, four hours; on the second, five hours; on the third, five hours and a half.

The Hall was decorated with flowers, and amongst the mottoes set out on large scrolls were the following :—

OWEN ROE O'NEILL—"Redouble your blows, and the battle is won."

SWIFT—"By the laws of God, of nature, of nations, and of your country, you are and ought to be as free a people as your brethren in England."

GRATTAN—"I have entreated an attendance on this day, that you, in the most public manner, may deny the claim of the British Parliament to make laws for Ireland, and with one voice lift up your hands against it."

WOLFE TONE—"I have laboured to abolish the infernal spirit of religious persecution by uniting the Catholic and Dissenter."

EMMET—"Brothers, march, march to glory; in your country's cause unite."

O'CONNELL—"There is no statute of limitation against the liberties of a people. Ages may roll over, yet their rights remain."

MITCHEL—"When Irishmen consent to let the past become indeed history, not party politics, and begin to learn from it the lessons of mutual respect and tolerance, instead of endless bitterness and enmity, then, at last, this distracted land shall see the dawn of Hope and Peace."

DAVIS—"Let your purpose bide.
We'll have our own again;
Let the game be fairly tried,
We'll have our own again."

ALLEN, LARKIN AND O'BRIEN—"God Save Ireland."

BUTT—"The destinies, the mighty destinies, of our country's children are in our hands, and curse, oh! curse the man who sows dissension amongst us."

GALBRAITH—"Be united, so that by uniting they would get rid of what we would call the accursed Union."

PARNELL—"Let us cast aside all feelings of self-interest. Let us act only with a desire to benefit our country—to regain for her a place amongst the nations of the world."

Irish Race Convention.

FIRST DAY—1st SEPTEMBER, 1896.

The Convention assembled at noon.
    Mr. Justin M'Carthy, M.P.—Fellow-countrymen, I have the honour and pleasure to move that the chair be taken at this great Convention by the Most Rev. Dr. O'Donnell, Lord Bishop of Raphoe.
    Very Rev. Canon Shinkwin, P.P., Bandon, seconded the resolution.
    Mr. Davitt, M.P., put the resolution, which was adopted amid cheers, renewed again as his Lordship took the chair.
    The Chairman—Gentlemen, my first duty as chairman is to ask you to appoint honorary secretaries to this Convention.
    Very Rev. Canon Lynskey, P.P., Clifden—I have very much pleasure in doing a very perfunctory duty here to-day. It is that of proposing that Rev. Father M'Guire, C.C., Enniskillen ; Captain Donelan, M.P. ; Rev. Father O'Callaghan, C.C., Mallow ; David Sheehy, M.P., and Michael Davitt, M.P., be appointed honorary secretaries to the Convention.
    Dr. Ambrose, M.P., seconded the resolution, which was carried unanimously.
    The Secretaries laid on the table the Agenda of Resolutions sent in pursuance of notice of 20th August.*
    The Chairman—I shall ask Father M'Fadden of Gweedore to begin the proceedings with an Irish prayer. Ἀbracaió an ṫagaṅc Paṅáiṙċe ṡaet Óóiṙ Uṙṅuiġ aiṙ ṙoṙġailt na ṗéiṙe móiṙe.†
    Rev. J. M'Fadden, P.P., advanced to the foot of the platform and read as follows, the entire Convention remaining standing during the reading :

    In ainm an Aṫaṙ, aġuṡ a Ṁhic, aġuṡ an Spioraio Naoiṁ. Amen.
    Cuiṙling, a Spioraio Naoiṁ, ó'ár n-ionnṗuioe, aiclion cṙoiṡṫe oo éṙeioṁeaṫ, aġuṡ aṫain ionnta ceine oo ġráṫa féin.
    Rannṁin. Cuiṙ ċuġainn oo Spioraio, aġuṡ cṙuṫóṫaṙ iao.
    Fṙeaġṙaṫ. Aġuṡ aṫnuaóṙaió tu aġaió an talṁan.
    Ṡuiṁiṙ.
    A Óhia, oo ṫeaġaiṡṡ cṙoiṡṫe na g-Cṙeioṁeaṫ le lonnṙao an Spioraio

---

    * These resolutions will be found set out at end of Thursday's proceedings.
    † "The Parish Priest of Gweedore will say a prayer at the opening of this great Convention."

Naoṁ; cadaiṗ ṫuinn iṅṗ an Spioṗaṫ ceaṡna, ṡo m-blaṗṗamaoiṗ an ceaṗc, aṡuṗ in a ṗoláṗ-ṗan ṡo m-beiṫeaṫ ṗioṗ-ṡáiṗṫeaṫaṗ oṗṗainn : Cṗe Íoṗa Cṗíoṗc áṗ ṫ-Ciṡeaṗna. Ωmen.*

The CHAIRMAN—Before any other business is done I have a joyful message for the Convention that ought to be delivered at once. Centuries ago, when the two Hughs fought bravely for Irish freedom and freedom of conscience, as well as later on in the days of the Confederation of Kilkenny and of Owen Roe, Ireland had no more helpful friends than Paul V., Urban VIII., and Innocent X. Well, once more

"There's wine from the Royal Pope
Upon the ocean green."

This great Convention was summoned to end Irish dissension, and I hold in my hand a gracious message from the illustrious Pontiff Leo XIII., just received through the distinguished Rector of the Irish College, Rome, in which his Holiness prays that dissensions may be ended. When you have heard the message in Latin and English, I shall leave it to the spontaneous act of the assembly to manifest its gratitude for such an exalted favour.

ROMA.
BISHOP OF RAPHOE, DUBLIN.
SANCTISSIMUS, BONUM SPIRITUALE ET TEMPORALE HIBERNORUM EXOPTANS, FINEM DISSENSIONUM PRECATUR.
KELLY.

In English :—
THE HOLY FATHER, YEARNING FOR THE SPIRITUAL AND TEMPORAL WELFARE OF THE IRISH PEOPLE, PRAYS FOR THE END OF DISSENSIONS.

The favour of such a Prince should not long remain without acknowledgment, and I wish to be empowered, if it be the will of this Convention, to send back the following message in the name of the Convention :—

MONSIGNORE KELLY, COLLEGIO IRLANDESE, ROMA.
Conventus gentis Hibernicæ Sanctissimo gratias agit amplissimas de verbis benignissimis, quæ uti favorem eximium, pacisque augurium felicissimum, una voce omnes accipiunt delegati.
EPISCOPUS RAPOTENSIS PRAESES.

In English :—
The Irish Race Convention begs to express its profound gratitude to the Holy Father for his most kind and salutary message, which all the delegates receive as a signal favour, and as the happiest augury of peace.

Now, gentlemen, there is a letter from his Grace the Archbishop of Toronto, which the Rev. Father Ryan, St. Michael's, Toronto, his delegate, is here to read to you. The letter is one which I am sure you will all hear with pleasure.

---

* " In the name of the Father, and of the Son, and of the Holy Ghost. Amen.
"Come, O Holy Ghost, replenish the hearts of Thy faithful, and kindle in them the fire of Thy love.
" Versicle. Send forth Thy Spirit and they shall be created.
" Response. And Thou shalt renew the face of the earth.
" LET US PRAY.
"O God, Who, by the light of the Holy Ghost, didst instruct the hearts of the faithful, grant that by the same Spirit we may know what is right, and ever enjoy His consolation : through Jesus Christ, our Lord. Amen."

Rev. Dr. RYAN—His Grace not being able to come to this Convention, wished me to read this letter to the Convention to-day :—

Toronto, August 13th, 1896.

REV. FATHER RYAN, RECTOR OF ST. MICHAEL'S CATHEDRAL.

My Dear Father Ryan—As it is quite out of my power to assist at the great Irish Convention to be held in Dublin in the beginning of September, I hereby depute you to attend thereat as my representative. You know my views on this Convention—its necessity and its purpose. Those views were substantially expressed in my letter on the subject addressed to the Hon. Edward Blake in October last. It was felt then, as it is now, in order to obtain Home Rule or any other measure of justice from the Imperial Parliament, that the Irish National representatives should close their broken ranks, and re-establish amongst them unity of aim and action. The Convention was suggested as a means of effecting this desirable and necessary union. The earnestness and alacrity with which this idea was taken up by the Irish people at home and abroad proved that some such Convention was felt to be a necessary means of restoring unity to the Irish Parliamentary representatives, and that it was expected to be also an efficacious method of perpetuating that unity. The Convention is now a great and memorable fact. May the kind Providence of God direct and control its deliberations, and may this assemblage of Irishmen be the starting-point of a great patriotic movement that will find its issue in complete success for the cause of Home Rule, and in a glorious victory for the just liberties and rights of a sorely-tried and long-suffering people.

Believe me to be, my dear Father Ryan,
Yours very truly,
✠JOHN WALSH,
Archbishop of Toronto.

Mr. DAVID SHEEHY, M.P., then read the following :—

Irish National Federation of America.
Secretary's Office, Room 26, Cooper Union, New York, August 19th, 1896.
TO THE CHAIRMAN OF THE JOINT COMMITTEE OF THE IRISH NATIONAL FEDERATION AND IRISH PARLIAMENTARY PARTY, DUBLIN.

Dear Sir—But for circumstances over which I have no control, resulting from a recent injury which has confined me to bed, I certainly would be with you as a delegate to the Race Convention soon to be held in Dublin. As a sincere friend of the movement to secure Home Rule for Ireland by constitutional means, I would like to offer a brief plea for unity, and to present a view of the present situation of affairs in Ireland as it appears to one placed, as I am, beyond the influence of the differences which now exist there, and which threaten to wreck the cause. It is but charitable to suppose that those who are directly responsible for the situation have been unable to realise the consequence, or to see beyond the exigencies of the petty and personal strief in which they are engaged. Those at a distance, who are free from every influence beyond the one wish—to accomplish the greatest good for those of the Irish race who have remained in Ireland—can certainly grasp the situation fully, and are the better able to suggest the remedy. The Irish who have been sent into exile for various causes, and are now scattered over the face of the earth, have kept green, under every vicissitude, their love of the old land, and have throughout evinced no less interest in the welfare of those left behind. Every appeal from famine and other distress has ever been generously responded to, and the contributions in the past by funds to improve the political and national condition of Ireland have been unprecedented as to the amount given and the extent of time through which the interest was maintained. It may be truly claimed that, but for this aid from abroad, Ireland to-day would be little better than a desert waste, and all trace of the Irish race would have disappeared long since, as the country became settled up by a foreign people.

With the growing dissensions of past years in Ireland a large majority of the Irish people abroad have passed from a state of despair to one of apathy and of indifference. But while those who have given deeper thought to the situation have time and again been discouraged they have not lost faith in the future. The Race Convention now to be held is the outcome of this confidence, and the delegates who attend from abroad have been selected as the fit representatives of those who constitute the most thoughtful element amongst the Irish race outside of Ireland. These men, therefore, have a right to a respectful hearing and to expect the honest co-operation of all who claim to be advocates of Home Rule. One great object of the Convention is to enable everyone to throw aside past differences, all of which have had, to a great extent, no better foundation than misunderstanding. If it be true, as is held, that all, regardless of other differences, hold in common a desire to advance the interest of Ireland, then all can meet in this Convention without the slightest loss of self-respect. Support comes from the Irish people, and not in the interest of a single individual. It is therefore equally incumbent that he should honestly co-operate and contribute his best efforts to formluate some plan of organisation and policy for the future which will remove the condition from which he has suffered, and to which all may in common subscribe. But rest assured that the man who will not accept such an invitation is no friend to Ireland, and looks only to his own personal ends; his occupation would be gone if the Irish people were again united. Let him bear in mind that by his neglect of duty at this crisis he will place himself beyond the pale of sympathy when called upon on some future day to receive the verdict which will be passed inevitably upon him by the Irish people at large—an unenviable distinction will rest upon him.

The time has passed for all sentimentality, as it has seldom happened in the history of Ireland that a more important crisis than the present has presented itself. Home Rule cannot be gained at present without a united people to make the demand, and without it Ireland can have no future. While it is perfectly natural, and even essential, that individual differences of opinion should exist as to the proper mode of accomplishing any public movement, yet, as soon as a course has been determined upon by a fair vote of the majority, the limit of individual opposition has been reached. Unless this principle be fully acknowledged and a loyal co-operation be rendered afterwards to the will of majority, political success must fail in any movement. If an organisation cannot divest itself of such a stumbling block it should cease to exist. In truth it must be stated that the impression exists with us that the present condition of affairs in Ireland is to be traced directly to repudiation, or want of appreciation by a limited number, as to the vital importance of political success in accepting without question the will of the majority. Unless the people of Ireland are blind from partisan zeal, and the leaders are indifferent as to the future welfare of the country, all must now realise that the only remedy rests in throwing aside all past differences of opinion when faults have existed on all sides, and the nearest approach to unity of the people must be brought about at whatever individual cost. If this end be not accomplished at the coming Convention as the result of general co-operation by compromise and by individual sacrifice for the common good, then may God help Ireland. The end of all aid and sympathy from abroad will have been reached, and the universal verdict will be that the Irish people are no longer worthy of name or country. The Irish race will pass away to other lands, to be absorbed by every nation of the globe, and in a limited time the traditions, history, and language of the dear old land will have disappeared, and be as much something of the past as those of the ancient Greeks and Romans. I will be with you in spirit, and will look forward with profound interest to the result of your deliberations.

Yours very truly,
THOMAS ADDIS EMMET, M.D.

Mr. SHEEHY, M.P.—There are other letters, but they are so numerous that it is impossible to read them all. Therefore, they will be handed to the Press.*

The CHAIRMAN—Men of the Irish race, there is only one way in which I may hope to return thanks for the unique honour which this chair confers upon me. It is to launch at once on this magnificent Convention the business that has brought you here from the four shores of Ireland and from many lands beyond the seas. To you, gentlemen, our kith and kin, come home from abroad, we who live in the Green

---

* These will be found at end of this day's proceedings.

Isle say from our hearts in the sweet language of your fathers, "Cead mille failte." In your love for Ireland you are here from the great Republic of the West, where so many millions of our people have built up for themselves a position and a name, and whence in times of trial has come to us the most generous support for every National demand. You are here from self-governing Canada, one of whose great Prelates first suggested this Convention to end our dissensions. You are come from friendly Nova Scotia and Newfoundland. You are come even from Australia, which has always vied with America in support of the National cause. You are here from Africa, where, in our days, to the South it promises to rival the Northern splendour of fifteen centuries ago. Then the never-failing Irishmen of England and Scotland are here; and lastly the tried men, priests and people, who live in the old land, in long array, from every county and every shore. You have come from near and far, at great inconvenience and expense, to work for the old cause, and to banish from our midst the bitterness of strife, filled with the idea that love of our motherland implies co-operation, and love, and friendship, and forbearances among ourselves in her cause. In my time I have seen the young family outcast on the roadside from the home the strong man had built; I have seen the priest dragged to prison for trying to shield the victims of such wrong; I have seen thousands of little boys and girls of from nine to twelve years hired into agricultural service far away from the homes where they ought to be at school; I have seen throngs of young people leaving the old and weakly behind, and hurrying to the emigrant ship; and I have often asked myself: Will the emigrants ever come back? Will they ever send us back the power to change these things and to undo these wrongs? Well-picked men of our race are here to-day from every land of the Irish dispersion, and with God's blessing before they go back the foundations will be laid broad and deep of that victory-compelling unity which this great Convention was called to promote. The unseemly dissensions which led up to the adoption by the Irish Party of a resolution to take counsel of the Irish race are only too familiar to need any reference from me.

But in the last days of June this year an event occurred that of itself should demand the summoning of this Convention. That event was the publication of the report of the Financial Relations Commission. I do not refer to the separate reports, however important, signed by different groups of Commissioners; not even to the marvellously reasoned conclusions of one who above all others sustained the cause of Ireland on that Commission. What does the Report of the Commission itself say, with an approach to unanimity that is unparalleled in such things? What have the experts and custodians of the British Treasury endorsed? They find that this poor country at the very least is over-taxed between two and three millions a year. That is the rule, that is the administration for you of the stranger, and to improve my argument, let me say, if you will, the well-meaning stranger. When we talked of a genial climate, a fair soil, teeming seas, an intelligent people, and said there was something radically wrong with the system under which our population fled the country, and our cities and industries decayed, we were answered back that this might be tolerable as Irish sentiment, but that the Parliament of Westminster knew how to make even justice prevail in its dealings with our country not less than in its treatment of any English county. At last the truth is out. This poor land, that shares so little in imperial expenditure, is despoiled by over-taxation. Her financial life-blood has been drained away until, from the industrial standpoint, she has been reduced to the condition of a perpetual invalid, while the neighbouring countries grow and prosper. Did the system against which we contend ever receive such a blow before? Let it go to the democracy of these countries and to the friendly peoples of the world that the existing system stands convicted of a monstrous wrong. It is the kind of wrong that all can appreciate, and for that very reason the report of the Financial Relations Commission, I venture to say, is an epoch-making event. It is a Nasmyth hammer with which to crush argumentative opposition to Home Rule.

But at a time when the National strength ought to be conscientiously applied to wield that hammer let us see that some of ourselves do not waste the needed energy or put the machinery out of gear. If we had now the united party of 1880–1890, speaking with one voice in the Imperial Parliament on behalf of Ireland, ere this the leading men of both English parties would have been forward to acknowledge that the finding of the Commission is a huge outstanding fact that compels immediate attention from any statesman who will not deny the plain axiom that justice to the governed is an obligation of Government. Therefore, it is my opinion that if we do not now unite to press the unanswerable claims of our country, history ought to deal with the dissentients more severely than it does with the wars of clan on clan some centuries ago, or the divisions in the National ranks within living memory, when our people in '47 and '48 were slain in hecatombs by famine, and by pagan political economy, while two or three Irish parties contended for the National allegiance. There was far more to divide good Irishmen then than there is now. And an event has occurred that ought to remake the whole Irish situation in the eyes even of English parties. Every pledge given against Home Rule is greatly in need of reconsideration in the light of the astounding financial wrong to Ireland that has been revealed, or rather proved conclusively this very year. The existing system is one of spoliation, and it is beyond the wit of man to devise any adequate remedy for stopping our current loss—not to speak of dealing with accumulated restitution—that will not comprise the establishment of self-government in Ireland.

We care not from which English party the Irish party extracts that right. We shall ever be grateful to the men who first emblazoned our cause on their banners and carried it successfully through the House of Commons. But Home Rule is now in money alone valued for us at a minimum English estimate of $2\frac{1}{2}$ millions a year, and I say we owe independent opposition to every party that refuses that refund and the political machinery for its profitable public use. That is one suggestion for uniting again the ranks of Irish Nationalists; and I believe that if the Convention will issue some such declaration on the subject as submitted in more than one of the resolutions on the paper, much will be done towards promoting the unity we desire, even though we have not in this hall, I deeply regret to say, the advantage of the co-operation of all the Home Rule members. I go further, and say that by stating anew what the Nationalist policy really is we can, through this Convention, make it so well understood that the public opinion of our race will, after a little, be everywhere at its back, and, despite delusive cries, require unity in the pursuit of it. Our political creed is an old one by which we mean to cling so long as God gives us strength to work for Ireland ; and we have the men who have observed the constitution of the Irish Party, and who by their record in days of stress have shown that they possess the ability, the courage, and disinterestedness to give effect to Nationalist principles at any cost to themselves. Depend upon it anything that can be said against the independence of the Nationalist Party under Mr. M'Carthy or Mr. Dillon, might as well be said against it in the years that followed the cementing of the Liberal alliance under Mr. Parnell. The truth is the practical working out of independent opposition or independent support has its difficulties at every stage, and nothing appears easier than for any Nationalist member to make out some kind of case against his neighbour over any understanding with an English party.

As an outsider I may be permitted to express a few thoughts further on the subject. It is the sense of the Convention that no man or set of men should be at all put in competition with the interests of Ireland. If that be so, the cause of Ireland must, *a fortiori*, be our standard in dealing with English parties. Therefore, the principle of independent opposition in our time is opposition to every party that won't grant the demands of Ireland—above all, the demand for national self-government, which we look upon as comprehensive of all others. Then, when any one party adopts your programme, the opposition as such ceases, and co-operation begins and continues, unless there is some failure in making good the compact. But, before either party adopts your programme on Home Rule, how far will you help them to pass other useful reforms ? When one adopts it, how far will you help the other to pass useful legislation, or impede them as a means of forcing your National views ? Again, in regard to the party that stakes its fortunes on your cause and shares your victories and reverses, if they fail to carry Home Rule through both Houses of Parliament, will you allow them to go on with English legislation either on the principle of mutual help or on the hope of improving the chances of Home Rule at an election ? Again, what grievances in legislation or administration inflicted by a party favourable to Home Rule would amount to a sufficient reason, on National grounds, for defeating them in Parliament or at the polls ?

These are some of the questions that must inevitably claim solution at the hands of our Parliamentary representatives ; and, in the nature of things, it seems to me there is only one rational way of solving them. Our members go to Westminster with a distinct mandate to wrest Home Rule by just means from Whig or Tory indifferently, and in the councils of the party, after mature deliberation, to determine how Ireland and the Irish cause requires the decision to be cast in the circumstances of each emergency. They make mistakes like other men. But do we expect in our time to have abler or more devoted representatives ? I think not. Only, besides consulting their constituents often and fulfilling their covenants with them faithfully, they must work together in

Parliament in the spirit of their pledge, standing as one man, and speaking with one voice, and making our country respected before those who, so far, love not our cause. Without this discipline Mr. Parnell's splendid political genius could have done little; with it, under God's blessing, a just, wise, active, and bold policy is sure to succeed. No Englishman or set of Englishmen can keep Home Rule in the front of politics. What can and ought and will win the Irish cause is the united effort of the Irish race at home and abroad. Minor reforms are important. Some of our grievances clamour for redress. But they must not take our attention from the National remedy which a Parliament representative equally of every class and creed and interest in Ireland can supply. It will be seen hereafter that the Englishmen who are most friendly to Ireland in this respect are also the wisest friends of England. But we may be forgiven if, in her straits, our sympathy and interest be concentrated on our own poor country. In the single department of education, simply because the views of Ireland's representatives have been ignored, the primary education of the people was cast on lines that left our emigrants, as a body, without the least manual or technical training to compete in America or Australia with other nationalities drilled from childhood in the aptest ways to earn a livelihood, and after half-a-century of protest, we are still without a university for the Catholics of Ireland.

They say these grievances are now to be redressed. I hope they are; much better late than never. But if the redress comes, mark the time. It comes far too late; and until you have native government every other grievance will have to be agitated for perhaps half-a-century before a halting remedy is applied, and we will be always kept behind in the march of human progress. Now, we think this is a fate to which we ought not tamely submit. The mixed race that has sprung from this soil, with the blood of Celt and Saxon, Dane and Norman intermingled, has a mission of its own, a genius and ideal of its own, virtues and endowments of its own, faults and follies of its own, which give it a distinctive character in every land under the sun; and we want Ireland, the cradle-land and nursery of our race, to be guarded with loving care and tended with filial devotion, and developed by native genius. It is next to useless to argue our cause unless we stand united behind our arguments. Despair of winning anything by argument has driven poor Irishmen to deplorable deeds, for which an inhuman punishment has been exacted. Perhaps the report of the Financial Relations Commission will make the case of the poor political prisoners better understood. In any event, if this Convention proclaims the National policy on a basis broad and strong, and demands fidelity and discipline in carrying it out, the Irish people will be once more united, and, God giving it, no power shall be able to resist the justice of the Irish cause.

The CHAIRMAN, rising again—As regards the procedure, I have to announce to you that there are several resolutions and groups of resolutions on the agenda paper, and some resolutions have been handed up that are not on the agenda paper, and what I intend doing is to take the agenda paper in order, and, in the first place, I invite Mr. Webb to propose the series of resolutions that stand in his name. When these resolutions are seconded *in globo*, they shall be put separately one by one, beginning with the first for discussion, or amendment, or approval, or rejection ; and as the debate goes on I shall try to find what other resolutions submitted to the Convention are germane to those that come first, so as to allow the whole discussion to go on together. One word more, which I know is unnecessary. In the Convention on Tara in ancient Erin, the representative Irishmen there assembled enjoyed privileges which members attending a modern Parliament might well envy. But any violence or insulting language was severely banned as being unworthy of an Irish deliberative assembly. I am sure that, while the delegates here will freely use their right to speak their own views, and the convictions of those who sent them, on unity or dissension, or policy, or public organisation, or party, or leaders, or finances, the manly, self-respecting, high-toned spirit of the past will be perpetuated in this great Democratic Convention of Irish representatives.

Mr. ALFRED WEBB—My lord and fellow-delegates, ladies and gentlemen, it is impossible not to feel deeply moved in laying these resolutions before this great assembly, the most widely representative of Irish feeling at home and abroad that I have had the honour to attend. Men come and go ; the *personnel* alters from generation to generation ; yet the National movement ever renews itself, and urges forward deep and strong in our day as in that of our fathers. I bring these resolutions forward as a basis for discussion, trusting that movers and seconders will be found to introduce them separately and seriatim. They so fully express my sentiments, my longings, at this important crisis, that there is little need I should with many words stand between you and them, and really important and representative speakers. Let me, however, express the spirit with which they have been prepared, and in which I trust they will be discussed. We assert the nationality of our country—dearer to us than life, essential to her progress, essential to her well-being, essential for union within her shores, essential to a real union with Great Britain. We in this land are not necessarily two nations. There is not a righteous interest that every man, woman and child within the four seas of Ireland does not share in common. The strife between us and England, which has prevailed through the ages, and which will prevail so long as the attempted stifling of our aspirations cries out to heaven, is unnecessary. We all desire its termination. Ireland is qualified to be the best friend England ever had. We can never forget, and shall never forget, the thousands of England's sons and daughters, who, especially of late years, have proved themselves our most sincere and devoted friends. We desire, forgetting past differences, to extend the hand of fellowship to all willing to aid in the regeneration of our country. A united party—a party in which the views of all will be considered, but which can be relied upon to act as one, will be the best means to that end. For the maintenance and efficiency of such a party effective discipline will be necessary ; neither constituencies nor the country at large will rest satisfied with pledges, professed in the letter, broken in the spirit. We feel for all who have been led into evil ways by a state of things in which justice is "sold, denied, or delayed," and every other feeling is obliterated in commiseration for brutal treatment—for treatment meted out by no other western nation to political offenders—for treatment which in the light of recent events startingly brings into relief the fact that there is one law for the Englishman and another for the Irishman; one law for the rich and titled, another for the ordinary citizen. We desire to press forward in the work of making the lives of the masses of our people— whether in town or country—better, happier, and brighter. We desire that education should be brought fully into accord with the religious feelings of our people. We desire that Irishmen should have the same rights in the matter of county and municipal government as the people of Great Britain. We are determined that the inequalities and wrongs of the present system of taxation shall be altered. We believe that the preservation of the ancient language of the country tends to raise the thoughts of our people, to open for them an inspiring field of mental culture, and to make them better citizens. These are the sentiments that I feel sure will animate our discussions, and that will be voiced in the resolutions that will be passed. This Convention is a supreme effort for reconciliation and unity. We trust it will prevail. But if, unhappily, it should not, none, either at home or abroad, will be absolved from the duty of carrying on the work as best they may, of throwing in their lot with and aiding to the best of their ability that body of men which show themselves most ready to forget the past, to bury differences, to join heart and hand for Ireland, and who thus prove themselves likely to be most powerful in forwarding the sacred cause of their country's redemption. I beg to introduce the following resolutions:—

(1) REUNION.—"Seeing that divisions amongst Irish Nationalist representatives paralyse to a great extent their power of serving Ireland, cast discredit on the country, and tend to alienate the support of the Irish Race and to destroy their confidence in the efficacy of Parliamentary action, we record our firm conviction that it is of the first importance to Ireland that the Nationalist representatives in Parliament should be reunited into one Party; and, in the spirit of the recent resolution of the Irish Party, we declare that, 'In our earnest desire to accomplish that result, we are prepared to meet on fair and equal terms all Nationalists who will join in the attempt to reconstitute a united Home Rule Party, in which every supporter of the movement shall be cordially received and justly considered, regardless of all past differences, and having regard only to his capacity to render service to the common cause.' We are glad to observe in the composition of this Convention and in the spirit shown throughout the country, marked evidence of a growing tendency to reunion, and we invite the Irish Nationalist Party to take such further steps as may to them seem calculated to promote the cause of reunion."

(2) UNITY.—"That we recognise as the essential element of the existence of an effective Irish Party the hearty co-operation and cheerful subordination of each individual in carrying out the Party policy, as settled (after free discussion) by the judgment of the greater number. That while we are glad to observe that on grave questions there have been but few intelligible differences of opinion in the Irish Party, and none difficult of reconciliation by reasonable men willing to agree, we most strongly condemn those public disputes regarding minor questions of persons and tactics which have so gravely impaired the power of the Party. We solemnly call upon every man belonging to the Irish Party, in answer to the prayers of our people all the world over, to forget old differences, to sink personal feelings, and to act for the future as good comrades and fellow-soldiers in the spirit of this resolution and in the support of that party unity on which the fate of Ireland so largely depends. We ask the Irish Party to take such steps as may in their judgment be found necessary to the establishment of unity and discipline in their own ranks, in accordance with the resolutions of this Convention; and we assure them of our unfailing support in the execution of this essential task."

(3) HOME RULE.—"That this Irish Race Convention reasserts the immemorial claim of IRELAND A NATION. We declare that England is governing Ireland wrong-

fully, by coercion, and against the people's will; that each year proves afresh the futility of the attempt; that Irish evils mainly flow from alien, irresponsible, uniformed, and unsympathetic rule; and that no policy, whether of severe repression or of partial concession, can allay her rightful discontent, or will slacken her efforts to obtain a Legislature and an Executive making and administering laws for Ireland by Irishmen on Irish soil. We declare it the prime duty of the Irish Parliamentary Party to continue to maintain its absolute independence of English Political Parties, and thus to preserve its freedom to give an independent opposition or an independent support to any Party, as may seem best in the interests of the National cause."

(4) AMNESTY.—"That, while hailing with satisfaction the release of some of the Irish Political Prisoners, we are indignant that relief has come so late, after their health had been broken by long years of suffering. We condemn the brutal treatment which England, while boasting herself to be the advanced guard of freedom amongst the nations, inflicts on political prisoners sentenced for offences arising out of Irish grievances. We mark the contrast in feeling and in action exhibited by England towards the Irish prisoners and towards other political offenders, as for instance, the Johannesburg Committee and the Jameson Raiders. We call for the immediate liberation of all the remaining Irish political prisoners still enduring the horrors of penal servitude, and we request the Irish Parliamentary representatives to press with insistent urgency for their release."

(5) LAND.—"That the Irish landlord system and methods have tended to impoverish, exterminate, and expel the Irish race, and have thus been the fruitful source of misery, discontent, violence and disturbance in Ireland. That the last Land Act, while bettering the condition of certain classes, fails to give the vast majority of the Irish tenantry that security against excessive rents and confiscation of improvements which is essential to their well-being and to the success of any scheme of land purchase; fails to give necessary powers for the enlargement of too small holdings by the compulsory purchase of grass lands from which the people have been driven, and fails to make adequate provision for the restoration to their homes of the evicted tenants, to whose courage and endurance such benefits as the farmers of Ireland have obtained are largely due, and whose case must ever appeal to the sense of honour and gratitude of their fellow-countrymen. We condemn the lateness of the period and the shortness of the time allowed for discussion, and the indecent threats of withdrawal, by which legitimate debate was curtailed; and we declare that the Act cannot be accepted even as a temporary settlement, and that the only hope of the tenantry rests in a united and determined Parliamentary Party, backed by a great agrarian combination, watching the operation of the Land Laws, exposing cases of injustice, and demanding a full measure of reform."

(6) TAXATION.—"That we rejoice that the evidence taken before the Financial Commission has at length made too clear for argument the injustice under which Ireland has been so long and is still labouring in the matter of Imperial taxation, and we record our grateful thanks to Mr. Sexton for his arduous and most successful labours in this regard. We call upon the Irish Party, at the earliest moment, to press upon Parliament our demand for the redress of past wrongs, and for the relief from present unequal burdens imposed by the representatives of rich and powerful Britain upon weakened and impoverished Ireland."

(7) LABOUR.—"That, while we hail with satisfaction the improved condition of those labourers for whom homes have been provided under the Labourers' Act, we regret that the great body are still without decent habitations and plots of land. Notwithstanding recent improvements, we claim that, whilst maintaining due supervision, the procedure should be further shortened, simplified, and cheapened, the appeal to the Privy Council abolished, and the Act made more widely useful; and that the Irish labourers shall be given the same franchise for the elections of Guardians as is possessed by the English labourers; that we recognise the just claim of urban labour to an improvement in the laws as applicable to the housing of the working classes of the towns, and we sympathise with every effort for a reasonable reduction in the hours of daily toil."

(8) LOCAL GOVERNMENT.—"That we condemn the non-representative and irresponsible system of Local Government in Irish counties by Grand Juries, and the narrowness of the franchise in Irish boroughs; we demand the immediate application in Ireland to Local Government, in all its branches, of those principles of democratic control which have been so fully carried out in Great Britain."

(9) EDUCATION.—"That for Catholics we demand perfect equality in the law and administration in the matter of education—primary, intermediate, and university—and the recognition therein not only of the national spirit, but also of the highest educational right—namely, the religious training of youth in accordance with the priceless principles of religious liberty and freedom of conscience; we demand the establishment of a University which shall afford to the Catholic people of Ireland educational opportunities equal to those enjoyed by the favoured minority of her population in the University of Dublin; we ask for a practical extension of technical education in agriculture and other industrial arts on a system adapted to the special needs of Ireland, so that her children may be better fitted to develop the resources of their country."

(10) GAELIC LANGUAGE.—" We hail with satisfaction the successful efforts that are being made at home and abroad to revive and extend interest in the preservation of the Gaelic tongue, and we urge upon all those who can further the interests of this movement to give every help and encouragement to the preservation and study of our ancient Irish tongue by the children of the Gael."

Rev. Dr. RYAN, of Toronto, rose to second the introduction of the resolutions 1 to 10—My lord, chairman and gentlemen of the Irish Race Convention, I deem it a great honour to be invited to address this magnificent gathering of the men of the Irish race, and I consider it an especial privilege to be asked to second these resolutions. Now, gentlemen, before I speak to these resolutions I would like briefly to define clearly and distinctly my position and the position of my fellow delegates before this Convention and before this country. I am here essentially in a representative capacity. In the first place I represent the Archbishop of Toronto. I think, gentlemen, you will admit that that has been abundantly proved by the letter of his Grace which I have read to this Convention. I am here secondly as the representative of the Irish people of Toronto, and it will suffice to tell you our methods, our democratic methods, in electing delegates to show you that I and my fellow-delegates are truly and honestly the accredited and authorised representatives of our country. Bear with me while I briefly tell you how the thing was done. The parishioners were asked to assemble and discuss the consideration of choosing delegates, and so they did. Then, electors were chosen from different parishes of the city of Toronto, came together, and in the same free and untrammelled assembly discussed and considered those elected representatives. These are our ways of electing delegates in Canada, and, therefore, we, perhaps unworthy—that is not for us to say—we are the duly elected, authorised, and accredited representatives of the City of Toronto. The same method was observed in all other Canadian cities, and, I believe, in the cities of the United States, and, therefore, I wish to emphasise the fact that we come here as duly authorised and accredited representatives of the Irish race in America. But now, gentlemen, a word on these resolutions. Perhaps it may seem a little hazardous to begin so early in the day in this discussion—for I wish to tell you, gentlemen of the Convention, that we come here perfectly free and independent. I take these resolutions as they have been read, and I wish the Convention to clearly understand that. They have been read *in globo*, they will be taken up afterwards in particular, and proposed and seconded, and put to you for discussion, amendment, or rejection, as you may think fit. Therefore, I take them in general. The three first resolutions, perhaps, more nearly concern the foreign delegates than the domestic considerations in the others, of which the people at home are the best judges. The first resolution seems to me to embody what were the ideas of the man I represent, the Archbishop of Toronto. He said: "You understand my mind thoroughly on this question." He has written it, and I have read it for you—"Tell them, in brief, that I agree with all my heart in Home Rule for Ireland; that I believe Ireland has a right to make laws for Ireland; that I believe Ireland will not only be more prosperous at home, but will be a greater strength to the Empire if she has the Home Rule to which she is entitled. We say here, as our Premier in Canada lately said: 'We in Canada', he said, 'are a loyal people because we are a free people.' "And tell them further," said the Archbishop of Toronto, "that as Ireland has the right to Home Rule in a native Legislature, so has she the power to obtain Home Rule. And that power, say it," he continues, "that power to obtain Home Rule is a united Irish people and a united Parliamentary Party." Therefore, coming here I find these resolutions that seem to me almost in the very wording to express the ideas and thoughts of his Grace of Toronto.

Now, my dear friends, we come not to any party, to any man. We come to Ireland, to the Irish people. We come to the Irish nation, and we speak to the heart of the Irish nation. We care not for party, and we care not for persons. That is perhaps your affair, and you have the intelligence and the power to settle your own affairs. But we say this, as coming from abroad, that in every representative political action there must be a party, and in every party, to have it truly representative, there must be freedom of private discussion, but there must be, too, strong insistence on the practical principle of majority rule, and following sharp and fast on the insistence on majority rule, a loyal obedience to the authorised expression of the people's will. These are, in general, the elements of any successful and united party. Now, friends of the Irish Race Convention, I say we come here not to dictate, we come here to suggest, we come here to advise, we come here independent, and that independence we shall preserve. We are not committed to any man or to any party, much less are we controlled by any man. We come in the cause of Ireland, and we stand by the Irish people, and what the Irish people in their united strength may seem best to do, that the Irish abroad will stand by, and that they are determined to maintain. Now, in conclusion, I would say this as a Canadian representative, that we, perhaps, have some special right to be here, for you know that Ireland has appealed to Canada. Ireland appealed to Canada for sympathy and moral support, and the answer was two historic resolutions in our free Dominion Parliament of Canada. One of these resolutions was proposed by a representative and leading man of one party, the Conservative Party. It was proposed by the Hon. John Costigan, or as we call him familiarly in Canada—though he has been for a long time a politician—we call him the "honest John Costigan." He proposed the first resolution of sympathy for Ireland in the Canadian Parliament, and again Canada answered. Then another resolution was proposed by the Hon. Edward Blake, the then leader of the Liberal Party in the Canadian House of Commons. And again Ireland spoke to Canada—this time for financial aid—and we gladly, and immediately, and generously responded according to our means. And the third time Ireland appealed to Canada—this time not for moral support, not for financial aid—she asked for more. Ireland asked Canada for a man, and we looked round about and we selected one of our ablest, bravest, and best—a knight without reproach, and we know him—the Hon. Edward Blake; and we answered your appeal and sent you a man to help you in your Parliamentary work and warfare. But now it is Canada's turn to appeal to Ireland. We do not seem to ask for much, my dear friends, yet indeed it is much. We appeal to you to be united. I know very well that reunion will cost some sacrifice— some personal sacrifice—but if I read the story of Ireland right I find that Ireland has been a sacrificial country and the Irish a sacrificial people, and I know that that spirit of sacrifice would cause them to sacrifice themselves for their country's sake. Now, it may be necessary to have personal sacrifices, and great personal sacrifices. But oh! the cause is mightier, the cause is greater than any individual in the country, and therefore we appeal for this unity, and men of the Irish race, let not our appeal go unheard. It is a reasonable appeal, it is a righteous appeal, it is a holy appeal, and let us go back to gladden the hearts of our people and be able to tell them that the Convention has indeed attained its end. Not completely—we are not fools enough to think that, but as our distinguished and able and eloquent chairman— and I am glad he is chairman—says, all we can hope to do now is to lay the foundations broad and deep and strong, and therefore to give hope to our people—hope and aspiration for the future—that we may depend upon it now—that we shall have what the Archbishop of Toronto wants —the unity of the Irish people at home and abroad, and in that cause as our able chairman has said, a united Irish people at home and abroad must compel unity at home. And that is the power, and the only power, that can lead us on to victory for the cause we love so well—Home Rule for Ireland.

The CHAIRMAN.—The introduction of the resolutions has been proposed and seconded, and now Mr. Justin M'Carthy is going to speak to the first resolution.

Mr. JUSTIN M'CARTHY, M.P.—My lord and fellow-countrymen—I am anxious to say a few words, and they shall be only a few, in support of this first resolution which you all have before you. There is no need of my taking up your time with any lengthened address, because the magnificent and convincing speeches you have heard can have left no doubt on the mind of any man here as to the course he is bound to pursue for the sake and in the cause of his country. No Convention ever held in Ireland, or that could be held, could have opened more auspiciously than this Convention to-day. We began with that most gracious and benignant message from his Holiness Pope Leo XIII. We had the wise and powerful letter of his Grace the Archbishop of Toronto, and we had the letter of my personal friend, and the friend of many here, the Irishman who bears the illustrious Irish name of Thomas Addis Emmet. I do not know how any Irish Convention could be opened more auspiciously than by messages such as these. Now, we have two powerful motives in calling this Convention. The first is to bury the past, and to take counsel together and make resolve for the future. These two results are to be brought about by the common consent of such representative Irishmen as are gathered so successfully in this hall to-day. Now it may be asked why did we—why, that is to say, did that section of the Irish Parliamentary Party to which I belong —why did we put ourselves forward to bring together this Convention? Well, for one reason. Because we are numerically by far the strongest Irish Party, and therefore, we felt that it became us to hold out the hand of brotherhood and friendship to other Irishmen. I am bound to say, and I am sure I speak for all my friends, that if any such appeal had been made to us by any body, however small, of Irish Nationalists, we should have welcomed that appeal and made the most practical response to its application. But we thought we were bound to come forward as no such appeal was made to us, and say to all Irishmen who believe in Home Rule, and work and hope for its success, we thought our duty was to say to them, "Come in and work with us on the old lines and on the old principle, that the majority shall decide the course of political action. Come in and join with us. We ask for no open act or act of penitence; we are willing to believe you were actuated with the best motive, but only let the dead past bury its dead, and now come in and work with us once again in harmony for the cause of Ireland."

Surely that appeal ought have been promptly and generously responded to by other Irish Nationalists. It may be even yet. I am not going to anticipate any evil result or failure. Now let me remind this meeting what was the course in the old days when we turned out Government after Government, and made it plain to every English Government that without the consent of Irish National members nothing could be done in the House of Commons. What was our policy then? It was this. At any crisis we held a meeting of the Party. There were many divisions of opinion in these consultations. Every man, even the youngest raw recruit, gave free expression of his opinion. We debated every question out, and then we took a vote, and the decision of the majority ruled the whole Party; and many a time, and not before the division in the House of Commons was taken, the Irish Party after a debate for hours in the Parliament in which all manners of opinion were expressed, the Irish Party went into the division lobby as one man. Now, we want to restore that condition of things. We want to get all Irish Nationalists to work on that same principle. But let me tell you, that human wit can discover no other way for conducting a Parliamentary movement to success but on the principle that the party shall be bound by the decision of its majority. Debate as we will amongst ourselves, when a vote is taken we must become as one instrument and one man again. It is my belief, and the belief, I hope, of all of us here, that a Convention such as this will be able to enforce that principle again. If you enforce that principle we shall be only too glad to welcome back any fellow-Nationalist who may have differed from us for any reason— we shall welcome him back, and be prepared and glad to work with him until the end is gained. But when the principle of the command of control by the majority is not recognised, then he indeed must be a sanguine man who could say he saw a chance of the near success of the Irish Nationalist cause.

Mr. THOMAS HUNT, of Melbourne, Australia—My lord, ladies, and gentlemen, I come before you to-day with a message of peace and with a request for national unity. I have heard of people going through fire and water to serve their country. I may claim to have gone through a portion of the latter element, for I may tell you that to pass through the Red Sea will give you more notion of what a reward there may be in future for those who are alive in Ireland. I came here from a free country, blessed with one of the freest constitutions in the world—I have come here representing the people of Victoria, and the only reward I shall look forward to—I suppose I shall not myself see the day when Home Rule is granted—is that some descendant or friend of mine may be able to point to this, one of the noblest historic gatherings that ever assembled, and point to me as one who took a small part, indeed, in the deliberations of one of the finest assemblies that ever I had the honour to address. One or two things suggest themselves to me principally as auguries, and good auguries indeed, for the future. One is the circumstance that this gathering is presided over by the eminent gentleman who left nothing for men like myself to say, because he has sounded faithfully and fearlessly, and with great ability, which all of us admire, the true key of national unity, and coming from a democratic community myself, and caring very little for individuals, and who were in the front or in the rere in the great battle for Ireland, coming to you with this message I say, that it augurs well for this great gathering that you should be addressed in the tone and spirit that you were in the beginning; and it is a further augury for your success that we have had bestowed on us the blessing of the Head of the Church to which, I presume, most of us belong. Another thing I may be allowed to allude to, and that is the pleasure it affords me to see so many of my fair countrywomen adorning this hall. I am proud of that circumstance, and I hope to be able to carry back to my friends in Victoria the proud message that they, by their presence, have contributed largely to unity in the Irish ranks. I disclaim possession of the gift of eloquence of some of your great countrymen who have kissed the Blarney Stone. But I hope to be able to see that stone before I leave Ireland, and after I get back to my people in Victoria I shall then for the first time in my life be able to claim some of that eloquence that people who have kissed the Blarney Stone are supposed to acquire. But I have been connected with politics in America. As a little boy, in '58, with my father and mother, I had to become practically an alien to my countrymen, for the reason that there were no opportunites for a growing up family. I was born in the historic county of Tipperary, and left there thirty-eight years ago with very poor prospects indeed. We, Irishmen and descendants of Irishmen in Australia, may be said to number one-fourth of the population. In that respect we were necessarily handicapped in the race for prosperity, and also by the fact that the other three-fourths had had better opportunities of technical and other instruction than we had. But, notwithstanding all the difficulties, I am a very poor specimen indeed of the many Irishmen who have forced their way to the front in Australia. But I am proud to say that in my small way I performed my duty as a man, and never forgot where I was born and the land that I love. Whilst I say that, it is only natural, coming from a free country, that I should love the soil of that country as I do. In that country indeed it is very rarely that disloyalty to the silken connection with the British Crown is heard of. But if this disloyalty to the

Crown is spoken of in any way it is not by Irishmen, but by somebody else, thereby showing that, given the same conditions of life and the same opportunities in Ireland to govern ourselves by and for the people, I say there would be no more loyal or true race, a race that would tend to build up, consolidate, and solidify the empire you now depise.

    I don't want to trench too much on your time, as I am, as you may imagine, naturally of a modest disposition, coming from the country I do, and scarcely knowing your habits in this, as appears to me, almost a foreign country, but I wish to say that since I came here I am exceedingly pleased with this beautiful historic city of Dublin, and, as compared with many of the cities on the Continent and elsewhere that I have had an opportunity of visiting, there is not a sounder political atmosphere—certainly a purer moral atmosphere—in the world, but it is for us here assembled to try and make the political atmosphere purer. I believe it is quite within your power; but coming from a country where we are small in proportion to the population, I think it right to tell you there is not a man in this assembly has a stronger feeling as to the rights of minorities. I would coerce no man to fall into our ranks even for the cause of Home Rule. I would not coerce him in that direction, but if our National Party is to be a factor in bringing about Home Rule, and if there is to be a National Government in Ireland at any time, we can get it not by internecine struggles. We can't get it, as has been said to day, by bringing up the dead ashes of the past. We must consider those who are opposed to us, and while not desiring to force our own opinions, we should be generous to those who are in a minority, because by that means—those are the only means—we can conciliate them and bring them into line in the direction we desire. I have belonged to a political party, and confidentially I may refer to one issue on which I took the right on a public platform to say in opposition to the party—that I would do my own small best in the direction of securing the right for the people to whom I belonged, to educate their children in a Christian fashion. I held that right individually, but if the conditions in Victoria were the same as they are here, I would advocate in my own party the necessity of enforcing education in the direction I required; but if my own party determined that the lines I was advocating were lines that they could not accept, I honestly say I would keep my mind on that point, or retire from the party altogether. Except with that spirit there can be no party government—and let me say, that party government here is somewhat different to that of our country, because we fight party against party for local political issues, while in this country you have only to fight the foreign enemy to restore your freedom. I fear again I am presuming too much upon your indulgence, but I prepared no speech and I prefer the impromptu to the carefully prepared speech. I think I may be excused if I refer to one or two other topics which touch this resolution—in fact series of resolutions.

    At least 200 delegates met in an Hibernian Hall in Melbourne, representatives from every town and hamlet in the country, and I was chosen to attend on their behalf as their delegate at this great Convention. I came here as free as the atmosphere, so far as I am concerned, not bound in any way to any individual, no matter what might be said

E

outside—and, perhaps, there are some outside who are willing to traduce instead of praise men who came here for the unselfish, devoted, and, I might say, noble purpose of even trying to assist the people of Ireland to secure the restoration of that independence of which she was robbed. I was also asked, coming through South Australia, to represent the people of that colony, nearly as large as the whole of Europe. We have in the six colonies six legislatures independent of one another, while in all, there is not a population equal to the decimated Irish population. There are something like three or four millions of people in the group of colonies having separate and independent legislatures. Each works out its political destinies. They are progressive, and in the matter of reform they conduct themselves as respectable citizens. Surely this spirit of democracy would be brought about if we had a United Ireland. On behalf of the people I represent, I ask for unity, and then Home Rule must necessarily follow. Let me, then, have a small recompense for coming through fire and water to reach here, and I say that no other mission in the world would have brought me to undertake such a journey. My wife, who is an Australian native—I do not mean to tell you she is a black, because that would be creating a false impression—she said to me when she learned of the object of my intended mission: "You must assuredly go." I felt proud of that encouragement, and nothing more fully fortified me than, as a small recompense for the journey I have undertaken, coming from the remotest part of the earth, to see that unity will take place amongst the people. Home Rule for Ireland, which was unfashionable some time ago in Victoria, is quite fashionable now. Not only had Irishmen espoused the cause of their brethren at home, but by their action they had won many friends from the English amongst whom they lived. They all agreed and admired the liberal spirit in which some Englishmen had turned to the just cause of Ireland when once the prejudice was removed from their eyes, and when they became just in their better feelings.

Rev. DENIS O'CALLAGHAN, Boston—Most rev. chairman and fellow-countrymen, the city of Boston, in the old colony of Massachusetts, merits, I think, a word before this presence and before this illustrious assembly of Irishmen, gathered from far and from near to consult together on Irish affairs. No one, I think, at all acquainted with National affairs abroad during the past two decades of years, to go back no further, will deny that Boston—and when I speak of Boston, I think I can well include all the New England States (New York is able to reply for itself)—has ever failed in its duty of granting support to the National cause and upholding the hands of Ireland's children on their native heath. I feel justified in saying, from a thorough knowledge of what the Irish people in the New England States, and in Boston in a special manner, have done, that among all the States of our fair Republic, Boston has ever held, and holds to-day, a good second place. Where in my city has not the beat of the National pulse ever been felt, and the hearts of the people not depressed or joyful, whenever news came from across the waters of the success or failure of the Irish cause? There are some fellow-countrymen, I feel, on this platform to-day, and perchance among you, who may well recall the time, in the crisis of Irish National affairs, when the affairs of Ireland were more or less in the balance, how the clergy of the Archdiocese of Boston, under the leadership of their illustrious and distinguished Metropolitan, assembled in council together, and sent across the waters words of cheer, and also substantial aid, to help the cause of Ireland. And, fellow-countrymen, the thought occurred to me to pay a visit to my native land on the occasion of this Convention, and I want to say here, in allusion to our distant friend who crossed the waters of the Red Sea, who proclaimed himself a Tipperary man, I proclaim myself a child of Rebel Cork. But, as in duty bound, I called upon our illustrious Most Rev. Archbishop John J. Williams, and said to him: "Your Grace, I have been requested by some of the patriotic Irishmen of Boston to come and attend this Convention." The illustrious prelate—and here, in this distinguished presence, I will say no truer Irishman walks the American soil—said to me, raising aloft his venerable hands: "Go, in God's name, and if you can say a word for unity amongst Irishmen, you will have done more than anything else, as a man, for Irish affairs." And in this connection, whilst speaking of his venerable name, allow me to join in connection with it the name of another Irishman—an Irishman, in one sense, more true, because born on Irish soil, venerated wherever an exile Gael has gone—I allude to him whom all Irishmen mourn, the late distinguished and patriotic John Boyle O'Reilly. Three days before he died I walked with him in the streets of Boston—Washington Street, I think—and our conversation was on Irish affairs. It was some time before his sad death, before disunion came amongst Irishmen, and the fair flag of unity was held still aloft, and turning to me, he said: "Father, it is an honour and a glory to-day to be an Irishman in the clubs of Boston." "And why is this?" said I. "Simply because the charge seems to be cast aside that Irishmen cannot be united once again, and they are proud, those who had previously kept their Irish origin concealed, they are now proud of their countrymen in Ireland." But from the time, and from that sad time, when Ireland's flag went down by disunion, apathy and deep-seated discouragement had taken possession of the people of Boston and of New England. But they have commissioned me, gentlemen, to come here and tell the reason why they feel so. Their hearts are still warm for Ireland and Irishmen, but they are discouraged and they are saddened by the dissension which prevails at home. It is patent to them that a hopeless disunion prevails amongst Irishmen, and it is patent to the enemies of Ireland as well, and they cry out: "Oh! my God, will this continue?" And they say: "May the watchful spirits and guardians that watch over the towns and hamlets of Ireland prevent it from taking place;" and they say: "May the martyred spirits, the martyred souls for Ireland's faith and Irish freedom, prevent the dire accomplishment." And hence they said to me: "In our name, say to the men of Ireland that if Ireland wants prosperity—if it desires peace—if, in the days of the near future or the remote, they desire Boston's aid and Boston's co-operation—then must they believe in and live up to that ancient maxim, as old as the hills: 'United we stand, divided we fall.'" Such are the convictions of the people of Boston, and I can only say, in their name, that when union prevails amongst you once again, they will stand forth and rally round the Irish flag, just as they have ever done in the days of the past.

Mr. MOSES CORNWALL, Kimberley, South Africa—My lord bishop and gentlemen, I assure you that I rise with a feeling of pride, mingled with fear, to address this glorious gathering of Irishmen, many of them from distant parts of the world, assembled here for the noble object of trying to restore peace and harmony in the distracted ranks of the Irish Parliamentary Party. Pride, I say, because for the first time in my life I have the opportunity and privilege of addressing my countrymen in my native land, and fear lest I might fail to place before you the sorrow and shame which the unhappy divisions existing amongst men that ought to be united have brought to the hearts of those I represent in distant Africa, and other parts of the world. A short time ago I was honoured by my fellow-countrymen to represent them at this Convention. I told them I would attend, not as a Dillonite, Healyite, or Parnellite, but as an Irishman, and that statement met with the unanimous approval of those present on that occasion. It is, my lord, incomprehensible to Irishmen abroad why men professing to have the same object at heart should be divided into different sections and factions—quarrelling amongst themselves about non-essentials, and disgracing their country's cause. These quarrels and factions alienate the support of thousands of Englishmen and Irishmen. I do not know what is the experience of those gentlemen representing Irishmen in other British Colonies, but my own has been a sad and bitter one. Many colonists holding high and honourable positions whom I have the honour of knowing, and who up to recent times were ardent Home Rulers, have changed and modified their opinions, not because they think it would not be right and proper to give Irishmen the right to make their own laws in their own land, but because they feel that if ever the right were conceded these wretched quarrels would be increased and even intensified. I appeal to all who come here, not as partisans but as Irishmen, to say if these gentlemen are justified in thinking so? It is a mistake to consider that this feeling is confined to Englishmen alone. Thousands of Irishmen like myself, who have spent their lives abroad, and others who equally love Ireland though they never set foot on its green shores, but who have heard from their parents' lips the story of her wrongs, have grown lukewarm in their support of Home Rule. I may tell you, that the overwhelming majority of the Irishmen of South Africa are in favour of Home Rule. Living in a land where every man has equal rights, and fair play, they are loyal to the Queen and Constitution. Irishmen in past times have filled some of the most important positions in the colony, and at the present time I need only name Sir Thomas Uppington and Lord Rosmead, the Governor and High Commissioner, who is an Irishman and a Home Ruler. The people there believe that the people of Ireland should be granted the right to make their own laws in their own land—a right which every free people should enjoy, and which has been conceded to nearly all colonies, and that all matters appertaining to the Empire should be discussed in the Imperial Parliament, where Irishmen should have a proper proportion of representatives. The Irish people in the Colonies would never consent if they had a voice in the matter to be deprived of a share in that mighty Empire, in building up which our countrymen took such a part, and which has afforded a home to numbers of our race. The Colonies and India do not belong to England alone.

They belong to Great Britain and Ireland, and he would be a poor Irishman who would willingly forego a right to his share in such an Empire. We also believe that the granting of Home Rule would enable a local parliament to develop the resources of the country and encourage industries, and do many other things which are now utterly neglected by the Imperial Parliament through want of time to attend to them, as well as from a want of knowledge to understand them. We also believe that the granting of Home Rule to Ireland would bring together men of different views and religions who now keep aloof from the movement. We believe, above all things, that Home Rule would bring back to our country the peace and happiness for which Grattan, O'Connell, and Parnell, and innumerable Irishmen fought and struggled, and for which men of our race will continue to struggle, until this boon is granted, but which will never be achieved until we put an end to dissension. Let us only be united, and let us prove to the world that we are fit and determined to achieve our independence, and no power on earth will in time prevent us from achieving our object. I will not detain you any longer. There are a number of other gentlemen here who, by their experience, are better qualified to speak to you. I thank you very kindly for your patient hearing, and I have much pleasure in supporting the resolutions before you.

Mr. CHARLES H. BROMBY, North Tasmania—My lord and brother delegates, I have been sent from an island so far away that it is not even marked upon that large map of the world which decorates the card of admission here to-day; but though far away, I can tell you that the hearts of Irishmen there beat strongly with love of their native land; and their children, who have never seen Ireland, and will, perhaps, never see it, are brought up with the same love of country as they themselves who have been exiled from this soil. In some ways it seems to me that the island in the seas so far away further resembles our own island at home in many respects. They resemble each other certainly both in physical appearance and also in the beauty of their women. The people there also resemble the Irish people in this, that they are as fond of a little friction when they come to deal with political questions. We fight and go for one another on such small questions as a railway for north or south, or east or west, but if we have this friction there, we did not commence differences until we got our own Parliament, and we had our friction afterwards. In that country, where Smith O'Brien and John Mitchel spent many days and years, owing to their love for Ireland, the people joined together to obtain a free Constitution. Now, I must tell you flat and plain that we in that country are astonished, and feel hopeless of your cause, when we see the way in which Irishmen at home are going on. The children of the race abroad see that the principal men are Irishmen, that the Governors of the Colonies are Irishmen, that the judges are mostly Irishmen, that the two first Speakers in the House of Commons in Victoria were Irishmen, and they are astonished that the people at home do not join together to gain the freedom of their country. Having said this, I may be allowed to make one or two practical suggestions as to how we out there think it ought to be done. In the first place, of course, it is the majority which ought to rule. I need not insist further upon that. But, as there are those who have followers in the Irish Parliamentary Party, and as it is of the greatest importance to gain them over to act like one man, I would suggest that in treating with them, in speaking of them, or in writing of them, you should do so with a kindly spirit—treat them as though they were one day to be your leaders and friends. We in Tasmania—and I think in this I can speak of Australia—do not care whether it is Dillon, or Redmond, or anybody else, so long as he is appointed by the majority. If, however, you cannot persuade these men to come back, then there must be an appeal to the constituencies. The people of this country are the best judges of the last resort. So go amongst the voters who vote for those men who will not have majority rule, and endeavour to persuade them not to vote for those men in future. I say that the man who will not abide by the decision of majority rule is as great an enemy of Ireland as if he were an English Unionist. All the shouting in the Leinster Hall will not do if you are not prepared to agitate, agitate, agitate. Go, then, amongst those constituencies who have returned members who will not have majority rule, and tell them of the words of wisdom you heard here to-day from my lord the chairman and other speakers, and, if you do but work hard, I feel confident that at the next General Election a different result will be attained. Looking through your resolutions, every one of which, of course, must have your full support, I have only seen one single word there with which I couldn't agree, and it is where one of the resolutions makes [reference to "the Conquest of Ireland." My lord, Ireland has never been conquered. If the resolution said "The origin of English rule," I could understand it. And how did that rule begin? It was through dissension. It was not a conquest which brought in the Normans. It was one of your own princes who sold his country because he did not agree with the majority. I need not tell you the history of your country. You know that when any misfortune was brought upon her it was brought upon her by dissension. I shall only say in conclusion that if Ireland is only united once more she can make England tremble, as she made her tremble before, and it will not be long before she will have won back her long-lost rights.

Very Rev. Dean HARRIS, Toronto—My lord chairman, ladies, and gentlemen, there is a possibility of inflicting too much of a good thing upon an exceedingly patient audience, and if we bring no further consolation home with us across the sea we will carry the assurance that Ireland had presented to us the most forbearing audience that ever we addressed. As Father Ryan has said, we are not representative of any particular section or any particular party. We are not purchasable commodities. We come here sons of the soil free and independent, and when any section of the Press or any body of men say that we are nobodies, in the name of God where will you find an honest man? If the Hon. John Costigan is a nobody where will you find a great man? We come twenty-three strong from Canada. I make no boast of this to you, but I mention it as an indication of the strong feeling of Irish patriotism that animates us—each and every one of us is paying his own expenses. We come at considerable sacrifice of time and convenience ; and we are here to do what we possibly can to patch up the differences that exist amongst the Irish people. For six months in the year, in the country I come from, the northern lakes are so bound by one solid mass of ice that sometimes they put their railroads across the ice and rush their heaviest trains across it. But there is a certain season in which this ice begins to break up ; it forms into fragments, and then a child of two years old could not stand upon it. Where you have a solid, compact body of united men you can bear any load that is put upon you ; but when you are broken into fragments you are as the melting ice. I come from the banks of the Welland Canal, where, fifty-four years ago, there were three thousand of our fellow-countrymen engaged in digging that extraordinary canal that extends from Lake Erie to Lake Ontario. That canal is not inferior in its construction to any canal in the world. The banks of that canal were honeycomed, and are to-day, with the graves of our buried countrymen, and we, their sons, have come to appeal to you in the name of God to close up your ranks. We come with kindly feeling towards Mr. Redmond. We come with kindly feeling towards Mr. Healy. We come with kindly feeling towards Mr. Dillon. We are not here, gentlemen, to question their motives ; we have not come to dictate any policy to you ; we have not come to intrude upon your private affairs. We have come as respectable beggars to ask you, in the name of God, to form yourselves into a solid body, and be as you were five or six years ago. Whatever may be the acrimonious feelings and divisions amongst yourselves we know them not. We believe in our hearts that the three divisions that exist amongst you are composed of honest, intelligent, and brave men. We all recognise that this meeting has to do what it possibly can to draw these three together and make them into one, so that as the husband and wife are two in one, the Dillonites, and the Healyites, and the Redmonites may form three in one. More than this I have no right to say to you. The Canadian delegation includes our chairman, the Hon. John Costigan, and our secretary, Mr. Cronin. We have with us Hugh Ryan, perhaps, the largest contractor in the Dominion of Canada, a man who has come here at great sacrifice ; and when, therefore, any section of the Dublin Press shall say that we are nobodies we throw the lie back in their faces. Have we not the right to expect from all parties courteous treatment ? Are we not entitled to fair play when we come from thousands of miles away ? What right, therefore, has any body of men to stigmatise us before the people of Dublin and the people of Ireland as nobodies representing nobody ? I, for one, am in a position to say that myself and my colleague from the banks of Niagara were elected by the Irishmen of Niagara to bear to you Irishmen a message of peace and brotherly love, and the petition that you will do what in you lies to stand together man to man until in the end we have accomplished the great end for which we have been working—Home Rule for Ireland. On this platform to-day you have a distinguished example of the power of burying differences. You have here one of the most distinguished Protestant gentlemen from Canada, the Hon. Mr. Blake, the leader, the head, and the chief for many years of the great Liberal Party of the Dominion of Canada. You have here an equally distinguished Catholic gentleman, the Hon. John Costigan, a member of the Queen's Privy Council in the Dominion of Canada, and of the Executive body that governs that country. These gentlemen have fought face to face against each other for thirty years—for thirty years they have never laid the shield or buried the hatchet, but when it was a question of doing anything for Ireland they stood together shoulder to shoulder and hand to hand. If, therefore, this distinguished Prostestant gentleman and this distinguished Irish gentleman have given this example to the parties that are divided, and if they have proved the possibility of union on a common platform, what is the reason that Parnellites, Dillonites, and Healyites cannot come together on this platform also? My lord bishop, I thank you very much indeed for your courteous reception, and the ladies and gentlemen for the hospitable, kindly and generous brotherhood they have extended to us. We want to go back to our own people—we never may put our foot here again; forty-nine years ago I was born in Cork—the city that John Mitchel, in Steinway Hall, described as the home of rebels, of fair women, and of handsome men—so we want to go back, perhaps, never again to see you, and we want to tell our people, from platform and from pulpit, and on the public streets, that the delegates from Canada met with a kindly, hospitable reception from the people of Ireland, and that we are grateful for it. One word more. A gentleman said to me, in my own city, "If they don't now settle we may despair of Ireland." "Despair," said I, "Never." "Despair of the people that have fought for centuries. So help me God, so long as there are three Irishmen living I will never despair of them."

Rev. PATRICK LYNCH, Manchester—My lord and gentlemen of the Convention of the Irish Race, the words I shall address to you will be brief indeed. Other gentlemen are anxious to speak, and I shall take up but very few minutes of your time. Now, it seems to me that the main reason for the assembling of this Convention is to promote union amongst the people of Ireland themselves. If the people of Ireland were united they would stamp out dissension amongst the Parliamentary leaders in twenty-four hours. Gentlemen, this is the message which those who sent me here charge me to deliver. I speak as a Lancashire delegate, and the Lancashire delegates are here to-day to speak for a half a million of the Irish race in England. In the town of Manchester we have a much larger population of Irish either by birth or by blood than there are in the cities of Cork and Limerick combined; and if in this magnificent gathering the cities of Cork and Limerick possess weight, as unquestionably they do possess weight, then I say Manchester, with a larger Irish population, ought to possess an influence as great. My lord and gentlemen, for the last twenty years we in Lancashire made ourselves political pariahs before the people of Ireland. In the elections for Poor Law Guardians, of members of the City Council, in the election for members of the County Councils, in every public gathering where the Irish vote could tell, the great principle that moved us to record our votes is the question, "Is the man an Irishman? Is the man friendly to Home Rule and the cause of Home Rule?" If he was, he got power and place by the votes of the Irishmen of Manchester. Last November I saw the blank walls of one of the wards of the city of Manchester placarded, calling upon the Irish voters to vote for a certain candidate for the City Council because he was a friend of Ireland and a Home Ruler. Now, you all know that the Manchester City Council cannot grant Home Rule to Ireland; but I think you will agree with me when

I say that this mode of action—the tactics of the Irish in England—are extremely wise. It is by keeping Home Rule so prominently forward, and by making it the polestar of every other public question, that we have driven home to the minds of the people of England the justice and honesty of Home Rule. I ask you to agree that the voice of Manchester ought to have weight in an assembly of this kind. What I say of Manchester is equally true of all the great towns of Yorkshire, of England, and Scotland. In the ordinary state of political things in England, both parties are nearly equal, and it is the Irish vote that comes in the determiner of the political scale in England. You in Ireland may give your vote for Home Rule, but in Ireland you are simply the wooden shaft of the spear. It is the vote of the Irish people in England that makes the steel end of the spear. [A Voice—"What about Scotland?"] I include Scotland with all my heart. Now, gentlemen, we are happy and proud to see representatives here from every country in the world almost where the Irish race are found. We have gentlemen here from America, from Canada, and from Australia, and we have a large number from the dear old land at home. Now, gentlemen, I think that if ever there was a truth it is this. America may send gold in abundance to help the cause, Canada may do the same and give wealth in like manner. You here at home may be as united as you will. England, if England pleases, can keep you down as she has kept you down for the last seven centuries. I say distinctly, America may give gold, and you at home may give help for unity, but if Home Rule is ever to be won it will be won more by the force of the Irish in England than by any other factor which assists in its winning. Having said this, I would not discharge my duty if I did not deliver in full the message which those who sent me here to speak for them commissioned me to deliver. It is this. They are becoming restive at the continuance of the dissensions in Ireland. If dissension merely existed amongst a half-dozen or dozen of the Parliamentary leaders they would give it but little thought, but when dissension exists amongst the people it is this that dismays them in the cause of Ireland. Their message, therefore, to you, representatives of the Irish race at home, is this—"Close your ranks, stand together like men, shoulder to shoulder, and we, the Irish in England, will vote our last man, and spend our last shilling, and fight your battle to the last ditch on your behalf."

Mr. PATRICK DUNLEVY, Philadelphia—I have come here from the "City of Brotherly Love," bearing no malice to anyone, but peace and goodwill. I need not tell you that it is the Quaker City of the United States, and in that relation I have great pleasure in supporting the resolutions of the Quaker gentleman of Dublin. I would remark, by the way, that I have been delegated to come here from an organisation through which all the money that has been raised in our city for the last sixteen years for the Irish cause has come, and, to all whom it may concern, "I can read my title clear." I have been much impressed with this land of my birth since I first set my foot upon it a few days ago. It appears that, after forty-five years' absence, I have not forgotten the faculty of perpetrating Irish bulls. I have been much impressed, and particularly so here to-day, as it reminds me of the series of gatherings and public demonstrations and meetings that we have held in our city since the days of the Land League movement up to a few months ago, in favour of the Irish cause. The character and importance of this meeting can be testified to by the eminent and prominent gentlemen who are here on the stage to-day. Without boasting, I can say that our city has marched in the forefront of Ireland's freedom from the beginning until now. We have never failed in responding to your appeals; and your very last appeal from the distinguished gentleman who has addressed you, Mr. M'Carthy, we generously answered it. But the unfortunate dissensions that sprung up among you here were carried across the water to our fair land, and permeated some of our best workers in the cause. But time has worked wonderful changes; and I say to you to-day that in leaving the shores of America for this Convention, I was clasped heartily by the hand and bid God-speed and success by the men who differ with me. I can, without presumption, say to you that I represent Parnellites, Healyites, and Nationalists to-day. I can say to you that their wish and their prayer is for unity, and I trust in God that here in this collective representative Convention there is wit and wisdom, statesmanship, disinterested love of our land and of her cause, sufficient to rise superior to all difficulties, and find a way out of this miserable condition. Do this, and I can go home, and with renewed energy and renewed effort, turn to the work of restoring confidence, and with that confidence will come again our support; and with a united front, and pressing home the essential question of Home Rule, it is but a few years, I firmly believe, until you will enjoy it.

Rev. Dr. FOLEY, Nova Scotia.—My lord and gentlemen, I think that this Convention has commenced with very happy auguries. We have received a letter from the workingman's Pope—the democratic Pope Leo XIII.—and the most rev. chairman of this meeting is an Irish Bishop who talks tersely, directly, like a man, and with a courage that has placed the men of his race always in the forefront of the battle. I see around me gentlemen who are famed the world over, and I am convinced that their political sagacity will crown with success the cause of Home Rule, imperilled though it may be. That this Convention, gentlemen, meets at the instance of a Canadian Archbishop is for us Canadians an object of legitimate praise, but that it meets for the purpose of proclaiming to all Irishmen of goodwill the joyous tidings of unity and peace, is a matter of higher import and of more heartfelt congratulation. I am not too sanguine when I say, though I be an Irishman, that round the world ring the confident congratulations of the Irish race. They are confident that to-day is the starting-point with a revivified Irish nationality. We have heard in our country reports of disaffection and disunion, but remember that they emanated from the Press that has ever striven to extort a verdict against Irishmen, and we did not believe them in their entirety. Yet we knew that the embers of discontent were smouldering; that sooner or later they might develop into a consuming blaze, and leave only ruins where once stood the fair fabric of the Irish National Party. This we knew, but our only hope is that this Convention—the wise counsels of this Convention—may prevail in effecting a complete reunion. We are not here to-day, ladies and gentlemen, either to speak of or to criticise the past. We are here simply to look to the future, and it seems to me that no man, no matter in what light he may regard this Convention, can reasonably deny our right and privilege to say a word at the present juncture. I have been sent here by the Irishmen of Halifax, and instructed by them in the most solemn manner not to say one word of a denunciatory character against any gentleman who has upheld the fame and loyalty of the old land, against any members of the Irish Party who have, to quote the words of Mr. Gladstone, made the cell a national shrine and the prison garb a dress of the highest honour. And we, the delegates from Nova Scotia, ask you, "Will you not send us back with a message that may re-awaken the old-time enthusiasm, and convince us that the principles for which Irishmen are battling are greater than any man or section?" An Irishman of Halifax said to me the morning before I started: "When you go to Ireland, tell them, for God's sake, not to spend their days speechifying, but get down to some practical business. Tell them to lay down some commonsense platform on which all Nationalists can stand." And we are sent here not to identify ourselves with any party. We come from a democratic country, where the rule of the majority prevails, and we wish that the will of the majority of the elected representatives of the Irish people should prevail in the administration of Home Rule affairs. We stand by the principle of majority rule, and any man who obtains a majority of one vote, be he any member of the Irish Party, no matter how he may be called, will have our support in the National movement.

The Irishmen of Halifax behind me beseech you to bury the carrion of dissension that stinks in the nostrils of decent men. Give us a guarantee before we leave this Convention that we may on public platforms and in the Press plead your cause without indignity and without subjecting ourselves to the taunts of men who would say that Home Rule is a mere fanciful speculation. What joy was ours when the hereditary English statesman made a speech in which he said:—"The flowing tide is with us." What joy was ours when unity brought us to the verge of triumph. But the old drama was once again enacted, and Irishmen were divided. Halifax and Nova Scotia are one with you and your struggle for right, for the promotion of your industries, and for the shaping of your own destiny. They beg me to tell you that if they are prosperous, if they share in the blessings of a Christian civilisation, if they stand together irrespective of politics in the determination to shape their own destinies—it is as the result of union. Our Archbishop—to show what a democratic city it is—our present Archbishop, the Most Rev. Dr. O'Brien, enjoys the distinction of being President of the Royal Society of Canada, a society that contains some of the most prominent scientific and literary men in the country. Our Lieutenant-Governor rejoices in the good name of Daly; the Mayor who preceded the present man had the Irish name of Keeffe; and I mention these matters to show the true democratic character of the country where the majority must prevail. I am convinced that you will send us back to Halifax with a message to gladden the hearts of Irishmen who are confident that this Convention will shield our country from the destroying rays of internecine dissension. Close up your ranks. Do not, I beg of you, cause us to hang our heads for shame. Do this, and I tell you on their behalf that you will have the material and moral support of all Irishmen of good will. You will have the admiration of your enemies, and of all who can appreciate the work of a united and determined race. I hope this Convention may be able to place on the National Registry this entry:—" In the month of September, 1896, in Dublin, the Irish Party was regenerated in the saving waters of unity by the Canadian Archbishop, with the greater Ireland as its sponsor, and was given for its legitimate parents the majority of the representatives of the Irish people."

The CHAIRMAN—There is a telegram from Bolton, England, which I will ask Mr. Davitt to read.

Mr. DAVITT, M.P.—The following telegram has just been received :—

> The members of the National League of Great Britain send greeting to Ireland's sons assembled in council, and pray that God may bless their deliberations, and bring peace and unity to Ireland. May the first thought of all be Ireland over all. God Save Ireland.

Mr. KENNEDY, Wellington, New Zealand—My lord and gentlemen, you are aware that I come from probably the most remote country represented here to-day, a country that is as large as Great Britain and half of Ireland combined. Our population is small, only three-quarters of a million, and the Irish population in the colony is only one-seventh of the whole. We therefore know what it is to be in a minority. Now, the question upon which we are sent here is the question of unity. If there is any other mode of ruling a country than the rule of majority we would like to know it. New Zealand was the land of experimental legislation. We tried many lines of action, but we never discovered any other means of ruling except the rule of the majority. A celebrated politician had said, "The privilege of the minority is to become a majority." We have a representative Parliament on the widest possible scale, and there is no particular love between the two parties—the "ins" and the "outs"—and the minority tries to become the majority. We appeal to the Irish people to sink their differences, and if they find in the course of time that any of their members go wrong, then let them go down to the people and oust them. The majority must bind the minority. We Irishmen in New Zealand are ardent Home Rulers, and there are other men who are not Irishmen who sympathise with the Irish cause; but they now point to the divisions amongst Irishmen, and Irishmen are not only discouraged, but they are made a laughing-stock by those dissensions. I was, therefore, sent to Ireland to point out the absolute necessity of unity and majority rule.

The CHAIRMAN—There is a telegram from Quebec, which Mr. Davitt will read.

Mr. DAVITT, M.P., read the following telegram —

> Hon. John Costigan, care Chairman, Irish National Convention.—Represent us. Meeting Irishmen to-night unanimously resolved send Convention brotherly greetings, heartiest sympathy. Pray God bless your labours with much success in interest of union of Irishmen at home and abroad in the grand cause of Home Rule and fair play to Ireland.—FELIX CARBRAY, Chairman.

Rev. GEORGE F. MARSHALL, Manchester, New Hampshire—My lord, ladies and gentlemen, I do not appear here for the purpose of making a speech. Enough has been already said to convince every honest man in this gathering that our purpose here, and our purpose in coming across the ocean, was to try and induce divided Nationalists in Ireland to throw aside their dissension and disunion and to work all together once more for our dear old country. We have come here to urge upon you to cast aside your differences and endeavour to form once again a grand united party, such as we had a few years ago—a party that would suffer dictation from nobody, and that would compel that despot, England, to give Ireland relief from the oppression under which she is suffering. I do not come here to speak on behalf of the one party or the second party or the third party. I appreciate the men who belong to those parties. I give them credit each of thinking that they are on the right road. When I was leaving the United States and now, I may say, I had and have an open mind as to which of the three parties was the best to obtain Home Rule for Ireland. It is for you to decide, and to decide by giving a majority. And when you have given that majority you should stand by that majority, giving towards the minority all deference, but, at the same time, seeing that that majority shall rule, and also insisting that the gentlemen who shall be elected by that majority shall have perfect control of the party, as the potter has control of the clay in which he works. I say that party should be in his hands in that way, and that he should insist they should all work together to advance the interests of Ireland, and endeavour to take away the shame attached to our dear old land—that shame which discord, dissension, and disunion have brought upon her. Say to your leader when you have elected him: "You were elected for a certain end; for that you must fight, sinking all minor differences for the common good." Let us see such a state of things, and then we can demand our rights from one of the greatest powers on earth. Years gone by it was a hard thing to build up an Irish party, but as years rolled by the party, once started, grew and grew until it became one grand united party, and even until it was courted by English parties. We want a party now on the same lines. We want a party now that will work firmly and steadily on the same lines. It is of no importance to us, delegates who have come across the ocean, whether it is the tried and true John Dillon who will lead the party; it is of no importance to us whether it is William O'Brien or Mr. O'Connor who will lead the party; it is of no importance to us whether it is Mr. Healy who will lead the party. No; but it is of the utmost importance to us that one man shall rule, that his rule shall be strong, and that it shall be obeyed; in fact that he shall rule, as we say in Irish, with láṁ láiḋir. We were told before we left the United States that our efforts would be of no use, and that it would be useless for us to interfere. Yes; but I did not believe those statements, and I do not believe them now, when I see in the chair of this historic gathering a descendant of the O'Donnells. I have confidence in a Convention composed of such men. Here we have a man who comes to the front as the friend of Ireland presiding at this meeting, and brings new confidence and new strength to our country; and with this new confidence and new strength, I hope we shall be able to go back to our friends across the ocean and tell them that there is a fair prospect of union, and that after all what was going on was only a little row and a little skirmish, and that the shame which dissension and disunion brought upon Ireland will shortly be wiped out.

Very Rev. M. A. CLANCY—I, too, have been sent with a message of peace and goodwill and reconciliation from the iron-bound coasts of Newfoundland to the fair Green Isle of Old Erin. Though I cannot boast of representing any very large number of Irishmen, or any very large country, as far as population is concerned, nevertheless, though we are only a small section of people, we are animated with the same impulsive love of Ireland, the same great desire for Ireland's freedom that the most bold-hearted in Ireland can possibly feel. You do not know, and you cannot feel the burning shame that comes into our faces when we are told over and over again : " What good are you Irishmen doing at all ? What is the reason that for even one sacred moment, when in that moment you might possibly touch the goal of liberty, you cannot be united amongst yourselves?" My colleague and I from Newfoundland come here to implore you to grasp our hands in brotherly love, that we may be united as one man in the demand for Home Rule. But as the most necessary thing you must be united amongst yourselves, and I fancy that from this great Convention must go forth a mandate, strong and powerful, and irresistible, that will command unity amongst the Irish Parliamentary Party. A great deal is said about majority rule. All of us who live in self-governing countries, such as Newfoundland, must admit majority rule, and although we are a very small number of people we can manage our own affairs. No doubt we have occasionally a little friction, but it is only now after Home Rule has been obtained. Before this Convention assembled I believe an effort had been made to unite the various sections into which unfortunately our party is divided. These approaches were made by men who had been previously in a kind of way political enemies. They were not very cordially received, however, but there should go out from this Convention a mandate insisting that those now separated should come together and be of one fold. There is very little use, after all, in harping all the time on this unfortunate want of unity. No doubt, within a very short time since, we who followed the debates in the English House of Commons often lamented and often groaned for one brief hour of blind old Dandalo. We wanted the master hand and powerful mind of Charles Stewart Parnell. Not many more words do I intend to address to you for the present ; but I am reminded here to-day of a story I read a great many years ago when the *Nation* was the people's voice. It is the story of the revolution in Spain in the year '42, and the hero of this story said—" Neither Christina, nor yet Don Carlos, and let our rallying cry be ' Liberty for Spain.'" And I will say likewise—" Neither Healy, nor Redmond, nor even John Dillon, but let our rallying cry be 'Liberty for Ireland.'"

Rev. EDWARD S. PHILLIPS, Pennsylvania—Most rev. chairman, fellow-delegates, ladies and gentlemen, I did not intend when leaving my home in America to make an address at this Convention, for I believed, as most Americans believe, and what most Irishmen know, that there is if anything too much orating in Ireland. I came here not to make a speech but to do something. I was not born in Ireland. I would like to have been born in Cork or Tipperary after the reputation these two worthy children have given of these two places. I may say, as we are all giving something of our pedigree, that my parents were married at the foot of

Nephin Beg, and if they remained there a short time I would not have been born in America, and as our young friend, Dr. Foley, said, it is no fault of mine if I am not an Irishman. I came here to represent the most intensely patriotic organisation in America—the Ancient Order of Hibernians, representing directly about ten thousand anthracite coal-miners in Pennsylvania, and the particular district from which I have come as a delegate is Lucerne. Therefore, I have a right to speak on behalf of Irish unity. I have been told by my fellow members of the Ancient Order of Hibernians to counsel unity if necessary, and it is not necessary to speak of unity, but for God's sake to do something for unity and for Ireland. Gentlemen, we have heard a great deal about unity. That word "unity" is magnificent all the world over—in America, Australia, New Zealand, South Africa, Great Britain, and Ireland, when it is on paper, but I have not yet heard one suggestion as to the means of promoting unity in Ireland. I have heard, with which I must disagree, one delegate say tyranny is necessary among the bosses—among the leaders. Gentlemen, I think that there is a great deal of trouble in the ambitions of leadership, and I hope that out of this Convention there will arise one whom Ireland can trust (A Voice—Sexton). I can't discountenance the magnificent work of the present chairman. I admire him for the work that he has done, and as all the speakers have said, and the magnificent orator from the North of Ireland, O'Donnell, has said, Ireland is greater than any man, Ireland is greater than leaders, and if the leaders be at fault then the people should know how to right the wrong. The people should be the law, and should rule. I live in a country in which there is government of the people, for the people, and by the people, and every time I'll swear by the people, because with the people all united it makes no difference about leaders—the country cannot go wrong. If, gentlemen, out of this Convention will come something good for the people of Ireland, for the proper representation of the people of Ireland, I care not who is leader, I'll go back to the patriotic Order of Hibernians (Board of Erin) and tell them I did not come in vain to the land of my fathers.

The CHAIRMAN—The proceedings of to-day will close with another speech. We have had a great advantage of hearing at considerable length the splendid messages that have come to us from our friends abroad, and the delegates of the Convention have had an opportunity of digesting a good deal of the proposals that are put forward upon the agenda paper; hence, it is my purpose on to-morrow, please God, while allowing to the utmost of my power all the latitude of discussion, to make a good way through the agenda paper. I hope to-night you will be able to consider the resolutions, and, therefore, while taking occasion to-morrow to explain thoroughly your views with regard to them, I think it would be possible for you to come to a conclusion, and, if necessary, to a division on them, without very long debate. I may mention that in connection with resolution (1), of the group "A," on looking over the paper I find resolutions "L" and "M" germane to it, and they shall be taken early to-morrow in conjunction with it, and likewise the resolution of which notice has been handed in by Father Flynn, Waterford, which very probably he will move as an amendment to the resolution that appears first on Mr. Webb's list.

Mr. JOHN FERGUSON, Glasgow—My lord and fellow countrymen, after the magnificent addresses which you have been listening to, and particularly after the address delivered by the distinguished ecclesiastic who occupies the chair, and under whose presidency I am proud to-day to speak, I feel that it is, indeed, too much at this late hour to ask you to listen for more than a very few minutes to the words I would like to say to you. I come from a land once hostile but now united in friendship for Ireland. I come from a country where we had to fight for our political rights and political existence as Irishmen—a fiercer fight than any you have had perhaps in this or any country in the world. We have had Irishmen shot on the platform while maintaining our green flag above. We have had bullets through our windows to tell us of the hostile feeling of the Scottish people. That day has passed away, and we roused the spirit of Celtic kinship amongst the Scottish people, and to-day Scotland stands solid for Home Rule. My lord, my eye fell at once upon the words upon the scroll at the back of the hall, and I went back in thought twenty-three years to the great Convention. I looked at the crowded gallery here and I thought of the gallery in the historic Rotunda, when, under the great Isaac Butt, we met there, 1,200 delegates, the best Parliament Ireland had seen for seventy-three years. We were then defying the law, for let our American and Australian friends take this back with them, that in those days such a meeting as this subjected every delegate to imprisonment and fine; it was contrary to law to hold a delegate assembly in Ireland. But our grand old Irishman showed us how to break the law, and by-and-by they had to repeal it because we were too many for them. But in those days "God Save Ireland" would not have been placed upon the gallery of our Convention. We have advanced since then. The names of Allen, Larkin, and O'Brien—another name should be there, you know it—it is in Glasnevin. There should be many other names, but there should be another martyr added to the three; he came from Glasgow. The Convention reminds me of something that then interfered with unity in our ranks—one the broken remnant of the gallant Fenian movement, which had not yet quite made up its mind that the unconstitutional battle should be no longer fought. Let no man fear to name the Fenian Brotherhood. Has not William Ewart Gladstone, that distinguished Englishman, said —the words are not Ferguson's words, but Mr. Gladstone's words— "The depth and intensity of the Fenian movement has taught me the necessity of legislating to avert a danger from the Empire?" And said that greatest of all English statesmen, that highest-minded and purest man of all English statesmen, although he has often gone wrong, said he, "It has been said that they are the scum of the Irish race; but my friend Mr. Maguire's book shows to me that the Fenians are the very cream of the Irish race." That, my lord, was provoked by those who put up "God Save Ireland" at the meeting.

I apologise for the digression, and I go on with my subject. There was another element of dissension at the meeting; that element inherited the glorious traditions of O'Connell, the glorious traditions of the Young Ireland Party, and it was not prepared to turn aside from the simple Repeal of which we heard a good deal, and which gave us a good deal of trouble, even for Isaac Butt's grand scheme. But ultimately we conquered, ultimately we had a unity in Ireland for years ; and oh, fellow-countrymen ! what was the result of that unity? Look at its result. The Established Church—the Church in which I was born and to which I belong—the Established Church was disestablished and put into an honest and honourable position, in which it is now. And the landlords, the foreign garrison in Ireland, that plundered it of twelve millions per annum, that have wrought such havoc in the land of the O'Donnells—ah, we clipped their wings ! Two or three millions out of their income are to-day in the pockets of the Irish people. Not much, I admit, but still it is something. But better than all, we have established the doctrine that they had no right to any of it whatever. We sent a Commission up to the Highlands of Scotland which wiped out all the arrears—you have not quite got that far yet—wiped out all the arrears and took forty-five per cent. off the rent. But we established by our united action Land Courts in Ireland which asserted the principle that no man should pay rent for any improvements of his own or those of his predecessors in title. I admit that, because of your disunion and because of your want of loyalty to your principles and your party, that has not been carried out as well as it would, but now is the time for a forward march. We have taught these men that they must no longer gather where they have not scattered, or reap where they have not sown, and now is the time for a united forward march. Oh, brothers dear, we must not again by our dissensions lose the vantage ground we have won. I am told all round no good will come of your Convention ; it will be just a large crowd of enthusiastic people ; they will cheer unity, but another crowd could be got up on the other side to-morrow. Not a bit of it. God Almighty has made mankind thus—that although some men upon any given subject may be so prejudiced, may be so full of hate, or of love, that they are unable to see the broad principle of truth, yet the great majority of men upon any one question can be taught that *Magna est veritas et prevalebit*—we will make the truth prevail. I have been excited by the magnificent speeches, and have got into an enthusiastic spirit by the gathering of the nation and the sea-divided Gael on the platform. I want now to deal shortly with one question raised lately in England, and by the *Times* newspaper in particular. It says there are now only four and a half millions of people in Ireland, and that we are so weak that we cannot get what we want. The Celt is gone with a vengeance, and the *Times* boasted that the Celt would soon be as scarce as a Red Indian on the shores of the Manhattan. But in relation to the foreigner the Celt is just as numerous in Ireland as ever he was, and he is armed with a power he never had before, and Ireland can now be properly represented in the House of Commons. But, then, what if Irishmen have gone with a vengeance? They are armed with a hundred times more power in foreign lands, and wherever the English flag flies there, too, are found members of the Irish race. The Alabama claim would never have been pressed home but for the Irish population in America, and the Venezuelan question, which is giving England so much trouble—I venture to think that some of our fellow-countrymen have something to say to that. The Celt has gone away with a vengeance, but he is coming back in many ways. He is not coming back with the green flag flying over shotted guns, but he is sending the produce of his

F

adopted country into England and is breaking down her monopoly. Now, too, we can return eighty-six members of Parliament to the House of Commons. We are not loyal under the present circumstances, and we cannot be loyal under the present circumstances, but we offer England a chance of making us loyal. If we get a National assembly in Dublin to manage our National affairs, we are satisfied to have an Imperial House for the Empire, in which Ireland should be properly represented. Supposing England exposes itself to the world by muzzling our members, by putting them out—and I admit they have the physical power to do that—then where is the constitutional assembly? Under these circumstances, is not the Government in Ireland manifestly a coercion Government? England in these days cannot afford to rule Ireland with the sword; England must appreciate Ireland, and here we offer her the hand of friendship, but we must have national self-government.

> "Oh! brothers, gather close to keep
>   The land we'll win once more;
> Division were the direst curse
>   That darkens now our door.
> The God of Nations musters us,
>   And leads us forth once more;
> Now who can break what He has bound,
>   While each to each is true?

> "And when the nations onward march
>   In better days to be,
> Our Irish flag shall float
>   Amongst the banners of the free.
> Its colour then will speak of hope
>   Like sunshine's glistening sheen,
> And all the world be better
>   For our wearing of the green."

I have much pleasure in supporting the resolutions.

Mr. DAVITT, M.P.—The Convention will now adjourn until 11 o'clock to-morrow. The doors will be open for delegates at 10.30. The following telegram has just been received by Mr. John Dillon :—

> A meeting of advanced Ulstermen, held in Wolverhampton yesterday, wish you, for Ireland's good, to be firm and just in pressing for release of political prisoners. Please read to meeting.—JAMES HARVEY.

The Convention then adjourned at 4 o'clock.

[Of the many letters handed to the Press at the conclusion of first day's proceedings by the Secretaries, the following were printed. They are arranged in order of dates.]

Archbishop's House, Logan Square,
Philadelphia, July 10, 1896.

To MESSRS. THOMAS ADDIS EMMET, M.D.; JOHN D. GRIMMINS, JOSEPH F. DALY, AND OTHERS.

Gentlemen,—I am greatly honoured by your invitation to act as a delegate-at-large from the United States to the Irish Race Convention, to be held in Dublin on September 1st, 1896. Nothing but a sense of duty would prevent my acceptance of this honour. I have made appointments for Confirmation and other functions for

FIRST DAY—CORRESPONDENCE.

September, which render it impossible for me to be absent for the time required to attend the Convention. I wish it from my heart entire success, and shall not forget to pray for this object in the Holy Sacrifice.

Yours very faithfully,

✠ P. J. RYAN, Archbishop of Philadelphia.

Mackay, Queensland, July 13th, 1896.

TO THE PRESIDENT AND REPRESENTATIVES OF THE IRISH NATIONAL CONVENTION, DUBLIN.

Gentlemen,—We, the undersigned, on behalf of the members of the H.A.C.B. Society, No. 233, St. Patrick's Branch, Mackay, Queensland, congratulate the promoters of this Convention, and we hope that by its means the antagonism to Ireland's best interests will be entirely obliterated, leaving a united party, for without unity representation becomes a farce, and you cannot expect the support from Australians which otherwise we would gladly contribute to the cause of Home Rule for Ireland. Believe us that in Australia there are thousands of Irishmen and others who have watched with painful anxiety the constant bickerings of Ireland's supposed representatives. What concessions can you expect if by your own conduct you merit the opprobrium and laughter of your enemies? We know that the representatives of Ireland are as capable and intellectual as any other representation of like importance, but while this division in the ranks exists, so long shall Ireland suffer. It is with pleasure we notice the efforts of Mr. Davitt and others advocating the liberation of the Irish political prisoners, and hope their efforts will be rewarded. With our best wishes for the success of your Convention, we remain, yours, etc.

CHAS. FRAZER, President.
JOHN P. DOWD, Vice-President.
MICHAEL BARRON, Treasurer.
CHARLES MEZGER, Secretary.
D. MARKEY.

Adelaide, S.A., July 14th, 1896.

JOHN DILLON, Esq., M.P., Chairman.

Irish National Federation, 24 Rutland Square, Dublin, Ireland.

Dear Sir,—The members of the South Australian Branch of the Irish National Federation deeply regret that they are unable to appoint a delegate whose business engagements permit of his leaving for Dublin in time to take part in the Pan-Celtic Convention. At the same time they are unwilling to allow the occasion of a gathering, so important from its constitution and objects, to pass without expressing a hope that the cause of Ireland may be furthered by the deliberations of the Convention. Nothing is more desired by the sympathisers in South Australia with the cause of Irish autonomy than the reunion of its supporters at home. They feel that the greatest strength of their opponents lies in the division of the forces that fight for Home Rule, and that a consummation so devoutly to be wished for as reunion ought to be possible in the case of those of one blood and aim. From the visit of Mr. J. E. Redmond and his brother twelve years ago to South Australia, to the split in the Irish Party, the movement for Home Rule gained ground here. The Press of South Australia, reflecting local opinion, met the demands of the Nationalists with sympathy or fair criticism. But the division in your ranks at home checked the growth in our colony of sympathy with Home Rule. It has, to a great extent, diminished the power of your countrymen to help you by discounting, through the so-called object lesson afforded by internal dissentions, the effect of their advocacy of your cause.

The Irish, and the descendants of Irish in South Australia, still fervently long for the success of your efforts to establish an Irish Parliament to deal with purely Irish affairs. They believe that in local autonomy lies the solution of the Irish question, and the strength of the empire. With that obtained, the abilities and energies now spent in the fight for a change in the political relations of Great Britain and Ireland would be directed to the good government and development of the country, with promise of excellent results. But they feel that they can do little to increase the measure of sympathy extended to you here while the division exists in your ranks at home. They, therefore, wish you God-speed in your efforts, through the Pan-Celtic Convention, to bring about reunion. May your deliberations meet with success worthy of the great issue at stake, and of the self-sacrificing zeal and patriotic aspirations of those who take part in them.

Faithfully yours,
P. M'M. GLYNN,
President Irish National Federation,
South Australia.

Irish National Federation,
Auckland, N.Z., 18th July, 1896.

JOHN DILLON, Esq., M.P.

Dear Sir,—I have the honour, by direction of this branch of the Irish National Federation, to forward you the following resolution unanimously and with acclamation passed at last night's meeting :—

"That we, the Auckland Branch of the Irish National Federation in meeting assembled, in common with all loyal supporters of, and sympathisers with, the cause of Ireland at home and abroad, records its conviction of the paramount necessity for unity amongst the supporters of Home Rule, and desires in the most earnest manner to convey to the National Convention to be held in Dublin the unanimously expressed wish and hope of this branch that, ignoring all differences and prejudices, and disregarding all considerations, the result of the deliberations of the Convention may be a resolve to cordially join together in and maintain a lasting course of united action, upon which depends the success of the Irish Home Rule movement."

I have only to add my own prayer that our earnest wishes and desires may, as the outcome of the Convention, under Divine Providence, be consummated.

I am, dear sir, yours faithfully,
JOS. A. TOLE, President.
M. J. SHEAHAN, Hon. Sec.

Catholic Summer School of America,
Plattsburgh, N.Y., July 20th, 1896.

My Dear Mr. Ryan,—Many duties devolving upon me at the opening of the Summer School session have hindered me from answering your letter of invitation to act as delegate to the great Convention at Dublin, September 1st. I am sorry to say that it will be impossible for me to accept it, much as I may wish to do my best towards the realisation of our hopes for general unity of action in the great cause in which a people's interests are centered. I have been the prime promoter in bringing to Worcester, Massachusetts, for the 7th of September, a great demonstration of the temperance forces of Massachusetts, and it would be unbecoming of me to be absent. It would be like "Hamlet" without the Dane. As the success of the movement depends upon my personal endeavours, I have turned the matter over in many ways, and have come to the conclusion that it is absolutely necessary for me to remain at home for this event.

I hope that the distinguished delegates who will attend the Convention from all parts of the world will be successful in teaching Irish representatives the necessity of unity. In particular I hope they will impress upon them the lesson which we have learned so well in America—that majorities rule, and that all men should turn their interests to the common cause of mother country.

I appreciate very gratefully the confidence of the Federation in selecting me as one of its delegates at large, and I would certainly strain many points to act in that capacity to the best of my ability. You can realize, then, that it is a sacrifice for me to remain at home, but I feel that my remaining is demanded by duty to the interests I have gathered about me at that particular time.

Please accept my grateful thanks and honour, and believe me, in the hopes of unity, your friend,

[Rev.] THOMAS J. CONATY.

FIRST DAY—CORRESPONDENCE.

Buffalo, N.Y., July 28th, 1896.
JOSEPH P. RYAN, Esq.

My Dear Sir,—I beg to return my heartfelt thanks, through you, to the gentlemen whose names are signed to the invitation so kindly sent me. Please to convey to them the high appreciation in which I hold the honour they have conferred upon me, and assure them that nothing less than the inability to leave home at the stated time could prevent me from enjoying the proud privilege of representing the Irish National Federation of America at the Dublin Convention. I have lately added pastoral labours to my editorial duties, and the dual responsibilities will claim my close personal attention for some time to come. Again thanking the gentlemen named and yourself most heartily.

I am, very sincerely yours,

[Rev.] PATRICK CRONIN.

---

113 King William Street, Adelaide, 28th July, 1895.
JOHN DILLON, Esq., M.P., Dublin.

My Dear Sir,—I enclose cutting which will appear in the *Southern Cross* on Friday next. It was wired to me from Sydney, with request to post it on to you, so as to catch an earlier mail than if sent from Sydney. Our branch of the I.N. Federation in Adelaide sent on a letter of congratulation and encouragement last mail, and I have also written to Mr. Davitt. I sincerely trust that the Convention may be the means of uniting our people in an invulnerable phalanx to meet the common enemy, and I congratulate you on the high and responsible position to which you have been elevated. We regret very much that South Australia will not be directly represented at the Convention. Were my Ministerial Parliamentary duties not so imperative nothing would please me better than to attend.

Very truly yours,

J. V. O'LOGHLIN, V.P., I.N.F.

Extract from *Southern Cross*, Adelaide, re meeting in Sydney, 27th July, 1896:—

"THE PAN-CELTIC CONVENTION.—We have received the following telegram from Sydney :—An enthusiastic meeting *re* Pan-Celtic Convention was held Monday night at the Guild Hall, Sydney. Mr. F. B. Freehill occupied the chair. The speakers were the Hon. R. E. O'Connor, Hon. John Toohey, Messrs. J. P. Garvan, William Ellard, Jos. Carlos. The following resolution carried—' That this meeting records its unabated interest in the Home Rule movement, and urges upon the delegates to the forthcoming Pan-Celtic Convention that in order to secure the restoration to Ireland of her Parliament, it is essential that every legitimate means should be adopted to re-unite the National representatives under one leader.'"

College de Chezal-Benoit,
Cher, France, August 28th.
To JOHN DILLON, M.P.

Dear Sir,—I am honoured with being the mouthpiece of my Irish ecclesiastical friends here, who regret not to be able to sanction by their presence, but who at least assist by their prayers and wishes, the great and glorious Convention in which much of Ireland's weal is involved. Though estranged from the dear old land, like so many others who have tasted the bread of exile, our love of country remains ever woven round our hearts, as the love of our mother, and it is with our hearts and minds fondly straying over to green Erin that we watch and glory in our country's gallant struggles. Distance, however great, precludes us not from being keenly interested in her faith, in her language, and her future. We, too, can feel the misery of Ireland far away, and it is with hearts grieved even to sadness at the spectacle of her seemingly never-ending calamities that we pray God for her speedy happiness. Greatly we lament to behold the spirit of cursed revolt which seems to animate a few of our honest countrymen, and which is so hurtful to our National interests, whilst gratifying to every foe of Ireland's rights and Ireland's welfare. But we rejoice at length to hear Irishmen all the world over sounding the trumpet of peace, and with one voice blaming dissension and calling for unity. To effect this unity at such a momentous crisis, your immense reunion is undoubtedly the best and surest means. In consequence, it reflects no little credit and honour on its talented promoters, as well as on the numerous delegates who enhance it by their attendance. Besides, it lays the ground of a great and fervent hope—all a nation's rancour and bitterness crowding to a burying point, and that people—the most heroic and virtuous on the face of the earth—blended together both in views and aspirations, will then get ready for that other great day of which the Convention is the harbinger, and on which all the wounds of Erin will be healed and her tears wiped away. Divided as they are by their insane dissensions, all Irishmen concur in this one exalted sentiment—this one sublime sensation—their thirst after the hour and the ineffable desire of Ireland's freedom. Now it is that this hour is beaming with a cheering warmth and a seductive brilliancy, and any Irishman who refuses to sacrifice his parricidal passion and his bitter resentment on the altar of the Convention, which is the altar of his country, obscures the fair prospect, and must not only be "unnational," but unnatural. The great and respectable gathering will, we hope, be crowned with success, and thus, please God, Irishmen will henceforth stand shoulder to shoulder, and once again make Ireland a reunited National Ireland, and show the world "what Irishmen can do."

I remain, dear sir, in the name of my Irish Professors and Seminarists, yours faithfully in C. J.,

[Rev.] Daniel Buckley.

Ashley House, Staveley road, Eastbourne,
28th August, 1896.

Secretary, Irish National Federation, 24 Rutland Square, Dublin.

Dear Sir,—I deeply regret that owing to ill-health, and having been for the last ten days laid up with influenza, I shall be unable to attend the Irish Race Convention on the 1st September, as I am not yet well enough to travel, and my doctor will not allow me to do so for another week.

I am, dear sir, faithfully yours,

J. Eustace Jameson [M.P.]

---

12 Stories Alley, Leith, August 30th, 1896.

To David Sheehy, Esq.

Dear Sir,—Please submit the enclosed resolution on behalf of the Irishmen in Leith in the interest of unity and the Irish Parliamentary Party. Wishing you every success,

I remain, dear sir, yours truly,

Francis Donaghy.

Leith, 30th August, 1896.

At a meeting of the T. D. Sullivan Branch held to-day the following resolution was unanimously passed in view of the forthcoming gathering of representatives of the Irish Race in Dublin :—" Irish residents in Leith, Scotland, are desirous of impressing upon the people of Ireland the urgency of once and for all putting their foot on the neck of faction from any quarter whatever and we believe that the Irish people ; after duly considering all phases of what has been the cause of disunion, should ask the promoters of faction through their constituencies to retire at once from public life and allow their places to be taken by those who are willing to pursue such a policy as will best serve the interests of the Irish people."

T. Burke, 9 Albert Street, Cemetry Road,
Darwen, August 30th, 1896.

To David Sheehy, M.P., Dublin.

Dear Mr. Sheehy,—Circumstances prevent us from being personally represented at the great Convention of our scattered race, consequently we adopt this method of expressing our feelings. Speaking on behalf of eighty members of our branch, and on behalf of the Nationalist population of Darwen, we are solid for unity. Dissension now, as in the past, is, and has been, the curse of our country, her people, and her cause. Our one desire then is to see unity restored once more in the Nationalist ranks. Irish freedom must not be sacrificed for personal spleen; Ireland first, personal laudation and ambition after. No man should be allowed to bar the progress of unity and freedom. The eyes of all nations are focussed on your deliberations to-day. Aye, the very spirits of departed heroes who loved Ireland more than personal ambition, will be hovering over and about you. Sarsfield, Grattan, Flood, Curran, Charlemont, Fitzgerald, Tone, and Emmet, O'Connell, Mitchel, Martin, Meagher, Butt, and Parnell, they were all for Ireland. Therefore, in God's name close your ranks, show a bold front to the common enemy, and show the nations that the Celtic race are both worthy of and capable of managing their own affairs. God bless your proceeding, and God save Ireland is the wish of the Darwen Branch.

Signed on behalf of the Darwen Branch,

WILLIAM M'CARTHY, President.
THOMAS BURKE, Secretary.

House of Commons Library,
August 31st, 1896.

D. Sheehy, Esq., M.P., Dublin.

My Dear Sheehy,—Your card of admission to the Convention received on Saturday last.

I regret that on account of pressing private affairs I cannot at present leave London.

I hope sincerely that the issue of the Convention's deliberations will be satisfactory to the people of Ireland.—Yours sincerely,

JAMES O'CONNOR [M.P.]

The following telegram was also read :—

"To Chairman Irish Race Convention, Dublin. South Islington Branch, London, heartily wish success to Convention, and sincerely hope that lasting benefit to Irish cause may result from its deliberations. God save Ireland. CAINE, President; SLYNE, Vice-President; MISS LYNCH, Treasurer."

Letters regretting inability to attend and of sympathy with the Convention were received from Very Rev. Dean Beechinor, Launcestown, Tasmania; Messrs. Thomas O'Brien, Gormanstown; and C. M'Carthy, Neath, Glamorganshire.

SECOND DAY—2ND SEPTEMBER, 1896.

The chair was taken at 11 o'clock by the chairman, the Most Rev. Dr. O'DONNELL, Bishop of Raphoe.

Mr. DAVITT, M.P.—I have to announce that two delegates from America have arrived—General Martin T. MacMahon, of New York, and Mr. Michael Murphy, of New York. I have also to announce that I have received from Hobart, Tasmania, the credentials of another delegate from that island. The Rev. Father O'Callaghan, of Mallow, one of the hon. secs. of this Convention, is appointed to represent South Tasmania.

The CHAIRMAN—In the course of the proceedings yesterday a notice was handed in of a motion to limit the time of the speeches. Now, it may be well to see first what progress can be made without any such limit. Resolutions L and M* go practically on the lines of the first resolution proposed by Mr. Webb, and the convenient course, I think, will be to afford the gentlemen entrusted with those resolutions an opportunity to speak, if they are so disposed, on this first resolution of Mr. Webb's. There is another resolution which does not appear on the agenda paper, to which I referred last night, and which in a somewhat different form will be proposed by Father Flynn, of Waterford. I am not sure, but it may be an amendment to these resolutions, and if it be quite convenient for Father Flynn now, I think it will help the progress of our deliberations if he addresses the assembly in the first place.

The following resolution was under discussion when the Convention adjourned the previous day :—

(1) REUNION.—"Seeing that divisions amongst Irish Nationalist representatives paralyse, to a great extent, their power of serving Ireland, cast discredit on the country, and tend to alienate the support of the Irish Race, and to destroy their confidence in the efficacy of Parliamentary action, we record our firm conviction that it is of the first importance to Ireland that the Nationalist representatives in Parliament should be re-united into one Party ; and, in the spirit of the recent resolution of the Irish Party, we declare that : ' In our earnest desire to accomplish that result, we are prepared to meet, on fair and equal terms, all Nationalists who will join in the attempt to re-constitute a united Home Rule Party, in which every supporter of the movement shall be cordially received and justly considered, regardless of all past differences, and having regard only to his capacity to render service to the common cause.' We are glad to observe in the composition of this Convention and in the spirit shown throughout the country, marked evidence of a growing tendency to reunion, and we invite the Irish Nationalist Party to take such further steps as may to them seem calculated to promote the cause of reunion."

---

* All the resolutions on the agenda paper will be found at the conclusion of Third Day's proceedings.

Rev. P. F. FLYNN, P.P.—The amendment that I have to propose is worded as follows :—

"That this Convention select from the delegates here assembled a committee of arbitration consisting of home and foreign delegates, which committee shall be empowered to provide for the consideration and acceptance, if approved of by the Convention, a set of rules forming a common platform, upon which all Irish Nationalists may stand again united, and work loyally together as a whole for the good of our common country."

My lord, ladies, and gentlemen—I rise before this magnificent assembly to propose this, what I consider to be, the practical work for which this Convention has been summoned. Yesterday we had the advantage of hearing delegates from all the world over, I may say, and they all came empowered to act in this magnificent assembly, and I remarked that they scored a point when they said they came untrammelled, unpledged, unbiassed, and with only one idea, and that was a prayer and a request that the people of Ireland should be again united. We have heard, therefore, the prayer for unity, and each and everyone in this hall, his eye is hot to see a united Ireland again. Eloquence will not unite the people. Eloquence may please them and electrify them, but in order that the Convention may be able to say "*veni, vidi, vici*" a common platform must be established on which the people of Ireland shall be called upon to stand, as you have the power and the right to demand. If such a resolution as I am proposing be not adopted the delegates will go home, and they will be able to say, "I have come and I have seen," but they will not be able to add the magic words, "I have conquered, I have put down strife, and I have put down faction." The business of this Convention is to form a platform upon which all Irish Nationalists may stand together as of old, shoulder to shoulder, acting in concert, honestly, manfully, and practically, for the good of the country. It is not necessary, my lord and delegates, to enter at length into the necessity of a resolution or amendment of this kind. I think it will have the approbation of every one who is honestly inclined to see a united Ireland again. The factionists will not respond to your call. It was not supposed that they would respond to it, and we have evidence to-day that they ignore it with contumely. But you, the Irish people—you have the power and authority to say "go" and they must go, "come" and they must come. You are the masters of the situation. In you rests the power—on you lies the heavy obligation, of making the members and the people a united and compact body again. Are you prepared to do your duty? If you are I say unhesitatingly that you will adopt the resolution that I have proposed to you, and if you adopt that I think you will cut the ground from under dissension—you will have saddled the right horse, and all Ireland will know who are right and who are wrong. With these few remarks, I beg to propose formally the resolution or amendment that stands in my name.

Alderman W. J. SMITH, Mayor of Waterford—My lord and fellow-countrymen, it is with a great deal of diffidence I presume to come before an assembly of this kind to-day to second any amendment or resolution. But, impressed with the importance of such a gathering as this is, I, as a consistent Nationalist all my lifetime, considered on looking over the agenda paper yesterday with Father Flynn and some friends that there was nothing practical on it to make the Convention end in any practical purpose being accomplished. I was more impressed by that on yesterday evening when the delegate from Pennsylvania remarked that he had been listening all the evening and day to different speeches, but that he never heard a single suggestion as to the practical result of the Convention. As Father Flynn has properly said, eloquence is very good, but eloquence will not unite us. And as we have met here to-day for the purpose of unity I unhesitatingly appear before you to ask you to accept the resolution proposed by Father Flynn, or any amended resolution that may spring from it. I appear here to second that motion, as I said before, as an Irish Nationalist; I am no man's man. I never was any man's man. I was always in my humble sphere my country's man, and it is for that purpose I ask you here to-day to consider, calmly and quietly, the resolution that has been proposed to you, because, unless some such resolution or kindred one is accepted we will go as we came and end as we came. Gentlemen, it has been stated in canvassing this resolution that the different parties, amongst whom there is more or less friction, have been asked already to this Convention. They have been asked to this Convention, but they may naturally say that those who asked them had no power to ask them. (Cries of " They had.") I am only talking, gentlemen, on what is said. I am not expressing my own opinions, but I say when the mandate of this Convention goes out to them, I would then say that the man or the patriot—the man who professes to be a patriot, and refuses to respond to this Convention here to-day, will take on himself a responsibility more fearful than has yet rested on any of our members, and a responsibility which, if I know my own countrymen, those whom he is obligated to will make him answer truly for. Gentlemen, I am more impressed by this, because I come from a city which has taken no undecided part. The citizens of Waterford, for reasons satisfactory to themselves, and in which they are perfectly justified, have taken a certain course in this quarrel. I, as a citizen of Waterford, along with a great many others, have differed in that way, and we have a right to differ, but unless some mandate of the kind that we propose is sent forward to them, how can I or any other man ask a man who differs from me in politics, and who has a right to differ with me—and honestly differs with me—how can I ask that man to surrender and say: "You are right and I am wrong?" If you want to have unity we must go and meet them, and ask them to meet us. We must hold out the hand of fellowship to them, and say we have been differing, we have been disunited; now at last let these disgraceful differences end, and let us shake hands once more, and work together for our country's cause. We want no renunciation of principle, we want no recantation of errors. We may be wrong and they may be wrong. Let us come forward and say we are all working for the one end. The people are united. Unity is the one policy for attaining our right; it is the miserable dissensions and quarrels of those that ought to be ashamed of the quarrels that have led to disunion. I have taken a life-long interest in the fortunes of my country, and I say it is time now for the people to take up the power which they possess—take it into their own hands, and I reiterate the sentiments of Father Flynn when I say that the men who are our leaders are the servants and not the masters of the people. I am not actuated by any party or personal consideration. There is no man in this assembly respects the gentleman behind me more than I do; but no matter who they are or what they are if they stand in the way of their country's union, let them go. I won't detain you any longer; it is for you to say will you accept it or not. I ask you to accept it or some modified form of it. I understand this amendment will be opposed, and I ask you therefore, as a confederated body to-day, whoever proposes or criticises this amendment let him put forward some alternative. Let us have no carping criticism with no result. The proposer will accept any modification of the amendment. Let any other resolution be put forward, and there will be no warmer supporter of it to-day than me. Let us have some resolution of the kind, and not go away with nothing in our hands. Let us not make the Convention a farce and a fiasco. If we do fail in our efforts to-day it will not be my fault, and I'll go back home again regretting that the men who ought to be patriots and leaders of the people have not found themselves able to sacrifice petty jealousies for the common interest and honour of our poor country.

Mr. T. P. O'CONNOR, M.P.—My lord bishop and gentlemen of the Convention, this body has shown itself an extremely responsive and faithful echo to the sentiments which brought it into existence. It was brought into existence for the purpose of putting down dissension and re-establishing unity in the Irish movement. It arose originally from a letter of the Archbishop of Toronto, followed up by a resolution, to which I shall have to refer by and by, passed unanimously by the Irish Party calling this Convention together. And every gentleman who has addressed this meeting has made himself also the faithful and responsive echo of the feeling which the Convention represents, that feeling being a desire for putting down dissension and for the re-establishment of unity. Yesterday we had, I think, one of the most remarkable and striking manifestations that an Irish or any other political body ever saw. We had a number of delegates from almost every part of the world, every single one of them, if not Irish by birth, Irish by extraction or Irish by sympathy, bringing before, not only us, but the larger world outside, the great fact which we ought always to remember, and especially in moments of depression and discouragement, that the cause of Ireland no longer rests upon the comparatively small number of Irish people within the Irish shores, but rests on the wider and stronger basis of a world-wide Nation. But as that array of speakers from all parts of the world brought home to us our strength, it also brought home to us the means by which that strength can be properly utilised, and our weakness therefore removed, and the joint and unanimous appeal of all these gentlemen was that discussion should be put down and that unity should be restored. And, therefore, my lord bishop, if I were to approch the consideration of any proposal made from any quarter whatever in any other spirit than a spirit of trying to help to put down dissension and the restoration of unity, I would put myself at once in direct conflict with the dominant and overwhelming and passionate opinion, not only of this gathering, but of Irishmen wherever they are. And, therefore, my lord, I think I need scarcely assure this audience that I approach the consideration of Father Flynn's amendment in exactly the same spirit as he has spoken, and as everybody else has spoken—namely, a spirit of trying to find some means of putting down dissension and restoring unity, and I am bound to say this, that, apart from the object with which this amendment was proposed, it recommends itself to my judgment and yours, I am sure, from the character of the man who proposed it. There is not even in this large gathering a more honest, a braver, or a more sincere priest or Nationalist in Ireland than Father Flynn, who proposed this resolution, and I am perfectly sure that in the remotest recesses of his mind and of his conscience you could not find any trace or any desire, whatever, in proposing this resolution, but the desire to put down dissension and restore unity, and, therefore, I approach this amendment as an honest amendment intention, proposed by an honest mind for an honest end, and the one test which I shall apply to it is, will this amendment carry out the purpose which it intends or will it not? If it carry out the purpose then in heaven's name let us all support it. If it be destined to fail, to defeat the purpose of unity, equally is it our duty unanimously, or if not unanimously by an overwhelming majority, to reject it. Well, now, I shall test it.

A Voice—Give us the alternative.

Mr. O'CONNOR—If my friend will allow me to proceed with my argument I am sure I shall give it in a way to which no sane or susceptible man can object, and every opportunity will be given to accept or refute this argument. My lord bishop—I first must call attention to a single fact. I don't do it by way of complaint, but by way of elucidating the situation. In the first place, an opportunity was given to every man in Ireland—to every Nationalist in Ireland—to present to this Convention for consideration any proposal, or any amendment which he desired. And, of course, the object was to give to this body, which has most important if not supreme functious to discharge and fulfil, adequate opportunity of reading in print, and calmly considering any proposal that was made. Well, the proposal of Father Flynn does not appear in the agenda paper. That to a certain extent takes the Convention at a disadvantage, but that is not the complete history of this amendment. I am glad that calm and better counsels have prevailed. Better counsels will always ultimately prevail in such cases. But I feel bound to give this Convention the original form in which this amendment was handed up to the chair. And here is what it was——

Rev. P. F. FLYNN—If I thought it well to change my amendment and to put it in the form in which I changed it before this assembly, I do it for a certain reason. I did it that it might commend itself to every individual in the assembly. I found on consideration that it might be contentious in the way in which it was worded, and I want to avoid contention if possible. I want to have no friction, and, therefore, upon advice I changed the resolution, because I was informed it would obtain a more general support if I did so. Therefore, I say it is unfair—and I submit the matter to the chairman—I say it is unfair to animadvert to a resolution that I never proposed.

The CHAIRMAN—As Father Flynn's resolution reached me in its unamended form, and was seen here by a number of persons yesterday in its unamended form, including Mr. O'Connor, I don't think, on a strict point of order, I can rule against Mr. O'Connor reading the text.

But for the harmony of the Convention I suggest a middle course to Mr. O'Connor, and that is without reading the resolution as amended in its original form to give the Convention his memory of what it was.

Mr. O'Connor—Of course, my lord bishop, I shall immediately comply with your suggestion, and I will give, without even looking at the original amendment, my recollection of what it was, and Father Flynn will have an opportunity of correcting me if I mistake its terms by my recollection of it. The original amendment was that a committee of arbitration should be appointed from this Convention, consisting of seven members of what were called the three contending sections of Irish Nationalists—and I think the foreign delegates were to have a representation of ten—and that this committee should submit to this Convention a plan of action upon which all the three contending sections could ultimately unite and work together. I am very glad, I am delighted, no words can express my joy, at the withdrawal of the original form of the amendment, because it is a withdrawal from a position which I would have felt it my duty to condemn and reprobate in the strongest manner. It is true that there are two contending sections of Irish Nationalists. There is the Parnellite Party and there is the Irish Parliamentary Party. When you deal with the Parnellites they are entitled to demand, and you are compelled to admit, that they are a separate and independent party. They are wrong for being so. Don't misunderstand my position. They are entitled to call themselves a separate and independent party, and we are bound to acknowledge them. They have very good reasons as they may think, very bad reasons as you and I may think, but they broke the Party pledge, and a certain number of constituencies elected them after breaking that pledge. Therefore, they are entitled to be regarded as a separate and independent party. But we come to the Irish Parliamentary Party. What right has any man to describe it as consisting of two sections or two parties? Gentlemen, I am going down to the very root of this whole difficulty, and if this Convention is not going to end in emptiness, in laughter, and in contempt, it will have to go down to the roots of this whole difficulty. What right has any man to speak of two sections in the Irish Party? Let us see what is the constitution of that Party? Every single member of that Party, without exception, has signed the pledge to sit, act, and vote with the Irish Parliamentary Party, to be bound by the decisions of its majority, and either to loyally obey its decisions or to honestly withdraw from the Party. I put this point to the Convention. I say that every single member of the Irish Party signed that pledge; but I go further, and I say he was elected because he signed that pledge, and I say further, that if he had refused to sign that pledge he would have been ignominiously rejected. Therefore, the pledge of party unity and party loyalty is the whole foundation or right by which any member of the Party sits as an Irish representative. What follows from that? That to speak of two parties in our Party is to tear down and destroy, not merely—I will do nothing now to destroy the future—but I say that to admit or acknowledge or recognise, to treat as one of the high contracting parties, one section of our Party, instead of with the Party as a whole, it is to tear down the foundations of National unity now and for ever. (Prolonged cheering, the whole assembly rising to their feet and waving their hats. The demonstration was repeated a second time.)

Does anybody in the possession of the ordinary amount of human sense not devoured by some demon of prejudice and folly, does anybody suppose that we who have to bear the burden and responsibility of this movement approach any proposition from the point of view of personal rancour or personal interest? We would be not merely inhuman monsters, who were betraying their country, but such a phenomenon of insane folly as no political movement ever produced. If this movement succeed, and by your help, and in spite of foes within and without, it is going to succeed, if it succeed I don't know what personal glory its success would bring to us. But if it fail you may be sure that upon our heads the guilt and the responsibility will be laid. Therefore, any proposition for conciliation, concession, and union that has the appearance of safety and a stable future demands our cordial assent. Does that mean, however, that we are to lead you into a fool's paradise and ask you in the name of conciliation and concession to accept a proposition which would lead to the destruction, not merely now but for all time, of the principle upon which unity must ever be founded? I am very glad to see that Father Flynn has abandoned the proposition that there are two sections in the Irish Party. I am very glad of the reason he gave for it. I am sure the premier desire of Father Flynn was to do an honest day's work for Ireland. I do not impute any other motive to Father Flynn, and I am sure he will give me full right to discuss freely, and, even if necessary, to condemn some of the opinions he propounded, without meaning any disrespect, for he enjoys my personal respect. I am very glad at the second reason given by Father Flynn for abandoning his proposition. The second reason was that he had consulted his friends, and his friends advised the withdrawal of the proposition in the interests of the Convention. Aye, the reason was that he knew that the sovereign assembly, the power and magnificence of which he has publicly testified to, would, if the proposition of two sections in the Party was put before them, scout and trample upon such a proposition. Well, now, I come to the consideration of what are the methods and means by which dissension is to be put down, and now I will answer my friend who, in a somewhat premature— though naturally with the ardour of an ardent Irishman—in a somewhat premature spirit asked me for my alternative. Is this Convention sovereign or not? (Cries of "Yes," and cheers.) Is it a success or a failure? (Cries of "Success," and renewed cheers.) Is it a hole and corner, squalid, and petty little gathering? ("No.") Is it a miserable little affair or is it, as Father Flynn must acknowledge and gladly acknowledge, the largest, the most representative, and the most noble gathering of Irishmen that ever assembled together? I will throw some light upon the situation that I think will help to guide you in your decision. This Convention was initiated by a letter of the Archbishop of Toronto, and was called by a unanimous vote of the Irish Party. Every member of the Irish Party was one of those by whom this Convention was brought into being. Why is not every member of the Irish Party here? Gentlemen, I don't intend to lower my speech to the point of personal controversy, and I hope you won't do it for me. I am discussing no man, but principles. Why isn't every member of the Irish

Party here? If he had charges to make why is not he here to make them? If he had complaints to allege why is not he here to make them? If we be the dishonest and unscrupulous tricksters we have been declared to be a hundred times over, why are not these charges, taken from private and whispered conversations, from private letters, from newspapers that can be avowed or disavowed—why aren't they torn from these dark and narrow recesses and brought here into the light of day where we stand now before our fellow-countrymen? Furthermore, this Convention—I must recur to the point again and again, because it is the essence of the situation—this Convention was called by the unanimous vote of the Irish Party. Did every member of the Irish Party do his best to make it a success? Why, my Lord Bishop, is not it notorious that every device and every means, fair and foul, have been exhausted for the purpose of making this Convention not the great success it has been but an abject and miserable failure. I will not scandalise the enemy by telling all I know of the attempts that were made to destroy this Convention, especially in the full and satisfactory knowledge that these attempts have failed. They have been made and they have failed. Well, what was the first line of attack? The first line of attack was to withdraw from the Convention, and not come before it with any charge. The second line of attack was to try and prevent the Convention from being a success or a numerous body. But now we come to the third line of attack, the most insidious of all. Father Flynn is no party to it. From the bottom of my heart and conscience I acquit him of any share or any responsibility, or even any knowledge of the third line of attack.

Rev. E. MURNANE, Bermondsey, London—I rise to a point of order.

Mr. O'CONNOR—My lord bishop will keep order. The third line of attack is this—the Convention is here assembled; its power and authority are acknowledged by everyone.

Rev. E. MURNANE still continued to call out "Point of order," and was brought by one of the stewards up to the front of the platform. Mr. O'Connor sitting down in the meantime.

CHAIRMAN—May I ask your point of order?

Rev. E. MURNANE—My lord, I was unwilling to interrupt Mr. O'Connor, but I wish to ask your lordship (I have brought delegates here on the plea that every party was welcome to this meeting). I ask, therefore, my lord, whether you think that the speech that Mr. O'Connor is making is likely to bring about that unity that we have all come here for?

CHAIRMAN—It is not the province of a chairman of a Convention like this to say whether any speech delivered to the Convention is effective for its purpose or not.

Mr. O'CONNOR—My reverend friend was quite within his rights to try and interrupt me on a point of order, and he has been ruled out of order by the lord bishop who is in the chair; but our reverend friend was really making an argument, and what I suppose appeared to his better judgment a reply to my argument, in place of a point of order. And what was his argument? That I was controverting the principle that everybody was welcome to this Convention. Why, I am reasserting that principle, and my complaint is that though the doors have been opened as widely and generously as they can, men have not come here and accepted our invitation. Now, gentlemen, I go to the third line of attack on the Convention. My reverend friend is quite at liberty to differ from me as to the effect of my words. It will be for you to decide. But I come to the third line of attack, and what does that mean? The Convention, in spite of every effort to make it a failure, has been a success. In spite of every effort to make it small it has been unprecedentedly large. In spite of every attempt to make it disunited it has been unprecedentedly harmonious. You are here, I believe, of one mind. I believe I may go further and say that that one mind is the determination that party unity must be preserved by party loyalty and by majority rule, which is the only method by which any party, or any society, or any government can be kept together. I believe further that besides being of one mind you are of one purpose, and that besides being of one purpose you are also inspired by the resolve, the inflexible determination to make that purpose effective for the future of Ireland. Well, what does that mean? It means that you are determined, as I understand your convictions and your temper, not merely to assert your faith in the principle of party unity and party loyalty, but also to proclaim to all the world your stern determination to put down every man and every set of men who would stand in the way. You see, gentlemen, that that determination of yours, while it is full of hope for the Irish movement and for loyal men, is full of terror and danger for the disruptionists and wreckers, and, therefore, a removal of the greatest danger that ever threatened them would be the removal of your determination to put down all wreckers, and, therefore, the wreckers want to stand between you and your determination. Well, if a committee were appointed—a committee of arbitration—for the purpose of settling our differences on one platform, what would become of the Convention? Assume the committee was in the next room, I want to know how long the committee is to last—I want to know how long it is to sit, and when it is to report? When is the committee to be expected to report? It would be a pretty quick committee if it reported to-day within a few hours. We are not going to sit beyond four, and I don't think it could report before that. Therefore, it could not report to day, and would it report to-morrow? I do not think it could. Aye, but if it were a committee consisting of the right kind of men who were determined not to make this Convention effective, but to make it impotent, it would be quite ready to report on Friday, when the Convention would have disappeared as completely as the snow in summer. And so you see this great body, which was brought here for a great work, and is determined to do that work, would be in such a case dispersed without doing anything, and I say, therefore, that the carrying or acceptance of such a proposal would mean the death of the Convention. And, speaking in no language of exaggeration—speaking in no heat—but speaking from the depths of my conviction and consideration of this question, I declare it my opinion that the death of this Convention would be the death of the Irish Constitutional movement.

And now, gentlemen, I think I have dealt with the tactics and purposes, not of Father Flynn, but of those who are the enemies of this Convention. Gentlemen, it may be a hard thing to say, but it must be said, the one way to restore unity is to put down disunion, and the one way to put down disunion is not to treat it as an independent and equal power gaining authority by its treason, but to do what Father Flynn asks you to do and what the Mayor of Waterford asks you to do—to do your duty and show your determination that any man who violates his pledge or breaks up party unity will no longer have to deal merely with the majority of his colleagues but with a united and a determined and a manly Irish people. And now I may be asked if we have any plan for dealing with party dissension. My answer to that is this : Read your agenda paper ; read the first sentence of the first resolution. The first resolution, as you will observe, begins by expressing the great concern of this Convention at the existence of dissension. It goes on to hold out again, as we have done many times before, the hand of friendship and fellowship to every Nationalist who is now arrayed against us ; and then, as our invitation is not accepted, it goes on to say that we are glad to observe in the composition of this Convention, and in the spirit shown throughout the country, a marked evidence of a growing tendency to re-union, and "we invite the Irish Nationalist Party to take such further steps as may seem to them calculated to promote the cause of re-union." Or, in other words, you command your Irish Party, and you give them full powers to take any and every step that may bring about the re-union of the Nationalists of Ireland. What more do you want? Do you trust your Irish Party? If you trust your Irish Party, trust them all in all or not at all ; and if they are good enough to be entrusted with the liberties and the cause of Ireland they are good enough to choose the time, the season, and the means by which the Parnellites can be approached. Look at the second resolution for a moment, though I am a little out of order in alluding to it, but the amendment to a certain extent deals with the second as well as with the first resolution. What does the second resolution say? There again you call upon the Irish Party to be united ; you call upon them to observe their pledge, to preserve their unity, and you call upon them, voicing your opinion, to take such steps, if the pledge be broken, as to make the pledge respected by every member of the Party. Now, there is my alternative proposal. My proposal is to stand by the resolution on the agenda paper, which has not only expressed a wish for union, but it points out the body and means of restoring union. Now, my friends, one word finally. We are to-day at the parting of the ways in Irish politics. As this Convention decides the movement will live and grow, or fail and die. I make the distinction between our present movement and the Irish cause. Movements have failed before, but the cause of Ireland is green and immortal, and if our means and our methods fail we know very well what the spirit of our countrymen is. And what I put most solemnly and earnestly to Father Flynn and to every good and sincere man—can there be a more serious and a more terrible responsibility on any man or any set of men than to make our people think that the Constitutional movement has failed and driven them back into dangerous and terrible measures, and have former times repeated, and men again like those who walked out of English jails a few weeks ago—men decrepit and prematurely old. Is that to go on ? Is it to be repeated ? Are you going to send other Allens, Larkins, and O'Briens to the scaffold ? Are you going to send other Davitts to

G

Dartmoor, or have you made up your minds that this Constitutional movement shall get a united support, and in that way, in spite of treason and of malice, shall make the world once more resound to the tread of the united Irish millions marching on to peace and victory?

The Very Rev. JOHN O'LEARY, P.P., V.F., Clonakilty—My lord, rev. gentlemen, and delegates of this magnificent Convention, I wish to add a few observations of mine to what has been said by the eloquent member who has just addressed you. In regard to the resolution, or amendment rather, proposed by my friend, Father Flynn, of Waterford, I can fairly say that I have the honour of knowing Father Flynn for many long years, and enjoyed, I may say, perhaps, his friendship, I have to endorse everything said by Mr. O'Connor relative to the splendid ability and marked patriotic services and that well-known interest which he has always taken in the cause of Ireland. Having said so much regarding the proposer of this amendment I now come to deal with it on its merits, and will begin by saying that I fully agree with every observation made by Mr. O'Connor as to the insiduous nature of the attempts made to interfere with the harmony and success of our Convention. I trust I'll not be found to repeat in my weak way any of the arguments that have been so splendidly elucidated by him. There are yet a few remarks that occur to me on points in this amendment that Mr. O'Connor has not dwelt upon. Now, gentlemen, we are asked to appoint a committee of arbitration. I unhesitatingly say here to-day before you and before the whole world that this Convention is the committee of arbitration. We know the men who are here, their names have been in the papers; we know their credentials; we know their representative positions; we know many of us who have never missed a Convention in Dublin or Cork for the last sixteen years—we know who welcomed their honest faces at this assemblage as we did in the old days of the Land League and the National Federation. If there is anything to be arbitrated upon it is by this Convention it should be arbitrated upon in the open light of day. Gentlemen, I will not thrash out mere technical or constitutional questions as to how far we may constitutionally and legally sub-delegate any powers to any committee whatever. I will not thrash out technical things of that kind, but I will say to you that you could not possibly form any sub-committee whatever that would have a thousandth part of the influence and of the moral effect produced by those here assembled. In the second place, my dear friends, I take it for granted that at this period of our lives we are not mere tyros in politics. We know something about how committees are formed, and is not it a curious thing that when we have now the second edition of this amendment—the first edition has been dealt with—I saw it, and I would have dealt with it were it not taken from before me—but when we have now the second edition we do not find on that paper the name of a single man to whom we are to delegate this power. We all heard of the amendment of the Prime Minister who thought of his party making a leap in the dark, but there never was such a leap into nebulous tenebrosity as there would be if we were to form a committee—I hope my friend, Dean Harris, is listening to me—of veritable nobodies. They are the nobodies in reality, because there is no man or anybody put before us.

Now, gentlemen, if we were to find on that paper the names of a sub-committee of representative public men, and if we were to be assured, in the second place, by one who had authority to speak, that each and every one of these men would go into the same room, or into some other place in this city, and give their best efforts to the drawing up of this platform and bring it here before us, and if we were to be assured that at some date before this Convention was dissolved, and the delegates sent away to their homes to the furthermost ends of the earth, that this report would be presented to us, and if we were to consider it, I gentlemen, make bold to say that there is no man here present to-day who would be more anxious to stretch a point, if I could stretch it, in order to bring about unity and harmony in our ranks. I defy anyone to say I have not been as well in politics after the split as I was before the split, and I defy anyone to point to a bitter or rankling word I ever gave expression to, whether to Parnellites or to the new section, and therefore all my sentiments and the feelings of my heart would rise up to second and endorse the resolution proposed by Father Flynn. But, gentlemen, he gives us none of these particulars that you would require in the smallest little lawsuit if you brought a person into court. No bill of particulars, no names mentioned, no time mentioned. Gentlemen, we know what the result would be. It is not easy for the most rabid malignity of party to scoff at this magnificent gathering; but there is not a scoffer in the land that might not point the arrows of scorn at the deliberations of this bogus and hole-and-corner meeting. We are the representatives of Ireland and of the Irish race, and we are not privileged to speak. Yes, let there be a committee of arbitration as there is here to-day, and whether it be a man belonging to the party that left us unfortunately in 1890, or to that section that seems now as if they were about to leave us—if there be such a section—or whether it be any other man in this assembly, he will be heard here with any proposition that he makes; he will be heard with the greatest patience and the greatest consideration. And, gentlemen, are we to suppose that after the Irish nation and its best minds have been giving their best thoughts to this weighty matter for so many months and for so many years—are we to be told that there will be wisdom to be found in hidden and dark recesses, and that no practical suggestion can be made by an Irishman before his fellow-countrymen? Therefore, I say that no matter even if this amendment were proposed by an angel from heaven the trail of the serpent is over every word. What then, my lord and gentlemen, is it for us to do? It is for us, in my opinion, to vote down, if it be put to the vote, strenuously and manfully this amendment, which can possibly do no good, which will inevitably do harm, which will make us the laughing stock of our friends as well as of our enemies, and which will send this Convention away, if it should be adopted, *sine die et sine fructu,* send us away for ever without having done one particle of good. Gentlemen, I thank you very heartily for the very patient hearing you have given me.

Rev. WILLIAM MEAGHER, C.C., Clonmel—Ladies and gentlemen, as yesterday was for oratory, and to-day for work, I will be as brief as possible. I appear before you to support the amendment of Father Flynn of Waterford, and I will tell you that this is the fourth Convention I have attended in Dublin. This is not self-laudatory, but for the purpose of making known that I am an old soldier in the cause, and that I have from the beginning maintained the principle of majority rule. I am for no person. I am for the cause. I have suffered for Ireland, and so has Father Flynn. And I can truthfully say that Father Flynn has suffered more in the cause of Ireland than any speaker who has appeared before you to-day. Father Flynn's amendment was inspired by the purest and best motives. I was present at an assembly of honest Irishmen who, having read the programme of this Convention, came to the conclusion that it would be desirable in the interest of unity, in order to have our work complete, that a committee of the Convention should be freely elected yesterday. Father Flynn has not been honestly represented here. It was early on yesterday that Father Flynn drew up this resolution, and it was handed into the Chair very soon after the Convention had opened. Father Flynn wished to submit that it should be received at yesterday's proceedings, that the committee should have last evening to deliberate, and that they should have a platform this morning to submit to the Convention. That was merely in accordance with the licence of the agenda paper. The agenda paper stated that any member of the Convention could submit to the assemblage a resolution. Father Flynn, knowing how deep-rooted strife and dissension are in the land, and knowing that after passing quietly the resolutions on the agenda paper, and returning to our homes, we would hear next week that disunion had not been wiped out of the ranks, wished that a programme should be freely submitted for your approval, and it was for you to accept it or reject it. Father Flynn was then not dictating to the Convention. The resolution of the sub-committee would be submitted for your approval or disapproval, and it was in that spirit that Father Flynn proposed this resolution, and I believe I am within the bounds of truth in saying that there is not a purer or a more patriotic Irishman than Father Flynn of Ballybricken, Waterford. We must be brief. I hope, as we are here for unity, we will set the example ourselves to-day. Yesterday was a day that confused our enemies and rejoiced our friends. Yesterday was, in the words of the Immortal O'Connell, "a great day for Ireland." I hope as yesterday was, so will to-day be. I believe that when Father Flynn will appear before you again, the error that has gone abroad will be removed, and that you will consider more favourably the amendment that he has submitted for your approval. I have very great pleasure in supporting Father Flynn's amendment.

Mr. WILLIAM SULLIVAN, Bradford—My lord, ladies, and gentlemen, we have come, myself and my colleagues, from England—Irishmen living in the heart of the enemy's country—to try and do our part over here to settle Irish differences, as we have worked like men in England for this holy cause of ours. When we heard the amendment proposed by the Rev. Father Flynn, we were astonished that anyone should think that we were so blind as to accept any retrogressive motion of that kind. I do not know Father Flynn myself, but I fully accept all that has been said of him by his friends as to his good intentions. But we do not want good intentions—we want good judgment. Here we are split in atoms. When we go on public platforms in England, and endeavour to heal up the differences of others, what are we told? "Go and heal your own differences before you come to us." I come from a town where we had been described as miserable miscreants by some of those who had been members of your party. We had been called ignorant caitiffs also. Why? Because, at the last general election, we thought of Ireland before we thought of anything else. We put our foot down at the last election. We parted with warm friends because we thought Ireland required our help first and foremost, and we were prepared to make any sacrifice to that end. Well, Bradford elected Tories at the last election, including Byron Reid, who called Father M'Fadden a murderer. From that you will see it would have been a disgrace to us had we acted in any other way than the way in which we have acted. We have come here to get strength for the cause of Ireland, and also something that will give us strength to fight our own battles in Great Britain. We are not going to be burked or put aside. I have been sent here with my colleagues to take counsel as to the best means of putting an end to the dissensions that unhappily exist. I do not believe in describing the different sections as "ites." I am no "ite," but I am an item in the National movement, and I say there is no man outside of the Redmondites—no Irish member of Parliament who has a mandate to fight against majority rule. What is it we have to consider? I say to you, Irishmen living in Ireland, what are your differences? What are you quarrelling about? We are all supposed to be agreed upon one principle. We are all Nationalists. It has often been said there must be differences of opinion. We know that the rivulets flow down the mountain side, join the stream, and flow on to the ocean in one compact mass. Well, what I want to say, to this great gathering is that the groundwork of all unity is obedience to majority rule. We know these men may differ, but you men should know what we have to suffer in England when we find one Irish leader on a public platform at home blackguarding his colleagues and their enemies. As I have told them before, it matters not to us what your differences are. We don't want to hear them. Keep them to yourself, but fight the cause of Ireland before the world. You may have your differences, but do you imagine for one moment that the men who could not agree at the Round Table Conferences that had taken place to heal our splits—does anyone imagine that we are going to get it from a committee of this audience? There are twenty or thirty men in the audience that each of us may know. Who are the men we are to take for the committee? Are we to put on the committee the men who have been fighting each other? Who else are you to put on it? They are the only men that we know, and they are the only men we would trust.

Now, I say that the amendment spells delay, and delay spells danger, failure and damnation. If we cannot have wisdom in a multitude of counsellors at any rate we will try. When I think of the cause we are fighting for, when I think of the mighty issues that are at stake, it breaks one's heart to think that the men whom the Irish people have trusted are the very men who knocked the olive branch out of our hands. What we want is to keep the Irish people. We talk of the glories of the country, and we have heard our friends from America and Canada, all of them prosperous men, giving incentives to fight for the liberty of Ireland, to fight to keep the people at home, for if you want to see the condition of the people who have left our land go into the bye-ways and the slums of Liverpool, Boston, Chicago, New York, and Philadelphia, and see where our Irish girls have gone to. I say if there are curses that cry to heaven for vengeance, it is the curse that has fallen upon our pure-minded girls, who have gone from their pure homes, driven from the old land. Why were they driven out? Because of faction. I have seen the people leaving Queenstown harbour, the bone and sinew of the land. What becomes of them often I want to know? We want these people to stay at home. We were told yesterday by the most rev. chairman of the extent of the overtaxation of Ireland. The only way to put an end to that overtaxation is by getting Home Rule for Ireland, and the only way to get Home Rule is to have one determined and united voice from Ireland demanding Home Rule ; and to men who will not agree with the majority then I say, in the Yankee phrase, " Let them git," and they will have to git. We have men here from all parts of the world. We have men from England whose nationality burned bright, and we all appeal to you to be united, for we are all united in England. We don't know what you are fighting for. We have come here for a mandate, a mandate of peace or war. We appeal to every section of the Convention to act like the mighty streams that flow through your land. You have differing opinions, but like the rivulets that flow into the main stream, let each differing section flow into the main stream that travels on until our great cause flows into the broad ocean of Irish prosperity and liberty.

Dr. W. P. O'MEARA, Southampton—I, like the speaker who has preceded me, come to you from England, and I do not think that I would have said anything if it was not from a desire to draw out from the body of the hall the opinion of the delegates who remain there. I rise to support the amendment that has been moved by Father Flynn, and I do so for this reason. When I go back to Southampton, the branch of the National League called after the renowned Henry Grattan will demand of me what I carry home to them, what is the result of our Convention. And if I tell them that we passed such a resolution as the first resolution that is on the agenda paper, they will say to me, "What good is that?" We leave the matter in the hands of the Irish Parliamentary Party to deal with the sections that have sprung up in their own ranks. If the Irish Parliamentary Party had done their duty you and I would not have been here to-day. If the Irish Party, when they found men in their own ranks did not obey the pledge which they had signed to sit, act, and vote with the majority; if, when they found that they did not, they did not drive them from their ranks, then, I say, it is time that some other means should have been chosen. It is very hard for humble men from the ranks like myself to follow and try and controvert the arguments used so ably by Mr. O'Connor. But, nevertheless, I have got as much interest in the country as Mr. O'Connor, and I am sure every delegate in the hall has the very same right to express his ideas. Mr. O'Connor tells us that this Convention itself is a committee of arbitration. How can it be a committee of arbitration, when, upon his own admission, he tells you that members of Parliament who ought to be here, and who are members of the section who have created the discontent, he tells you that they have remained away?

A Voice—They ought to be here.

Dr. O'MEARA—It is no answer to tell me they ought to be here. I am perfectly well aware they ought. But the fact remains, and facts are what we have got to deal with, that a large portion of the Irish representatives have remained away from this Convention. If they have remained away, and they are men of influence and position and have followers throughout the country. If these men remain away, how can you get them to arbitrate; how can you say we are arbitrating with them now when they deliberately abstain from coming amongst us? In the same way the members of the Parnellite Party—I look around for any well-known representatives of the Parnellite Party, and I don't see any of them here.

A Voice—It was their own fault; they were invited to come.

Another Voice—Did you see the *Independent?*

Dr. O'MEARA—Yes, my friends, I saw the *Independent* to-day, and I thought it a disgraceful production, and it is a poor day for Ireland when a paper which describes such a Convention as this as an "assembly of asses" can be publicly sold in Dublin. I support the amendment on these grounds, that if these men will not come to us we, like Mahomet, must go to the mountain. We must go to these men if they will not come to us. If these men do not come to us we must go to them (loud cries of "No, no"). Do not misunderstand me. I do not mean to say that we are to sacrifice a single principle that we have stood by and fought for; but I mean to say that we must go to them, to meet them and try and get them to come into our ranks (applause and interruptions). I don't want anyone to misunderstand me in this hall. I am an ardent supporter of majority rule, and thoroughly convinced that any man who does not obey it ought to be kicked out of the party. But I think this is a time and epoch for conciliation, and the best course we can adopt for the good of the country and the good of the cause we all hold so dear is to support and carry the amendment moved by Father Flynn (applause, dissent, and cries of "Vote").

The CHAIRMAN—There are some cries of "Vote," but I think we might hear one or two more speakers.

Rev. P. O'LEARY, P.P., Castlelyons—My lord and fellow-delegates, you have heard a great deal of eloquence to-day. You have heard a great many very solid maxims put before you to-day, but we delegates as a body are not what you can call Ciceros—we are not all born to be like Demosthenes—but I think as a body the great majority of us have been born with a fair share of common-sense. Consequently, as we cannot pretend to a very exalted standard of eloquence, and also being possessed of only the ordinary amount of common-sense, and claiming no more, we do not come here to enter into dark and mysterious details of the subject. There is an amount of mystery about this business of unity that I confess I cannot fathom. An amendment has been proposed asking that we who have come here from the ends of the earth and every part of Ireland should now hand over to somebody else the very purpose for which we came here. Now, suppose you appoint a committee of arbitration of course the committee appointed will come before you and say: "Please gentlemen, tell us what we are to do." Gracious me, was there ever a committee of arbitration that had not to come before the people who appointed them, and get in black and white the lesson they were to carry out? Your committee will come and ask you to give them a programme and an agenda paper, and, of course, you will say: "Of course, we do not exactly know what we are to give you." Suppose we are anxious to show respect to those who have come from distant parts—from the ends of the earth—and we wish to appoint some of them on the committee of arbitration, they will ask us something like these questions: "Tell us," they will say, "is this dispute about Home Rule, because if it is we will settle the matter at once." But you will say: "Oh, no, we are all agreed as to Home Rule. Every one of us, even those most opposed to each other on other matters, are as one in support of Home Rule. In fact, even those most prepared to destroy each other, are in proportion most desperate advocates of Home Rule." The committee will say: "Gentlemen, what are we to do? You are all united on the question of Home Rule, and so there is no disunion at all." Their next question is: "Come to the point, does the difficulty consist of some point of detail; are you disunited as to whether it should be Home Rule or some other kind of local autonomy or self-government?" And you will say: "Oh, no, Home Rule is all right, and we are all united on the point." The answer is, "What is the row about then?" But then somebody will say, "Oh, that is a very deep question." It is an exceedingly deep and mysterious question. There is some awful dynamite business at the root of it, and if you touch it you will be blown up. So take care you don't touch it. I confess myself that that impression has been made upon my mind.

I came into this Convention feeling that the business was the plainest and most simple and open that could be, but when I have listened to the speeches on both sides I have asked myself is there not some terrible thing under this that I can't understand? So really and truly, as a delegate speaking to delegates, our duty here is to face this matter. What is the row about let us ask, as nobody else can give us an inkling of what it is about. Is it about majority rule? Not at all. They are all most terrible sticklers for majority rule. But I must confess that on that point of majority rule I am afraid there is a screw loose. What is the meaning of majority rule? That is the question. You remember the story about the animal in the wilderness. One man swore it was blue, another that it was black, and another that it was red, but they all swore what was true, because one saw it blue, another man saw it black, and another man saw it red. Now, I ask again, what is the meaning of majority rule? I have seen sometimes in the Press very strange expressions from men whom I consider excellent judges upon what majority rule means. I remember a man in the public Press protesting that he never would enter the Party because why should he for ever remain in a miserable minority. And now suppose I myself was a layman, and were elected a member of the Party that represents this country in the English House of Commons, and that this majority rule is proposed to me as the fundamental principle of the existence of that Party, and the source of its power—supposing somebody asked me: "What do you mean by voting, sitting, and acting with the majority?" These are three nice words, but, oh, how easy it is to slip between them. I am, of course, bound to obey the majority. Very well. I come to you and say: " I will obey the majority as long as the majority goes right. But is there any man on the face of the earth so stupid as to expect that I would obey a majority that is going to the mischief." Is that majority rule? What is a man in the minority to do?

A Voice—To obey.

Father O'LEARY—That is the point, and let the delegates pronounce their opinion out. If you examine the language you will find that there is a terrible mistake when a person says, "I will obey the majority as long as the majority is right." Imagine a man in the minority believing the majority is right! There is no such thing. Every man in the minority is fully convinced the majority is wrong. Therefore I say, and I think there are no delegates here but will agree with me, that the men in the minority are bound to obey the majority, even when the majority is politically wrong. Every man in the minority is bound, I say, to support the majority, even when the majority is wrong. There is no second word about it. If you minimise the principle, if you give the men in the minority head-room to slip away, then you whip the ground from under the whole business. Every man is bound to obey the majority, even if flatly politically wrong, and every man who won't do his duty is not wanted, except to make himself scarce. Now, I'll ask another question bearing upon this idea of delegation. I ask another question—Who are we?

A Delegate—The people.

Another Delegate—The majority.

Father O'LEARY—Hear, hear. We are the assembled representatives, duly elected and sent here from all parts of Ireland, and from the ends of the earth. As we stand here to-day, or sit here, we are the supreme court of the Irish nation. Now, the result of that fact is that we are now to lay down the law for majorities and minorities, and that we are bound to do it ourselves, and not to go delegating it to anybody. There is no question of delegation. What are you going to delegate? You are going to send three or four people from the different parties to approach certain people, and say, "Will you obey the majority?" and they will be delighted to say, "We will obey the majority when it is right," and so the delegates will come away with no other answer. Very well. Therefore there is no use delegating your power; keep it in your own hands; keep the bridle in your own hands. You are here assembled as the representatives of the Irish race. Do not let any man put his hand outside yours on the bridle. If you do you lose control of the seat, and leave the whole guidance with others. That is no Demosthenes eloquence. This is business. Do not mind eloquence; decide for yourselves, and keep the power in your own hands.

A Delegate—We are the power.

Father O'LEARY—There could be only one reason for delegating a question to a committee, and that was where details and mysterious calculations, which would take up too much time from a body of men, arise. In this question there was no such thing. It is the simplest question that ever was put before a body of men—viz., "Do your duty." The only real question to be deliberated upon by the delegates come together is not a question that regards personal feelings, animosities, and pique. The whole Irish race is to be represented here in this hall; delegates have to come from the ends of the earth at great trouble and expense in order to rub against the grain. Another question for us, as practical, commonsense men, who have come here, is this : I said that we are the supreme court of the Irish nation ; are we to enforce our decrees ? The proposer of the amendment certainly made his proposal in a most honest spirit. I differ with Mr. O'Connor on one point in regard to that proposal. He said that the amendment was changed because that, unless it was changed, it would be trampled upon and rejected unanimously. Now, I don't believe that Father Flynn changed his resolution with that motive. I disagree with Mr. O'Connor on that point. I believe he changed his resolution merely for the purpose of promoting unanimity, and, secondly, that he had no motive whatever in proposing the resolution first or in altering it afterwards, or in insisting upon it now, except the motive of shaping some resolution out of these deliberations—the very thing we are anxious for ; the very thing the people in the country are asking : Will the Convention do anything ? Will it do any good ? Very well. We have not, of course, a military force to carry out our decrees, but there are things that are stronger than a military force. We have at our disposal, at all events, the public opinion of the great majority of the country. Unfortunately, there is an element of dissension. There is a certain element it is not easy at first to grasp or realise. If I am a member of the minority, and happen to be a clever fellow, I can know how to manipulate a majority rule, and how to manipulate my friends and my influence in the country, to appeal to the crowd from the authority of the Convention. Very well. The practical question is, then : How is that to be opposed and remedied ? I want to answer that question. Eloquence is a very fine thing, but one practical action is worth all the eloquence in the world. If you lay down the law that every man in the minority is bound to obey the majority, even if the majority is wrong, lay down that law. There is no person in this assembly that will have any objection to that. I think there is no person in this assembly who will allow a member of the minority in the Irish Party to question whether the majority are right or wrong. Of course, during their deliberations, when the party are met in their Committee Room, then every man is bound to stand up and give an account of the faith that is in him. Every man is bound then to stand up and debate the point to the utmost extremity of his talent. But the moment the decision is given, and the majority goes against him, he is just as solemnly bound to bow his head and follow the majority, and do so in such a manner as that the country abroad will not get a single hint of anything that occurred within. He is bound to that solid obedience to the majority, that he has to follow them when he thinks that they are wrong, and to do so without offering complaint before the country in such a manner as that he would injure the cause of his country by his complaint.

What is the support the majority is to get ? In other countries that have their own Government, when the majority decides, the Executive Government of the country go forward armed to the teeth to support the majority. All the resources of the country are placed at the disposal of the majority. They have all the wealth of the country. The very moment the Tories get into power in England all the millions of English taxation are at their disposal. They have the army and the navy, and better than the army and the navy, they have the money. Consequently, if you wish—I am giving my own opinion on this point; it is a mere personal expression, and one that I give out from myself alone—if you wish the Convention of the Irish Race to have a result; if we wish to see that our majority will have its way, that the minority will have to submit; if we want to see that done, what is our duty? Our duty is to come out and support the majority, and the back of my hand to the minority. Let us ignore them altogether, and let them alone. We don't want them. We want our majority, and our majority are our representatives. And let me tell you, and I dare say you understand it as well as I do—we delegates have no masters here. The leader of our majority is our servant—the members of our majority are our servants. Those who refuse to come here, and even insulted some of our worthy delegates—those men are our servants, and they refused to do the duty that we appointed for them. They are all our servants. If a servant refuses to do the duty we have appointed for him we dismiss him, and we get another man in his place. If he does his duty, and does it well, we pay him. I assure you, I believe the whole question of unity is in that question of the paying. Our friends from foreign countries came here, and over and over again I listened yesterday to the most affecting, and the most heart-rending, and the most piteous appeals to the people of this country to unite. I would, with all respect, suggest to our friends from across the seas one idea. There was a certain man at one time who said he would give a certain portion of the people what weather they liked. They came together, and said that they came to him for the weather. He said, "What sort of weather do you wish?" Some said wet, some said dry, some said cold, and some said hot. "Oh, gentlemen," said he, "agree, and then I will give you whatever you want." That one word that I have heard throughout the country and across the sea for the last two years has caused me the most bitter vexation. I have heard it said by our friends in foreign climes, "Unite, and we will send you everything." How in the world can we be expected to do that unless our friends from foreign climes will change the principle a little bit? You come here from the ends of the earth to try and establish union in this country. We came here on account of the respect we owe you. Therefore, I think there is not a delegate that will not agree with me when I ask you to go back to your own country and say that, "The majority are united, and it is our duty to support the majority," and when asked about the minority to say, that they are nowhere. You come here in this glorious assembly, the most extraordinary gathering of Irishmen since the days of Cormac Mac Art. It is the most extraordinary assembly, as our most rev. chairman said, since Irishmen came together from all quarters of the country in the days of the great "Feis Teamhra." We tell our friends who come here that our duty is to support the majority, to give them the standing, and to give them the money. I will give them this guarantee, that if, as they once did, the hundreds and the thousands and the hundreds of thousands in cash come from Australia and America to the majority, you will find how

soon the minority will fall into line. Deire ξαċ αon ϝοιϝϛéιl αn c-αιηξeαʋ.*
That is the suggestion that I have to make, and it is a practical one. I
will ask every delegate from Ireland to send that message in the most
solemn manner away to America and Australia, and say, that the people
are united, for we are practically united, and then when you have the
money from those countries sent home to fill the war chest once again,
then, believe me, you will have a party that will be respected. That is
the suggestion I have to make instead of the amendment which has
been put before you.

Rev. D. F. MURNANE, Bermondsey—My lord, may I just say a
few words of personal explanation, and also make an appeal to this very
great gathering of our race? I am the representative of a branch—I
am the founder of a branch—of the National League in Bermondsey,
and therefore I am sure the esteemed president of that organisation will
not feel that in the question I asked him a little while ago I had any
personal feeling. But remember we have come here—we, the children
of Erin, have come back now to try and retrieve in some way the grand
traditions that our people have given to us. I confess that the speech
of the most reverend chairman gives us wonderful courage and hope,
for in it he spoke of unity, and there was not one word uttered by his
lordship that gave the slightest offence to the tenderest susceptibilities of any section of the Irish people. May I try to follow up the line
of thought of the delegate from Southampton. Remember that in every
place where the Irish people have gathered together there you would
have a little Ireland reproducing the traditions and the faith, and, I am
sorry to say, the dissensions and divisions of the Irish people at home.
May I say to you, personally, that I am in accord with the great majority
of this meeting. Surely we have not come here to push the interest of
any party before the cause of Ireland? Surely we are not going to
make a desert and call it peace? We have come here to make a golden
bridge, over which those who differ from us may approach us again and
reunite with us. Therefore, whether the platform is to be drawn up by
the committee, or whether this great Convention is to decide, will you
remember that the future will be very different from the past. In the
past it has been one section against another, but if it goes forth to the
world that a programme was drawn up and adopted by this great
gathering, surely you get full strength, and with the great power that
will be behind us we can begin anew in a far stronger way. Surely we
have come here to make peace with our divided fellow-countrymen, and
not to cut off a still larger number. This Convention will strengthen
the supporters of majority rule. It is difficult now to go into the
question of why those dissensions have arisen, and as to the differences
and jealousies that have existed. When I was coming to this Convention the words I used to the meeting gathered together to select a
delegate was that I was coming here on the understanding that no names
were to be mentioned, that no sections were to be referred to, and that
the whole object was to bring about unity amongst our separated
brethren. I told Parnellites and the men who followed Mr. Healy, that

---

* The end of every Gospel is money.

if they came here they would have fair play. I said to them that this was a question for the Irish people to settle, and not the leaders. We are in favour of a policy of independent opposition to every party. I implore of you, therefore, not to be of a partisan character, but let us say "Ireland above all, and God save Ireland."

The CHAIRMAN—I think it will accord with the sense of the Convention that one speaker, and only one speaker more should address you for the motion; and although it is not in right order, yet I think, as it is his desire, I am sure the Convention will hear a few words in support of his amendment before I take a division. I call upon Father Kennedy, late of Meelin.

Rev. M. B. KENNEDY, C.C., Blarney—My lord and fellow-countrymen, I have endeavoured to follow closely the arguments advanced in support of the amendment moved by Father Flynn, and I fail to find any reason why he and those of his opinion should not leave to the decision of this grand Convention the settlement of the question. Are we not specially selected by the Irish people for the purpose of bringing about unity amongst our countrymen, and are we to delegate our powers to a committee to go out of this Convention, whose authority a section of the party has ignored. Upon the success of this Convention—the most representative Convention of Irish Nationalists that ever assembled in Ireland—depends the future of Ireland for a generation. It is plain that for three or four years, owing to the noise and squabbling in this country, no progress whatever has been made; and if this Convention fails to bring Irishmen within one bond of brotherhood, and show them that it is the duty and the interest of all Irish Nationalists to strive together, we shall write ourselves down a fickle and brawling race, fit only for the lot of slavery and unworthy of the sacrifices made by our Irish friends abroad. Fellow-countrymen, if we were in earnest we should have no leisure for wrangling. Recrimination and squabbling over every petty point of policy are not the weapons of men who have an honest appreciation of the sacredness of the work on which they have entered. No Irishman who is worthy to have any share in this great National struggle will descend to clamour—to the petty squabbles of John Doe and Richard Roe. Well, if subjection and discipline and self-restraint must be the motto of those who elected us, and who, like us, have to fight in the ranks, surely it must work disastrously to the progress of our cause if we tolerate insubordination on the part of those who are our lieutenants and the trustees of the National interests in Parliament. Unless we compel them to yield a loyal acquiescence to the mandate of the ruling authority of the Irish Party, all our efforts to maintain an efficient representation at Westminster will be paralized. Speaking from his Metropolitan See in this city, a great Archbishop laid it down as the duty of Irishmen of his day that they should bend all their efforts to marshal and organise the elective power of the country so as to ensure a right direction being given to every available vote. But it is no longer to organise and marshal our forces into one grand irresistible army the country is summoned. It is now with some —happily a small minority of our fellow-countrymen—it is now with them every chieftain for himself, every section for itself, every malcontent for his own grudge, and Ireland in such a clash of interests goes to the

Saxon, where she went before, through divided counsels and the want of a central authority capable of enforcing obedience and directing the combative power and strength of the nation.

I say to you, fellow-countrymen, to quell dissension you must keep the story of the past in your hearts. Faction, and the spirit of faction, have robbed Ireland of many a glorious story in the past, and until that spirit has been exorcised from our midst it will continue to leave us at the mercy of those who can keep the future in their eye, and act up to the level of their destiny. In politics, as in the conduct of a great army, there is no such thing as strength without discipline and combined exertion. It is true we are twenty millions of people, counting our fellow-countrymen in America and elsewhere, but it is also true that if we were twenty millions ten times over our numerical tot would be politically powerless unless we proved our title to freedom by working unitedly and working untiringly for the noble object we have in view. Have we not one of the most powerful, one of the strongest countries on the earth to contend with, and here at home have we not a powerful and merciless class who traditionally, and for every selfish motive are opposed to us, and why squander any of our resources in bye-battles as to who is the best man in the Irish Party, or in petty squabbles for the leadership of the Party, bye-battles and squabbles that can only make our cause odious, and, what is worse than odious, can make it contemptible? By the details of our wrongs, and the fierce denunciations of injustice and oppression, we have created a public opinion in favour of our claim to legislative independence; we have roused and enlisted on our side the feeling of America and Australia and of Liberal England; we have at our back in this struggle the respect and sympathy of all honest men in Europe. What do I say? Degraded and weakened as Ireland at present is by dissension, we stand now upon a vantage ground that even Mr. Parnell had not. Because we have demonstrated by the conclusive evidence of triumphant experience that a Home Rule Bill can pass through the eye of the needle of the House of Commons. Well, if at this juncture we allow dissension to split up the country into as many camps as there are rival pretenders to the leadership, to a throne that is not yet vacant, we shall be only trifling with the men of other nations whose sympathies are with us, and we shall be abdicating for ever any claim to the generous aid that our exiled friends in America and Australia have been giving to us. Every evil that we have suffered, every misfortune that we have suffered for centuries past, is due to one cause that at certain periods of national trouble and distraction, we cease to consider ourselves as a nation of united brothers, whose first duty it is to exert our common efforts, not in recrimination or in mutual destruction, but to oppose the common enemy. Look into your hearts, fellow-countrymen, they were made for love and confiding friendship. What fatal power has changed their nature and converted them into the dwelling places of discord and distrust? Long ago it was the policy of the tyrant who divided that he might command. To-day it is the turbulence of a few who will not yield to the will of the majority. Well, let insubordination prevail, and to-morrow set in the chair whom it elects. How can he expect to have obedient or disciplined followers in the Party or in the country—he who raised himself into authority by deeds of disorder and undiscipline? If a rebellious minority should at length succeed in attaining to control, must they who have been vanquished by the leader of the present strife cease to contend for the supremacy? Has he not marched to power through rapine and plunder—has he not set at naught the democratic principle on which alone he can hope to govern—the rule of the majority? Is this drama of dissension then to go on for ever? No, no, in the name of the beating and resolved hearts of millions of my countrymen, I say no, no. Ireland has had, like every other land, her times of distraction and degradation. But she is rising—has arisen—from the nightmare of strife and dissension. There is hope on her brow; above all, there is resolve in her heart. And, ah! men of America and Australia, if you knew how much it nerves and ennobles the hearts of us here, and our countrymen, to find that we are not alone in the world, to know that high-souled freemen like the patriotic American priests and delegates who addressed us here to-day and yesterday pant for union amongst all sections of Irish Nationalists, and pray for it, for us, you would not grudge the pains you take for poor old Ireland. I, as one Irish priest, say to you—" God bless you."

Mr. M. O'MARA, P.L.G., Dundalk—I do not wish to make a speech, but I take the liberty of making the suggestion that there should be a limit to the time given to the speeches.

Rev. P. F. FLYNN, P.P.—My lord and brother delegates, I am extremely grateful for your giving me an opportunity of replying to the very strong and exhausting criticisms that have been passed upon my amendment. In the first place, I will take the liberty of saying that nearly every speaker who spoke against the amendment spoke as if I wished to take the decision of this matter out of the hands of the Convention. Gentlemen, I had no such wish, and, gentlemen, my amendment on the face of it told that most distinctly, and I am surprised that any one of the ability of my friend, Mr. O'Connor, and other gentlemen who spoke, could misconceive my meaning when I said, that a committee could be appointed by yourselves who would report to you—(cries of "When?")—report to you for your own consideration and your own approval, and you would be the masters of the situation. I therefore have not withdrawn the decision of this matter from the Convention. I came here, gentlemen, to promote unity if I can. There are two ways of promoting unity. One is by cutting off, and the other is by amalgamation. I don't want to cut off if I can help it. To cut off should be our last and final decision. The men who would be cut off have done magnificent work for Ireland. But I would hope that when they would reconsider their position they would gladly join our ranks again and act together once more. I, gentlemen, left out a part of the resolution which I handed to his lordship yesterday, and I have done that in the interests of peace and in the interests of union. I have done it because I thought it formed a more universal and less contentious platform. I introduced no names, I introduced no parties, and our Parliamentary representatives well know how committees are to be formed, and how they are to work, and when they have to sit, and how long they have to sit, and with all their cleverness and with all their ability, I defy them to fix a time when any committee would sit, or should sit. Mr. O'Connor is familiar with Parliamentary work, and he knows well that if the principle of a Bill be admitted, that Bill can be corrected and modified in committee. I asked you only to admit the principle of my amendment, and that you yourselves be your committee. I ask you to admit the principle of my amendment.

A Delegate—What is the principle?

Rev. P. F. FLYNN, P.P.—The principle is that we elect a certain number of delegates from this Convention who will draw up rules that will be approved of by the Convention. (Interruption and cries of "Withdraw.")

The CHAIRMAN—Kindly allow the speaker to proceed without interruption.

Rev. P. F. FLYNN, P.P.—I find here in letter M the following:—"That a committee, consisting of the following gentlemen, be appointed to amend the constitution of the Irish National Federation." Now, you can see the names in letter M. This committee will be formed—it will sit how long?

A Delegate—It will be rejected.

The CHAIRMAN—I have got written notice from Mr. M'Govern, of Gortmore, Dunboy, that the resolution is withdrawn—absolutely withdrawn. I wish to say it is withdrawn in favour of Father Flynn's amendment.

Rev. P. F. FLYNN, P.P.—I do not think, gentlemen, I have anything else to say except this. It has been stated that I made a great mistake in the original resolution by admitting that there were three or four parties in Ireland. The principal speaker who criticised me reduced them to two, and of those two the larger he divided into sections. I say, and the country holds, and it is my opinion, that that is a distinction without a difference. I believe there are three parties in Ireland to-day with whom we are going to unite. I, at all events, have endeavoured to explain my position. I am grateful to the gentlemen who spoke so favourably of myself and my character. I can say the same of them, and I am only sorry that I have not an opportunity of grasping the hands of every member of the sea-divided Gael, and uniting them once more in a common compact body to work for the regeneration of our common country.

The CHAIRMAN—I am going to take your voice upon the resolution and the amendment. The amendment goes first, and it just occurs to me to say, from all I have heard, that if it were a question of majority rule I have not heard a dissentient voice.

At this point Father FLYNN approached his lordship and spoke a few words to him.

The CHAIRMAN—Gentlemen, is there one here who has not heard of Father Flynn's services to Ireland? Out of love for unity and Ireland, and to promote harmony, he withdraws his amendment. (Loud and long continued cheering, the whole assembly rising to their feet and enthusiastically waving hats and handkerchiefs.)

Rev. P. F. FLYNN, P.P.—Gentlemen, I am most grateful for your applause, and I say, now that my action has met your approbation, I feel hope, and only wish it was in my power to do anything further for the restoration of unity; and I only hope that if there be any gentlemen who have the same feelings and ideas on this subject that I have, that if I could be their leader in the present circumstances I would ask them to follow my humble example.

The CHAIRMAN—I will now put the resolution, which is as follows :

"Seeing that divisions amongst Irish Nationalist representatives paralyse, to a great extent, their power of serving Ireland, cast discredit on the country, and tend to alienate the support of the Irish race and to destroy their confidence in the efficacy of Parliamentary action, we record our firm conviction that it is of the first importance to Ireland that the Nationalist representatives in Parliament should be reunited into one party ; and, in the spirit of the recent resolution of the Irish Party, we declare that—
' In our earnest desire to accomplish that result, we are prepared to meet on fair and equal terms all Nationalists who will join in the attempt to reconstitute a united Home Rule Party, in which every supporter of the movement shall be cordially received and justly considered, regardless of all past differences and having regard only to his capacity to render service to the common cause.' We are glad to observe in the composition of this Convention, and in the spirit shown throughout the country, marked evidence of a growing tendency to re-union; and we invite the Irish Nationalist Party to take such further steps as may to them seem calculated to promote the cause of re-union."

The CHAIRMAN—All within the barrier in favour of the resolution will say " Aye." (Loud cries of " Aye.") All against the motion will say " No."

There being no response :

The CHAIRMAN—I declare the first resolution on the agenda paper—in discussing which so much has been done to debate the other questions—unanimously carried by this great Convention of the race of Erin. Will you kindly cast your eye on the second resolution on the agenda paper as follows. The Hon. Edward Blake will speak to the resolution :—

"That we recognise as the essential element of the existence of an effective Irish Party the hearty co-operation and cheerful subordination of each individual in carrying out the party policy, as settled (after free discussion) by the judgment of the greater number. That while we are glad to observe that on grave questions there have been but few intelligible differences of opinion in the Irish Party, and none difficult of reconciliation by reasonable men willing to agree, we most strongly condemn those public disputes regarding minor questions of persons and tactics which have so gravely impaired the power of the Party. We solemnly call upon every man belonging to the Irish Party, in answer to the prayers of our people all the world over, to forget old differences, to sink personal feelings, and to act for the future as good comrades and fellow-soldiers in the spirit of this resolution and in the support of that party unity, on which the fate of Ireland so largely depends. We ask the Irish Party to take such steps as may, in their judgment, be found necessary to the establishment of unity and discipline in their own ranks, in accordance with the resolutions of this Convention ; and we assure them of our unfailing support in the execution of this essential task."

The Hon. EDWARD BLAKE, M.P.—Gentlemen of the Convention, the happy unanimity with which, after exhaustive debate, the first resolution has been carried encourages me in the hope that the second resolution may meet the same result. You have already resolved with reference to those Irish Nationalists who are divided from the great organisation which summoned this Convention, who are divided from the Party, and in the country from the majority of Irish Nationalists—you have already unanimously resolved to extend to them a cordial and generous and frank invitation to enter and move into co-operation with you in the sacred National cause. Reunion, as you have determined, is of the greatest importance to the cause of Ireland, and you as men of common sense know that where a common cause is to be fought in one arena, the division of those who fight upon one side into two armies is useless, wasteful, and destructive. Furthermore, the union in the nature of things must be a cordial union, a vital union, a real union, a union of will and of sincerity, which shall make one single organisation govern the forces, as all other complex organisations must be governed by the voice and morale of one single organisation. A merely nominal union, a sham union, really discordant, full of rivalries, instead of trying to find common ground of agreement, would be, and if it has existed, has been an intolerable situation. The sorest wounds that can be inflicted upon men are the wounds of their professing friends ; the most dangerous blows in the fight are those which are struck in the flank and in the rear. Numbers are important to an army ; therefore we are for re-union. Morale is more benefit to an army than mere numbers. A general it has been said is worth forty or fifty thousand men. Why? Because his presence and spirit inspire confidence, and produce that morale which makes every man do immense work.

Now, it has been said that we are not doing anything practical. I say we are doing business, and we are doing everything that is practicable. We began by the appeal which has been made to those who are effectively at the moment outside our ranks. We propose to deal in this second resolution, which I humbly support, with the principles of union—not merely the union which we seek to consolidate with them, but also that union which we wish to exist within our own ranks as they stand to-day. And, therefore, this resolution, in its first paragraph, describes that kind of union which this Convention is asked to define as the real essential union, which is its mandate to the people throughout the country :—

"That we recognise, as the essential element of the existence of an effective Irish Party, the hearty co-operation and cheerful subordination of each individual in carrying out the party policy as settled (after free discussion) by the judgment of the greater number."

I don't believe that there exists in the breast of a single member of this Convention a disposition to quarrel with the paragraph which I have just now read. Such a statement is true of all political parties. Our conflicts in this day, whether of peoples or of those who are representatives of peoples, are conflicts of opinion, conflicts of thought, conflicts of intellect, where the arena and the field is the field of thought. Men who are in general agreement as to great and capital objects towards which they seek to arrive, we must necessarily expect will combine for those capital objects, preserving a certain measure of independence of thought and action, with a view to influencing those with whom they co-operate upon all the minor details and tactics which are to be used in order to reach the attainment of their ends. Intelligent men, thinking men, yet though combining in the capital object, will necessarily have various shades of opinion upon these minor matters, and in politics, above all things, questions of tactics, questions of expediency, as distinguished from questions of principles—questions of time, of method, of manner, of opportunity, of place, of degree—are the commonest questions with which we have to deal. All these various elements have nothing to do with principle. They are very difficult, very complicated. Men will differ in judgment, but if they do not agree to subordinate their opinion to the opinion of the greater number of their fellow-countrymen, there can be no successful party action, there can be no taking even the first step towards the common end. Free consultation, wherever consultation can in the stress of battle be had, and after that consultation. where every man is free to speak his own mind, a decision arrived a : by the majority must be accepted by the others, not violating their consciences indeed, because if a capital occasion occurred in which a man believes that the whole future will be wrecked by the pursuit of that course, he need not vote for it, but withdraw quietly from the council.

So much for the case where consultation is possible. There are other cases in war, and there are other cases in the Parliamentary conflict, where previous consultation is impossible. Nobody who knows anything of politics but knows that nothing is more likely to happen than the unexpected in the course of a debate. On the floor of Parliament the general in command may find himself confronted day after day with an absolutely new situation. It was my misfortune at one time to lead a party, and I have often said to my friends—"Gentlemen, I will consult you whenever I can, and as often as I can, upon what I forecast to be the future, and that you should share my responsibility. Occasions may arise when no previous consultation is possible ; I will do my best according to my judgment, and then I expect you will stand by me as loyal men facing the enemy, whether in the flank or in the rear, and if upon the whole you think I am not worthy of your confidence, then court-martial me." While this is the rule in ordinary political parties, and a rule upon which I myself have acted—while, I say, that is the rule of ordinary political parties, and applies to ordinary political parties, does it not apply with tenfold more force in the case of Ireland? Ours is a case wholly exceptional. We are waging a war for a nation's cause, and our success depends upon our presenting to the world the spectacle of unanimity. At the best we are eighty-five men in the midst of a Parliament whose total membership is 670. We are few as we stand. Are we to be for ever divided? We shall be weakened, of course, by the loss of a few votes. But divided counsels are infinitely more deleterious than the loss of a few votes. Our enemies rely to-day, as they relied in darker days, upon our discord. You recollect that speech of Lord Salisbury, in which, with brutal frankness, he told the English people not long ago that all they had to do was to be patient a little with the Irish trouble, for that ever since the days of Strongbow all Irish troubles settled themselves by the divisions that arose. I say to you, take counsel from your adversaries. Be wise, and learn a lesson, before it is too late, from those jibes and taunts that are directed at you. These jibes and taunts are applauded by the enemies of Ireland. It is only the great majority that fails, and individuals are encouraged, and discord is said to be the best thing in order to render powerless the Irish race and achieve a continuance of that domination that it is our duty to overthrow. Now, I don't like quotations, but I will give you short quotations. They are from the speeches of two prominent men in the ranks of Irish politics, made at the grand Convention held in this city in November, '92, after the General Election of '92, and they refer to and deal with the situation which had been created by the unhappy split, and solved, so far as it was possible to solve it, at the General Election. The first reference that I shall read is by a man now unhappily retired from the service of the Irish Party because of those dissensions which we deprecate——

A Voice—Sexton.

Mr. BLAKE—Mr. Sexton said this—

"A united Irish people, a united Irish Party, has been substantially restored. The grand principles, the indispensable principles of conduct and action, have been the subject of our struggle. If those principles had been suppressed the Irish cause was lost. What were they? Let me recall them to your minds, and I ask you to fix them on your minds for ever. The first was that the Irish cause, the cause of Irish liberty and the fortunes of the Irish people, is supreme in its demand for allegiance, in its claim upon the services of every Irishman, and no other cause, and no other claim, shall ever be brought into rivalry or competition. The second principle was that the representatives of a people struggling to be free must firmly act together. They must act together or they will not win. The third principle is that in order that they should act together they must pledge themselves to discipline and obedience. The fourth and final principle in this code of fundamental and indispensable principles of the Irish cause is this—that the penalty for the breach of this solemn pledge is exclusion from public life. I say if these principles had been suppressed the Irish cause was lost. These principles were challenged; they were attacked and they were defended; they were defended and they were maintained; they have been maintained and carried to the front of our public life, and there they will remain for ever."

I am afraid that that promise has not been fulfilled, and, owing to the disappointment of these expectations the eloquent speaker, whose words I have read, has for the time felt himself forced to quit the arena and cease to give the country unexampled services that for many years he rendered to the cause which is dearer to him than life. Now, I want to read for you another extract or two from another speech delivered at the same Convention by another able and prominent member of the Irish Party, who has not withdrawn from public life, though, I regret to say, his presence does not adorn this platform.

"What, then," he asked, "should be the spirit in which we approach this occasion? I say in a spirit of reserve, in a spirit of recollection, in a spirit of due solemnity; and I say that if there were patriotic hearts in Ireland—I care not how extreme they be— to hail the coming of that day, they should rejoice and they should be willing to work in unison with their brethren, no matter what minor details have separated them. I decline the invitation to make current controversy in Ireland one long post mortem examination, and if we fail by our dissensions, by our divisions, to achieve the purpose which we all assert, history will not engage in a discussion as to a nice apportionment of blame, but will curse the folly of the men who, in the last and the declining years of the great statesman whose life is dear and precious to Ireland, spent the time in odious recrimination. True it is," he said, speaking of those upon whose conduct he was animadverting—the separated minority, "true it is, they rate themselves very highly, and adopt noble maxims. Did you ever know in the history of heresy and schism that one was ever started without maintaining that it alone had the true deposit of faith? Did you ever know any creed to be promulgated in any country that there was not something to be said in favour of? And accordingly I take my stand"—

as I take my stand this day—

"And accordingly I take my stand in regard to all the questions of the future, in regard to the Home Rule Bill or any other matter. I judge them by one fact— namely this, that they pledged themselves before conventions and the country to abide by the rule of the majority, and they have broken that rule. And why is it that they stand aloof from their countrymen? Is it a question of principle, some questions about the land or the judiciary? I say it has become the merest personal question. There are certain men who would rather rule in hell than serve in heaven; who would rather be captain of the Forty Thieves than a private in the regular army. If these nine statesmen came back within the bosom of their party—for it is their party—and had to debate in the forum and councils of that party with Mr. Sexton, Mr. John Dillon, or Mr. O'Brien, on questions of land or judiciary or of veto, I think they would very soon find their level and their match."

I agree with those sentiments; but they are not applicable to Parnellites alone. They are not applicable to Parnellites chiefly, they are applicable to other men and more modern situations. I apply them to-day, and to-day they are as applicable as that day they were. Well, now I say that it is better that there should be 71 really united men according to the principles that are stated in this resolution, than 82 divided against themselves. And better that there should be 60 than 71 so divided. Now, turn to the second portion of the resolution which points out and states—

"That while we are glad to observe that on grave questions there have been but few intelligible differences of opinion in the Irish party, and none difficult of reconciliation by reasonable men willing to agree, we most strongly condemn those public disputes regarding minor questions of persons and tactics which have so gravely impaired the power of the party."

You will observe that this resolution is framed, I am glad to observe, by Mr. Webb in the spirit which ought to actuate the spirit of this Convention, and deals with fundamental principles of action, and does not invite dispute as to the merits of individuals or minor questions. This paragraph deals with two great questions—with fundamental questions upon which we have agreed. Now, how are these questions to be treated to-day? Some of us would like, on such an unexampled occasion as this to vindicate ourselves from attacks on matters to which no doubt this resolution has reference. A great service was done for the Irish cause in the silence which has been observed in these conditions. It was believed that on the whole public disunion, scandal, and dissension, which is a fatal thing, should cease, and the effort was made perhaps too long to preserve silence under attack so as to minimise the atmosphere, the area and the acuteness of dissension. Gentlemen, will you allow me to say a few words as to Irish public service in Parliament. It is a service of sacrifice. We agree to forego the great opportunities of honourable ambition in ordinary politics. We accept no office; we accept no honours; we touch no remuneration. We are debarred by our voluntary action, by the inexorable conditions of your service, from the assumption of those active duties which many men feel competent and desirous to discharge. Our only reward is, that under these conditions, sitting in an alien, and, until lately, an absolutely unsympathetic Parliament, we agreed to act as we have acted, and did the best we possibly could for our country. Let me quote the words of Edmund Burke. Speaking to his electors, he said :—

"It is not to be imagined how much of service is lost, from spirits full of activity and full of energy, who are pressing, who are rushing forward to great and capital objects, when you oblige them to be continually looking back. While they are defending one service they defraud you of a hundred. Applaud us when we win, console us when we fall, cheer us when we recover, but let us pass on, for God's sake let us pass on."

He goes on to say :—

"Gentlemen, we must not be peevish with those who serve the people, for none will serve us where there is a Court to serve. But those who are of a nice and jealous honour, they who think everything in comparison with that honour to be dust and ashes, will not bear to have it soiled and impaired by those for whose sake they make a thousand sacrifices to preserve it immaculate and whole."

Now, if I rightly catch the spirit of this gathering, a spirit with which I highly sympathise, you are against entering into the squalid details of that past which you and I alike deplore. The chief accuser is not here. You have heard enough, and too much, for yourself and for the cause of Ireland in the Press and on the platform. I will not even go over the bead-roll of these accusations. I have ten or a dozen of the capital headings by which men in the forefront of the battle have been wounded —wounded also through the sides of Ireland in days gone by, and which have culminated in a course of negativing all party discipline, those who called for the abolition of the committee voting against its abolition ; those who called for the rise and progress of the Irish National Federation decrying it and trying to paralyse it; those who called for party meetings systematically refusing to attend and help the deliberations of the party ; those who called and pressed for the National Convention refusing to attend it ; the occasion seized upon the floor of Parliament to array men against party action ; to make rival proposals ; to flout the rightful authority of the chair, and to paralyse anything like united and determined party progress. That situation is intolerable. Mr. Sexton, whose words I have quoted, has left the ranks of your service on account of it. Mr. Webb, who moved this resolution which I am supporting, has also left the ranks of the Irish Party in despair. Others of us have thought it fit to submit to the arbitrament of the people the question and the situation before deciding upon our course ; and this Convention is called in order that the voice of Ireland might speak—that it may decide, not as against men or in respect of particular accusations, but decide and affirm what are regarded as the fundamental principles of unity and subordination, in order that it may invoke a general amnesty, a general shake hands in concert and co-operation, and in order that it may give directions to the Parliamentary Party to do those things which may be needful to maintain unity and discipline in the ranks. The resolution, as I have said, enters not into the merits of the disputes. Nor do I. It is the publicity of them, the time and the place, and the method of which we complain. It is the insubordination which you are asked to condemn. Some change is needful, lest there be a collapse of the Irish Parliamentary Party. God forbid that there should be such a collapse. Then what a change ! The next paragraph of this resolution states the change for which we entertain, we are determined to entertain still, a hope :—

"We solemnly call upon every man belonging to the Irish Party, in answer to the prayers of our people all the world over, to forget old differences, to sink personal feelings, and to act for the future as good comrades and fellow-soldiers in the spirit of this resolution, and in the support of that party unity on which the fate of Ireland so largely depends."

Our hearts are for peace, your hearts are for peace ; the keynote of this Convention is peace—a real peace, a genuine peace, founded not on the vain protraction of disputes and differences about the past, but forgetfulness of all that. Let us turn the bitter and shameful page, let us tear it and destroy it, and let us write a new page of unity and forgetfulness of the evil past and go forward again as comrades to a glorious future. The lessons are obvious, the utility is plain. I implore and entreat. In the course of this struggle some wounds, undeserved, may have been inflicted upon me. I freely forgive them all. I am fully sure that with every desire to say no unnecessary word, or do any unnecessary act in the heat and strain of this struggle, I may have been tempted into words which others may consider undeserved. I do not wait to be asked. I humbly ask pardon for any offence of that kind. This should be the occasion for the exhibition of peace, charity, and goodwill. Christians, although worshipping at other altars, we are united in worshipping the God of love, and acknowledge our trespasses and ask to be forgiven, as we forgive, and I am quite sure that the spirit in which this paragraph is framed must meet with the strongest support and sympathy from those ministers of the Gospel who adorn this hall by their presence. One word from a sweet singer of the land from which I come, though not the same division of it—Mr. Whittier—

> " Let us, then, united bury
> All our idle feuds in dust,
> And to future conflicts carry
> Mutual faith and common trust;
> Always he who most forgiveth
> In his brother is most just."

God grant our prayers may prevail in this great Convention—this supreme organised effort of Irish nationality. If our professions—genuine and sincere—are not accepted, if the platform which we have laid before you is not agreed to, shall this movement collapse? Shall we lay down our arms—shall we, of the majority, confess ourselves beaten? No, a thousand times no. Shall you abandon the ship, or shall you endeavour to organise a crew? Any tolerable situation must end by mutual agreement and good will, as, under the Providence of God, it ought to end. If not so; then how? By the same steps which have vindicated that principle of unity and discipline to-day to which the first paragraph of the resolution gives adhesion. Such were the genuine conditions which settled the terms of the Irish National Parliamentary service, and which shall give Ireland an army which, though somewhat reduced in numbers, shall at all events be thoroughly efficient, acting upon these lines by which an army, few or large, can hope to achieve success at all. With this proposal the closing paragraph of this resolution deals. You are asked to instruct and to strengthen the hands of the Irish Party in a contingency which we cannot leave out of count. We trust and hope it may never arise, but if it does it must be dealt with. We ask the Irish Party to take such steps as may in their judgment be found necessary to the establishment of unity and discipline in their own ranks in accordance with the resolution of this Convention, and are assured of the unfailing support in the execution of this direction. If this meeting interpret the duty of the Irish Party to ourselves, and to the people for whom they speak, so instruct them. Give us the duty. Yours is the duty of decision to-day. On your decision depends the future of this phase at any rate, of the movement, and if this phase fails, well we know that another phase, less hopeful and less pleasing to the Irish people at large, will have, in all probability, to be suffered before a constitutional movement will again emerge from the difficulties. I have not used words of any angry passion. I have not sought to excite your emotions other than those of which my own heart might feel. When a grave and festering wound has to be dealt with, it is necessary to probe it and see where the mischief is, and I hope I have not said any words stronger than were absolutely necessary in that connection. I have tried to set before you, in restrained tones, a plain issue, and God grant that you may be wisely guided.

Mr. JOHN B. O'HIGGINS, Boston—My lords and fellow-delegates, I bear with me a message from the Hibernian Knights. It is a message of good will and of well-done to honest John Dillon and the members of the Irish Party. I bear more, and I am sorry to say that it is a message that you won't like so well—a message to the rank-and-file of my fellow-countrymen. The members of my society say to you: "Have done with treason." They say that you have elected to a position in the British Parliament men who are traitors to Ireland. A month or two ago we held a small convention, what we call a gathering of the clans, and we had a series of resolutions prepared by men who have made many sacrifices in support of Irish liberty and in defence of the Irish cause. One of those resolutions denounced the man, who I am sorry not to see here to-day, in order that I could convey it to him—Mr. John Redmond, as well as the people who have elected him to the position he occupies. The other resolution dealt with one who I own has done good service for the Irish cause, and whom I also expected to see here, and they desired me to say to him that though his work was good when it was well done, nevertheless, he acted like the cow that pitched over the bucket of milk, and deserved to be punished accordingly. Like your noble friend, Father Flynn, the proposer of that resolution, owing to its having been stated that Mr. Redmond and his followers and Mr. Healy and his followers would be at this Convention, withdrew it in favour of union and harmony, now we find—or at least I do find—that delegates who have come across the Atlantic Ocean to speak on behalf of unity are called something like dupes and nobodies, aye, and we are called tourists from Canada and America. Why don't these gentlemen take a little tour of probably only thirty or forty or fifty miles, and come in here to hear what the people of Ireland have to say? Aye, and they refer to the men who have held aloft the flag as the people who filled their pockets with gold and sold Irish seats. Well, that was enough to show me those persons would not be here. Immediately on landing at the Cove of Cork yesterday morning I happened to get hold of a little newspaper printed in the Rebel City, and I noticed the expression upon it, "This so-called Convention of the Irish Race," and I said to myself "The serpent is in Rebel Cork as well as in Dublin."

Well, gentlemen, there is just one other message I have to convey to the Convention, and it is this, that we believe that you have been too easy with those recreant members of the Irish Party. We believe in exacting the most rigid discipline possible from the Irish members. And why? Because nearly a thousand years ago when a united Ireland was once before created out of chaos, there is no other way to do it except by the heroic methods of Brian Boru, and those methods were, that people who were not with him were against him and, were recognised accordingly, and I trust that the Irish Party, the National Party will recognise that there is no other way to deal with those people than to consider them from this moment against them, and act accordingly. And, men of the constituencies, I hope that when they do act you will be at their shoulder to a man and to woman also. It has been said that if the Irish Party did their duty there would have been no disunion. Well, I believe in my heart and soul that the reason why the Irish Party did not do their duty is because the Irish people had not done their duty just as well. A worthy soggarth from the South delivered a very sensible address before you to-day, and I will say to you in the language of the Gael, ᴅo ḃı ceaṗt aıse,* I will further say that in America, in speaking of the few intelligible differences of opinion in the Irish Party, we can hardly find a difference at all. The only thing that we can find is this, that there are not offices like that occupied by as good a man as ever adorned it to go around amongst so-called leaders. While you may call upon men belonging to the Irish Party, we over in America make a demand upon them; and here let me say, that while a number of patriotic and true-hearted Irishmen and descendents of Irishmen voiced the opinions of those whom they represent, and begged and appealed to you for union, the people whom I represent do not appeal to you; we demand of you to have union. And why? Some two years ago at a Convention of the Ancient Order of Hibernians in the city of Omaha, Nebraska, an effort was made to have a certain percentage of the large amount of money subscribed by the members sent to Ireland, and when we made an effort to have that motion carried, it was found that because of these little miserable and unintelligible differences amongst you people here, the Irish in America, representing that order, refused absolutely to do anything because they thought it would only breed further dissension. That is the reason why we demand unity— in order that the money which has formerly flown into the coffers of the organisation that is represented here to-day should again flow across the ocean, and so that even if they could not strike a blow for the dear old Ireland with our hands the money that we would send over would help to do it.

I have one other little message to convey. Looking over the faces of the men present at this Convention I notice that the youth of Ireland are not as well represented as they might be. No, because they are to-day out on the Western plains beyond the Rockies, performing in the streets of Boston and Chicago and other places; and what are they doing? They are hoping against hope that some day they will be able to return back and strike a blow against the oppressors. That is one of the reasons why they are not here. They are trying to show to England in their own small way that until she does justice to Ireland's claims, and recognises Ireland as an independent part of the United Kingdom—if you can say so much without speaking treason—we will work and toil, and build a cordon of fire about her—such a fire as has

---

*" He was right."

been built about her in South Africa and other portions of the globe where the hunted fugitive Irishman has found a resting place. I do not say that as a threat. I trust that they will recognise that we are a power, and not to be sneered at or scoffed at, and that it will hang over England as the sword of Damocles. I tell them also that the sooner they turn their foreign faction out of Ireland, and let the Irish people govern themselves, the better it would be for the peace of England and peace of her people. I believe the suggestion I made will be adopted, not only by the Irish Party, but by the Irish people, and if the Irish people are united with the Dillons, the Davitts, and the O'Briens, and the rest at the head of them, they are sure to succeed. I say—

"Knaves and traitors stand aside,
Foe to Ireland, ᵽúg an beaⱡaċ."

The CHAIRMAN—I think, in one way or other, this second resolution has been debated at considerable length, and unless there be any person present to speak against it I shall put it from the Chair, but before doing so I think it right to say that two resolutions have been handed in from different quarters, which I consider to be germane to the second resolution, and it would be right before putting the second resolution to give the gentlemen interested an opportunity of speaking if they are so disposed.

Mr. DAVITT, M.P.—This resolution has been handed in by Mr. Michael Howley, of No. 1 Branch Irish National League in Keightley, on behalf of Daniel Smith and William Moran, Edinburgh, of the John Dillon and W. E. Gladstone Branches I.N.L. of Great Britain:—

"That, owing to the miserable squabbles which have disgraced the Irish Parliamentary Party during the past six years, the cause of Home Rule, in our opinion, has been seriously imperilled, the influence of the party considerably lessened, and the hopes and aspirations of the best and truest of our people chilled and thwarted. Believing that the cardinal principle of unity should form the basis of the deliberations of this important gathering, we would respectfully urge when, after due consideration, its decisions have been arrived at, every effort should be made to impress on the various constituencies the absolute necessity of demanding the immediate resignation of any representative, no matter how marked his abilities, or how great his services, who neglects or refuses to abide by majority rule."

The CHAIRMAN—If any of these gentlemen who handed in these resolutions wish now to speak, I ask them to come on to the platform and speak to the second resolution.

There being no response,

The CHAIRMAN put the second resolution.

There was a general shout of "Ayes," and one person said "No."

The CHAIRMAN—It is carried with one dissentient voice.

Several persons called out that it was in mistake the delegate said "No."

The CHAIRMAN—I have been informed that the voice saying "No" was in mistake, and I declare the resolution carried unanimously.

The CHAIRMAN—Now, unless the gentlemen interested in the resolutions read by Mr. Davitt come forward to propose them, I shall assume that they are satisfied with the instructions which are given in the resolution No. 2, and, more markedly still, by the voice of this Convention, the Irish Party to take effective means to preserve thorough discipline in their ranks. Mr. John Dillon will now speak to the third resolution.

"That this Irish Race Convention re-asserts the immemorial claim of IRELAND A NATION. We declare that England is governing Ireland wrongfully, by coercion, and against the people's will; that each year proves afresh the futility of the attempt; that Irish evils mainly flow from alien, irresponsible, uninformed, and unsympathetic rule; and that no policy, whether of severe repression or of partial concession, can allay her rightful discontent, or will slacken her efforts to obtain a Legislature and an Executive making and administering laws for Ireland by Irishmen on Irish soil. We declare it the prime duty of the Irish Parliamentary Party to continue to maintain its absolute independence of English political parties, and thus to preserve its freedom to give an independent opposition or an independent support to any party, as may seem best in the interests of the National cause."

Mr. JOHN DILLON, M.P.—I have come here to-day to place myself unreservedly in the hands of this Convention. I came here prepared to answer charges if they had been made where they ought to be made—in the face of the people. I came here prepared promptly and without reserve to obey the mandate of this Convention, and if it had asked me to follow any other man in the sacred cause of Irish Nationality without hesitation, and I may add without regret, I would have accepted this course and would have shown that I could obey, that I could obey others, and that I knew what discipline meant. I have risen for the purpose of supporting the third of these resolutions, but with the kind permission of this Convention I think it might be fair to allow me to say a few brief words on the general questions which have been discussed, and, first of all, I am proud to see, and more rejoiced than I can tell you, that from the beginning of these proceedings, triumphantly successful as they have been, and fraught, as in my inmost heart I believe they are, with a rich promise for the future of Ireland, no single man from all this mighty gathering has attempted to question the supremacy of this Convention. And that I think in itself is a matter of first and most essential importance, no man has risen up to question the supremacy of this Convention, and when one looks back on the history of this Convention and considers the methods by which it was summoned, I fail to understand how any honest man could question its right to speak for the people of Ireland. How was this Convention called into existence? The suggestion came this time from across the ocean, from a great man, none the less Irish because he occupies a lofty position in the Church of another nation, and who in his person typifies some of the greatest, the most historic, the most magnificent glories of our race, that they have carried the dominion, the faith of Ireland, to far foreign lands at the other side of the globe, aye, and have occupied lofty positions higher than the position of princes in that great and illustrious Church to which I am proud to belong—though Christians of all denominations are welcome on this platform to-day, and in this hall. I say that this great man who first suggested this Convention typifies in his person also these glorious traditions of our race, that no matter where they are scattered, and no matter to what eminence they may be elevated, no matter to what Church they may belong, their hearts are still bound to Ireland and to her cause with an indissoluble bond which neither thousands of miles of ocean, nor long years of separation can tear asunder.

And I confess I must ask the pardon of the delegates assembled for being drawn by that consideration into a very brief digression—I confess when, in the early days of the preparations for this Convention, objection was taken to our opening the doors of the halls and platforms of this gathering of the Irish race to the spokesmen and representatives of Ireland's scattered sons in America, in Australia, in South Africa, in New Zealand, and wherever that race has been scattered by persecution and ill-government, I was astounded, I may say I was horrified, that there could be found a man on the soil of Ireland who, with the unparalleled and immortal record of the fidelity of Ireland's scattered children, could object to invite them into the councils of the nation, and to give to them that voice which surely they are entitled to by the glorious part which they have borne in the past struggles of our people. And in that invitation, in spite of objection, was included not only the men represented by the delegates from America and Australia, but the portion of our race who, throughout the years of our struggles and agony, have borne a place in the vanguard of the battle, and who endured scorn, outrage, and boycotting, and were often driven from the workshops and mines of Great Britain because they would not deny the land of their birth—the land for which, if need were, they would spill their blood. We were told that we sought to out-number the voice of the children of Ireland by the foreign delegates and the delegates from England. The men who held such views must be content to shut out from the future struggles the help of those men who had sacrificed so much. The scroll which hangs in front of me is the best answer to those who say the children of the Gael in England have no right to a voice amongst us. We are assembled here to-day, and have delegates from every branch of the scattered Gael; and I put it, has there been any attempt to out-number the representatives of Ireland, or has anybody been denied voice or vote at this Convention?

Now, I come back to the question how this Convention was summoned. It was summoned first of all by resolution passed by the Irish Party, nearly unanimously, many months ago, affirming that a great Convention should be called; and later on, when the preparations were more advanced, the body of rules under which you meet were submitted to a duly convened meeting of the Irish Party, and at that meeting every member of the party ought to have been present, and the rules and constitution were unanimously agreed to and passed by the Irish Party, and this resolution was adopted:—

> "That we cordially invite Mr. John Redmond and his friends to co-operate with us in a common, earnest endeavour to make the coming Convention an effective means of satisfying the widespread yearning of the Irish race for thorough union."

By that resolution we invited the Parnellites to come in, not only to this Convention, but into the Organising Committee of this Convention, and to act with the Irish Party in securing that their party in the country was fairly represented in this gathering. They did not do so. We could not coerce them, but what we did was to act in such a manner as to bring the conviction to the mind of every man who takes an interest in Irish politics throughout the world that we did our best in the direction of union. Well, not having succeeded in getting the co-operation of the

Parnellite party, we proceeded, with the approval of the Irish National Party and Irish National Organisation, in carrying out the arrangements for this Convention. And now I come to the point which I would commend to the common sense of the delegates present. I say that it does not lie in the mouth of any man who belongs to the Irish Parliamentary Party, and who deliberately stays away from a meeting of the Party, to declare that he is not bound by the act of this meeting. He can no longer truly say, if he pursues such a course, that he is acting with the party. And, therefore, I say that every member of the Irish Party without exception—they number seventy-one—is bound to recognise the constitution of this Convention as sealed with the approval of the whole party. And I was glad and proud to observe that in his powerful and eloquent speech, and he always speaks with power and eloquence—I have heard him under very difficult circumstances, and under a much more difficult circumstance than he occupied to-day—I allude to Father Flynn, of Waterford, for on more than one occasion in the streets of Waterford we stood side by side in very unpleasant circumstances. He always speaks powerfully, and I was glad to notice that at the outset of his speech he recognised in the fullest way the supremacy of this Convention, and the duty of every Irish Nationalist to abide by its decisions.

Well, I am sorry to miss from the floor of this Convention some men who ought, and I trust will, abide by its decision. If Father Flynn and other men in this hall recognise the supremacy of this Convention, and that it is in reality the voice of Ireland, has that been the attitude of all the members of the Irish Party? I am sorry to say it has not been that attitude, I regret that the foreign delegates and many other members of this Convention have been obliged to see this great assembly denounced as a hole-and-corner meeting—as a packed Convention, and as a meeting which was worthy of no respect and no consideration whatever. Now, I venture to say, regarding the proceedings of yesterday and to-day that there will be found very few Nationalists in Ireland who will stick to that view of this Convention; and if they do pretend to adhere to it I think they will find that the voice of Ireland has been heard here to-day, and that their view will find little support in Ireland. Now, in this connection I desire to say that I listened with great interest and great pleasure to the speech delivered by, I think, Father Murnane, who represents one of the London branches of the League. He advocated—and I could recognise in the tone of his voice an honest and an earnest desire—to bring about union in the Irish Party; and he spoke with an eloquence—characteristic of many Irish priests. He might remember, and I trust he will remember, that it was owing to the majority of the Irish Party and our action that he got leave to speak in this hall. For to men like him an effort was made to deny them the liberty of this platform, and shut their mouths on the ground that they were strangers and outsiders, and had no right to take part in this Convention. Well, my lord, this Convention is assembled—I challenge any man who has an honest mind, who takes up the constitution under which it has assembled, to say that there was ever called together in Ireland a freer or more open Convention, and I say we have been listening for many long and weary years to charges and complaints of the most complicated and ever-changing character. There is not a man, there is not a colleague who sits around me, who has not been denounced and abused by those who ought to be his friends. For my part I do not care how much any man may abuse me so long as he does not scandalize Ireland in the process. A certain section of the Press in this country is teeming with allegations and charges. My lord, I say that here to-day before the people of Ireland those charges should not have been made, or the authors of them should have been on this platform to-day or ought to be for ever silent; and I appeal to every delegate in this room, no matter what his views may be, whether he believes that I am right, whether he agrees with my policy or not, I appeal to him for the honour of Ireland, and for the sake of the public life of this country, to set his foot resolutely and strongly on a continuation of these scandalous disputes.

My lord, it has been said that personality and personal ambition stand in the way of the advancement of Ireland's cause. I stated before this Convention assembled that if it should be found, either now or at at any future period, that the Irish National members of Parliament—and I include now, for the purpose of this statement, all members returned to support the Home Rule cause—would assemble together and say, We will not follow Mr. Dillon, he has taken too active a part in previous bitter disputes—we will not follow this man or that man, but will select another man who has not taken part in this dispute, I say joyfully, and with a sense of immense relief, I would place my resignation in the hands of these men, and invite them, without regard to personal feelings, without regard to personality, and in the name of God and their country, to unite again, no matter who was made their leader. Some men seem to think that the position of being chairman of the Irish Party is very cheerful, under present circumstances even, and so attractive a position that a general struggle and scramble for it have been going on resulting in I myself out-distancing my opponents. Well, ladies and gentlemen, I assure you that, though after a brief experience, it is not all pleasure; and I do say this, that I cannot understand how any man who has a sense of fairness could attribute, under present circumstances, to any individual an inordinate ambition to get into the position unless it be that he argues from the condition of his own mind. But I repeat this offer from this platform to-day. Let the other men, whose names have been shibboleths of faction, meet me on this issue. Let the Parnellites and let the Healyites, if such there be—I am not aware that any member of the Irish Party is prepared to go before his constituents and declare himself a Healyite—let the Parnellites and let the Healyites, if there be any such—as Father Flynn suggested there are three parties in Ireland—let them assemble at any time during the autumn in Dublin and say, "Stand aside, Dillon; stand aside, Redmond; stand aside, Healy; and we will unite under another man," then I say I am their man, and I shall be the first to sign a pledge binding me to loyally follow that united party.

The fact of it is that in dealing with these matters we have been, to a certain extent, beating the air—fighting with phantoms. Charges and allegations have been made, and when you close with them to disprove them, like the figure in the ancient fable, they dissolve in vapour and cloud, and fresh forms arise before you on the path. When these matters are all analysed they come down to questions of personalities; and I say it would have been an everlasting shame to Ireland—a shame from which this assembly happily entirely saved the country—it would be an eternal shame if personal questions were allowed to tear asunder the national forces when they were face to face with the implacable enemies of their race. Let me say a word on the question of party discipline and union. What I would implore of this Convention— though indeed it is not necessary to make any appeal to them, because they have by their action shown how keen an apprehension they have of the true principles on which a party must be founded—what I would implore of them is this. We have in the complexities of contention and quarrels, to some extent, lost sight of those vital principles on which all parties throughout the world are founded and governed. If you break up and destroy the unity and discipline of that party you can have no progress. You have heard from a man who can speak with the authority of experience, as leading a great party himself (the Hon. Edward Blake), those principles which must rule and do rule all parties. If those principles as laid down by him apply to all parties, I say that they apply with a thousandfold force to the small body on whose fidelity and on whose unity in the very heart of the camp of the enemy the cause of Ireland rests. If it is the duty of Canadian or American parties to insist on unity and discipline, it is clear it is ten times more the duty of the little army of Ireland to insist upon a far more stringent discipline. We know that in the great parties of England, America and Canada there are many ways of holding men together which do not exist with us—many ways of influencing men who are inclined to go outside the party lines; and in those countries the fate of a nation does not depend upon the discipline of any one party. In England or Canada, and if the party is negligent or disunited the punishment comes surely and swiftly, and it comes in the shape of the other party, who drive them out and come into power in their place. But in the case of Ireland the situation is totally different. We have no other party to take our places. We have not got command of the Government of our country, and our differences and our disorganisations and our personal disputes are visited on the miserable country which has sent us to fight its battle. We do not make way for another party. No, but we open the gates to the enemies of Ireland, and the consequences of our divisions are written in the tears and the blood of our people, and the endless prolongation of her sufferings. Therefore, I say in the name of God and of Ireland, never forget to maintain untouched and untampered with the essential principles, which are the foundation upon which the Irish Party rests. I would ask what are those principles? They are embodied in the pledge, but not sufficiently clearly embodied to defeat the ingenuity of men who are very able and very ingenious, and who desire to escape. But the pledge binds men not only to sit and vote, but to act with the Irish Party; and I say deliberately that if it were to be considered free to men to defy on the platform and in the Press, as well as in the House of Commons, the deliberate judgment of the majority of the party, then I say the pledge becomes a mockery, a humbug, and a delusion, and you will very soon have not only three parties, but at least a dozen parties, each led by a leader of its own.

Therefore, what I claim to be the basis on which all party discipline and party unity and effectiveness must be placed is, that there should be given a loyal and earnest support by every member of the Party to the policy of the Party as a whole, and that the support should not stop even inside the House of Commons, but should be extended throughout the country. The illustrious Bishop of Meath some time ago in a conversation that he had with the late Mr. Parnell asked—" How did you keep the Irish Party together?" He replied—"I kept it together by enforcing the rule of the majority. I sometimes thought the majority was wrong, but the great principle was that we should act together." It has been said by one priest here to-day in a most eloquent speech that the minority should go with the majority whether the majority was right or wrong. Well, it is possible to conceive a case where a member of a minority could not see his way to do that. But he has a remedy. If his conscience will not allow him to go with the majority, I say, for the sake of his country, he should stand aside.

Now let me say a word or two as to the future. I think myself, and I have long thought it, that too much has been said in a despairing tone as to the present position of Ireland. Really to hear some people talking you would suppose that the whole history of Ireland since the Union was the history of a united and unbroken party until the year 1890. What are the facts of the case? There never was a united party in Ireland until 1885, and it is most instructive to anyone who has to deal with the present situation in Ireland to look back for a moment to the history of the formation of the united party of 1885. Here is an extract from a paper which is not a great friend of Ireland, but it is an interesting extract, and very much what is to be read in the same paper to-day—the London *Times*. This article was written in the *Times* of the 30th March, 1880, commenting on the general election that was then taking place. And during that election, as many men around me on this platform and in the body of the hall to-day will remember, Ireland was torn asunder by differences, Nationalist being pitted against Nationalist in many of the constituencies. And here is what the *Times* said :—

" It is not in Wexford county alone that Mr. Parnell's nominees are found unacceptable. He can scarcely fail to discover that no true, durable unity can exist among Home Rulers. They may agree to make themselves as disagreeable as they can be to Parliament, and may with one accord join in impeding public business at Westminster. But nothing can shape into a homogeneous party an unprecedented piece of political mosaic. Any trivial incident may break up and resolve into their original elements the motley collection of intimidated or coerced Liberals, Nationalists, Federalists, earnest lovers of Catholicism, and haters of the priesthood, true sons of Ireland and men who have no real connection with it. The compact lasts just as long as no strain is put upon it. But only let Mr. Parnell and Mr. Biggar endeavour to carry some particular point which they have at heart, and the world is pretty sure to see that the Home Rule Party is but a mob of politicians who bear no great love towards each other."

Now that was the way in which Ireland presented itself to England in the year 1880. What occurred? An election took place, and on 27th April the Irish Party met—that is to say, all who had been returned to support Home Rule, and at that meeting a question arose as to who should be the chairman of the new Irish Party that had been returned.

Mr. Parnell was proposed as chairman, and Mr. Shaw was proposed against him. The party divided, and Mr. Parnell was carried to the chair by 23 votes to 18—simply a majority of 5. What occurred then? In a short time the minority quitted the majority, and finally crossed the floor, and for four years the Irish Party was split, 32, I think, was the number of the Parnellite Party, and a considerable number of Irish Home Rule members opposed them from the opposite side of the house. Within the ranks of the Parnellite Party there were men who kicked over the traces, men of ability and position who objected to party discipline, and they finally disappeared out of Irish public life in 1885; so that during these years there was not unity, there was division; but there was a fight for unity, and what saved Ireland was this, that the principles and practice of a united party were never surrendered, but were held up before the people, and when at last an appeal was made after four or five years to the constituencies of the country then there was a united party, because the constituencies took the matter into their own hands, and they approved of the pledge and the whole machinery by which since that day the Irish Party has been governed. What I would say is this, that so long as those principles are stood by, and, above all, so long as here, in the face of this mighty assembly, they can be asserted and unanimously approved, it is nonsense to talk about despairing of the future of the Irish cause. Leaders may come and leaders may go. You change the *personnel* of your leaders and the *personnel* of your party, secession may occur, individuals may leave you, but so long as the great principle of unity is held up and insisted upon by the people, and so long as a united party is held to be essential to the effective constitutional fight for Ireland's liberties, then so long, I believe, Ireland will rally round that standard.

For my part my position in this matter is exceedingly simple and exceedingly easy. My principles are known throughout the country, I am for a disciplined party. I am for a united party, and I am for maintaining that unity at any cost. I am in the hands of this Convention; I am in the hands of the country, and ultimately in the hands of the Irish Parliamentary parties—Parnellite and Nationalist—if they will assemble and agree to follow any other man. My personality will never stand for a single hour, nor for a single moment, in the path of Irish freedom, nor will it be allowed to stand for a single moment to obstruct the reunion of Ireland. So long as I have a mandate from the people I will fight for unity against every man who assails it.

I come now to say a word or two on the third resolution. I need say nothing on the opening part of that resolution, which simply reasserts what is the first article in the creed of every Irish Nationalist, that is our separate national right. I shall confine the very few remarks I have yet to make to the second portion of that resolution, which says that—

"It is the prime duty of the Irish Parliamentary Party to continue to maintain its absolute independence of English political parties, and thus to preserve its freedom to give an independent opposition or independent support to any party as may seem best in the interests of the National cause."

That is a proposition which I believe will recommend itself to this great Convention. I do not believe that there will be any difference of opinion in regard to it. We hold that we have always maintained the same independence which was the doctrine and the creed of our party before 1890, but what I want to lay before you, and before the country is this. We do not seek to rake over again the ashes of old controversies, we have faced the country and this Convention with this fresh pledge that we recognise it to be the duty of every Irish Nationalist to maintain an absolute independence of English political parties. And if that be asked in the name of union, then in God's name we give it to the world as the first article of our creed and the first rule of our life in Parliament. But let me say this word in defence of the party with which I am connected. We have been charged, and from more than one quarter, with truckling to English parties. I don't believe that we have ever laid ourselves open to that charge, but it has been made, and I saw and read with astonishment a statement made in this city not a fortnight ago, that the object of my life was to make the National Party the tail of the English Liberal Party.

Now let me point out to you one fact. Some time ago one of the multitudinous charges made against us was this—that so subservient were we to the English Liberals that, when the cause of Catholic education in England was brought up by the Tories, we would turn our backs on the Catholic schools of England and would support the Liberals.

A Voice—You never did.

That charge was made. It was made in various places throughout Ireland—I need not recapitulate them, they will be in the minds of many men in this Convention—and it was made by members of our own party. Well, the time came for a decision, and I will say this, that there never was an issue on which the Liberals of England were more anxious and more eager to get the support of the Irish Party. It appeared, from one point of view, rather a hard thing for the Irish Party, seeing that the Liberals had lately passed a Home Rule Bill, and as they contend—I won't enter into an argument on the question—but, as they contend, they had been defeated at the polls because they were Home Rulers, that on the very first great question in which the Liberals were interested we should turn round on them, and, as they put it, "overwhelm them with an avalanche of a majority." And I was appealed to personally. I suppose I received two or three hundred letters from the Radical leaders throughout England, imploring of me at least to ask our party to withdraw from the House of Commons, and, as the cause of the Catholic schools was not in danger, not to humiliate the Liberals by increasing the majority to an overwhelming extent, and the Liberals in Parliament who had fought our battle appealed to me. Under these circumstances the Irish Party met, and would it be believed that the men who had charged myself and the men who work with me before Irish audiences with being prepared to betray the cause of the Catholics of England never took the trouble to cross the Channel and attend the meeting of the Irish Party when this great question was decided? And when this question was decided, what was the action of the Irish Party? The men who were concerned about the fate of the Irish Catholics and the possible action of the Irish Party in voting with the Liberals were not there, but we who had been told, and are now told, that we are the tail of the Liberal Party, we voted against the men who had offered us Home

SECOND DAY—MR. JOHN DILLON, M.P.

Rule, and we showed to the world by the greatest proof that any party could give that we stand as independent of all British parties on the floor of the House of Commons, at least as independent as any party that ever went before us. Yes, we voted independently, and we received the united thanks of the Catholic Bishops of England, and I hope, and I have some reason to hope, that when Home Rule comes up again the Catholic Bishops of England and the Catholics of England, who voted against Home Rule at the last election, will not forget our action.

And now I challenge any man to come again before an Irish audience and say that I was trying to make the Irish Party a tail of the Liberal Party. I faced the Liberal Party when the men who make these charges skulked in Ireland. I stand here surrounded by the men who, by their services and record, are entitled to speak, and in the name of the honour of their country and of her most sacred interests, in the name of the Christian faith they profess, and of the charity which they are bound to observe, I ask those who make these charges to come forward now, when they have a full and attentive audience, to make their complaints and state their charges, and if they have not done so, I ask them to be silent for ever, and to allow Ireland to go on undistracted by these petty, contemptible, horrible, and deadly disputes, which have dragged our sacred cause in the mire before the people of the world, and which I trust and hope it will be the proud privilege of this so-called "hole-and-corner" and "bogus" Convention to bury in an oblivion which no man will ever break.

Mr. DAVITT, M.P.—The Convention will adjourn until to-morrow, at eleven o'clock. We have received a number of messages from Queensland, Newfoundland, and other places, which I shall hand to the Press.

The Convention adjourned at four o'clock.

Letters handed to the Press :—

St. John's, Newfoundland, 17th August, 1896.

TO THE CHAIRMAN OF THE IRISH NATIONAL CONVENTION.

My Lord,—On behalf of the people of Newfoundland, we send to you through our delegates a heartfelt greeting, a warm word of sympathy and encouragement in the glorious work you have undertaken—namely, the gathering together of the various streams of National life in Ireland into a mighty and irresistible torrent of love and patriotism, which shall sweep before it all obstacles, and blend every drop of heart's blood that wells up in the bosoms of her sons into one great ocean of National unity and National strength. The delegates to your Convention bring with them to the hallowed shores of Ireland the mandate of the Irish people from the furthest corners of the earth. Wherever the sun shines upon the home of a child of the Irish race, from the frozen regions of the North to the burning sands of the tropics, from the distant lands of the East to the golden shores of the Pacific, from every clime, and every land, there goes forth a cry—a heartrending cry, an agonising cry, at the painful prospect of the unreasoning and patricidal disunion which prevails among the ranks of those who are in the van of the fight for the liberty and prosperity of our motherland. And you, gentlemen delegates, are sent by us with a mission of immense meaning. It is a divine mission in a sense, for it is to echo the voice of a great people crying out for justice and peace and unity, and as such, it is the voice of God himself. We send you not to entreat, or to sue for, but to command, a truce to these divisions and dis-unions, and a brotherly embrace and hand-shake of love and goodfellowship. The leaders of the National cause in Ireland are but the trustees of the Irish people, and they are accountable not only to the small remnant, who, surviving persecution, famine and emigration, still dwell within the shores of Ireland herself, but to the millions of her race who people the distant countries of the earth, and to whom every green sod and every ivy-clad ruin of the dear old land, are sacred and revered pledges, cherished in the deepest memories of their hearts' and guarded with a jealous anxiety against encroachment or desecration.

In this great Convention of the Irish people it is meet that Newfoundland should have a place, yea, and a leading place. Looking back over the annals of our history we see many a page lit up with the glorious record of her sympathy with Ireland in her times of trouble, and of practical aid in her times of want and hardship. We claim the proud vaunt of being the "Ireland of the West," the earliest colony of Irish emigrants in the western world. The nearest point of America to the old land. We stretch out our arms a thousand miles into the Atlantic ocean to grasp in the warm clasp of fellowship and welcome, the hand of our motherland, to bid her have courage, and rise triumphant from her bondage and become a nation among the countries of the world. We pray that God may bless this supreme effort for union, and that the setting sun of the nineteenth century may cast its golden splendour upon a prosperous, peaceful, and self-governing Ireland.

On behalf of the people of Newfoundland,

✠ M. F. HOWLEY,
Bishop of St. John's, Chairman.
P. J. DOYLE, Secretary.

Greymouth, New Zealand, 28th July, 1896.

TO THE CHAIRMAN OF THE IRISH NATIONAL CONVENTION, DUBLIN.

Sir,—The Irishmen of the west coast of the South Island of New Zealand regret their inability to send a delegate to your Convention. They, however, as requested, send the following letter to express their views on the object of the Convention. Irishmen at home and abroad are fully conscious of the many disabilities under which our native land suffers. We are likewise cognisant that these must be removed before our people can live in any peace and prosperity in the land of their birth. We, the children of Erin, have been driven into exile, and nearly every foreign land gives a refuge to many of us who, if our civil affairs at home were properly managed, would have been spared the many miseries resulting from expatriation. But we are aware that the future welfare of our native land, to a great extent at least, lies in the hands of her elected representatives. And what a power for good for Ireland have they not proved to be when they presented a united front in the British Parliament. That union secured for the Irish Parliamentary Party the respect and admiration of all the lovers of our country throughout the world. It obtained for it many measures of amelioration which could not otherwise be obtained. It brought joy and hope for the future to the sea-divided Gael ; and on account of it the children of Erin in all parts of the world, together with their many friends, cheerfully opened their hearts and purse-strings and contributed most generously to aid the good cause at home.

But now we regret to see that the demon of discord has managed to edge in between, and created disunion amongst the elected representatives of our native land, upon whom rested our highest hopes. Every mail scatters broadcast to the ends of the earth the fullest account of the bitter attacks and mutual recriminations made by the members of the Irish Parliamentary Party on each other. At this we, in foreign lands, hang our heads for shame and become very much disheartened. No men should know better, from bitter experience, than the Irish Parliamentary Party that "a kingdom divided against itself cannot stand." The history of our nation and our people points out more clearly than that of any other nation that nearly all our national misfortunes have arisen from division, disunity, and divided counsels. Cannot past experience bring with it a profitable lesson for the future ? We hope so, indeed. Shall division and divided counsels continue to prevail in the ranks of the Parliamentary representatives, and cause them, however well intentioned and individually patriotic, to do most effectively by their *modus agendi* what is most pleasing to the very bitterest enemies of our native land ?

Well, we hope that the happiest results will accrue from the Convention now assembled, and we shall ever look upon those as the enemy of our country and race who shall in any way mar the object for which the meeting was called. And as we believe that Home Rule is the key to the solution of all the Irish difficulties, it is the ardent hope of the Irishmen of Westland, New Zealand, many of whom are now in declining years, and who have always supported the cause of Ireland in her legitimate struggles for the amelioration of her condition, that Providence may cement in solid unity the members of the Irish Parliamentry Party, that so they may be able to obtain by their united efforts what the Irish race so much desire for their native land and what divided counsels can never attain. And may He who controls the hearts and councils of men guide you in your deliberations to so laudable an issue.

Signed on behalf of

THE IRISHMEN OF THE WEST COAST OF THE
SOUTH ISLAND OF NEW ZEALAND.

Croydon, N. Queensland, July 10th, 1896.

To JOHN DILLON, Esq., M.P., Chairman Irish National Party.

Dear Sir,—The Home Rulers of Croydon, wishing to be represented at the Convention of the Irish Race to be held in September next, have this day appointed the Rev. V. R. Landy, O.S.A., as our delegate. He will present duly accredited credentials signed by the Mayor, Mr. Tarbart, and other influential gentlemen. With an earnest prayer that the labours of the Convention will result in a complete union of the whole of the Irish race,

Yours faithfully,

JAMES HALL.

Devon Chambers, Hunter and O'Connell Streets,
Sydney, 28th July, 1896.

JOHN DILLON, Esq., M.P.

My Dear Dillon,—I regret that it has not been found feasible to send a delegate to represent New South Wales at the forthcoming Pan-Celtic Convention, to be held in Dublin on the 1st of September; but, although New South Wales will not be represented by a delegate, the interest which the friends of the cause take in everything that concerns the welfare of the movement continues in unabated strength. Some of the effects of dissension in the ranks of the Nationalist representatives of Ireland in the British House of Commons in regard to the progress of the movement are too obvious and deplorable to need mention. If the people of Ireland could only realise fully the effect of this dissension upon the friends of the Irish cause who reside out of Ireland, I feel certain that the people would insist upon their representatives once again presenting a solid, united front to the opponents of Home Rule in the British Parliament. It is simply impossible for those who watch the progress of the movement from a distance to understand by what process of reasoning any friend of the Irish National cause can tolerate the existence of rival sections in a National Party which has but one object—the restoration to Ireland of her right to Parliamentary government.

The resolutions which were carried at the public meeting in the Guildhall, Sydney, last evening (and which are forwarded herewith), were carried with the enthusiasm that has always characterised Irish Australians in regard to the National cause.

The proceedings at the fourthcoming Convention must attract the attention of all well-wishers, not only of Ireland, but of the British Empire, as no sentiment exists more strongly than that the concession to Ireland of free Parliamentary institutions would be the most effective means of not only restoring prosperity and happiness to the people of Ireland, but of strengthening the Empire itself. I can assure you that in no part of the world will the proceedings at your Convention be watched with greater interest than in New South Wales. There is but one sentiment expressed in regard to the Convention, and that is, that its labours may result in once more placing the Irish National question in the van of British Political questions, and that the long deferred hope of the Irish people may soon be realized with the attainment of a measure of freedom equal to that enjoyed by the British Colonies.

Yours faithfully,

FRANK B. FREEHILL.

St. Patrick's Society,
Cornwall, Ontario, 14th August, 1896.

Resolution moved by Mr. M. M. Mulhern, seconded by Mr. J. F. O'Neill, passed unanimously, and desired to be conveyed to the Irish Race Convention through Hon. John Costigan :—

"Whereas, a call has been issued for a Convention of Irishmen, to be held in the city of Dublin on the 1st of September, for the purpose of uniting the Irish people the world over in the cause of Home Rule for Ireland. We, the members of the St. Patrick's Society of Cornwall, being desirous of placing before the assembled delegates our firm belief in the principle of Home Rule, and believing that the united action of Irishmen, and those of Irish descent, at home and abroad, is necessary to achieve the end for which the Convention is called, we heartily endorse any action taken. Having watched with feelings of pride the rise and progress of the Home Rule Party under the wise and patriotic leadership of the late Charles Stewart Parnell, and noted the success attending their efforts, and firmly believing that the cause of that success was mainly due to the firm and united feeling that existed in the ranks of the Irish Parliamentary Party, ably assisted by the Irish people, both at home and abroad, therefore, it is with feelings of regret and humiliation that we notice that divisions have arisen since the death of the late lamented Irish leader, and we hail with joy the summons issued for a Convention of the Irish Race throughout the world to formulate a policy whereby the forces of the Home Rule Party can be reunited, and the dissensions that exist be healed ; and we hereby tender our sincere support and influence, both morally and financially, to further the aims of the Convention."

E. O'CALLAGHAN, President.

F. G. O'HAGAN, Secretary.

Message to the Convention from the Irish Home Rulers of Southern Tasmania, assembled in meeting at Hobart, requesting Rev. T. M. O'Callaghan to represent them ; moved by Rev. J. O'Mahony, seconded by Mr. E. Mulcahy, M.H.A., and supported by Rev. P. O'Reilly :—

"That this meeting views with sorrow the continued dissension in the ranks of the Irish Nationalist Party. That, though we consider it no part of our duty to dictate to our friends at home the proper course to be followed, in order that this dissension may be healed, yet, living as we do in a democratic community, we desire to impress upon our delegate, and through him urge upon the Convention that, in our opinion, the majority should rule ; that this is the only way in which the existing breach will be closed, and dissension will in the future be avoided."

Telegram to John Dillon, M.P., Dublin :—

"Success Convention ; Irishmen Rockhampton urgently recommend unity—
KELLY, GILLESPIE, WYNNE."

SECOND DAY—CORRESPONDENCE.

P. O. Box 419, Pretoria, S.A.R., 9th August, 1896.

Jas. F. X. O'Brien, Esq., General Secretary, Irish National Convention, Westminster, S.W., London.

Dear Sir,—At a meeting of Irishmen, held here on 21st ult., the resolution, which I have much pleasure in enclosing herewith, was passed, and I was instructed to send the same to you to be read at the National Convention, which is to be held in Dublin in the first week in September next. It expresses the sympathy of the Irishmen in this town with the view of the reunion of the Irish Party, and they sincerely trust the purpose for which the Convention has been convened will be accomplished.

Yours respectfully,

M. C. Hayes, Hon. Secretary.

At a meeting of Irishmen held in Pretoria, South African Republic, on Tuesday, the 21st July, 1896, the following resolution was unanimously carried :—

"That this meeting of Irishmen assembled in Pretoria deeply deplore the dissension that still exists among the Irish Party, and express hope that the coming 'National Convention' will unite all sections of the Irish representatives, and erase for ever the evil elements of dissension and discord."

Alfred James Flynn, President.
James Paul Geraghty, Vice-President.

Committee :

T. Cunnama.	Henry Dunn.
T. Geary.	J. V. O'Brien.
W. H. Barry.	W. Nixon.
Edward Farrell.	Thomas Lee.

W. C. Hayes, Hon. Sec.

THIRD DAY—3RD SEPTEMBER, 1896.

The chair was taken at 11 o'clock by the chairman, the Most Rev. Dr. O'DONNELL, Bishop of Raphoe.

The CHAIRMAN—Mr. Davitt will read some correspondence.

Mr. DAVITT, M.P.—I am requested to announce that the Convention of the Irish National League of Great Britain will assemble at 10 o'clock to-morrow in this hall instead of Saturday, as first agreed upon. The following cable has been received by his lordship the chairman :—

"MOST REV. DR. O'DONNELL, Chairman Irish Convention. I hope that, in the interests of countless thousands of the young people of Ireland, the result of your deliberations may be unity, complete and entire, amongst your Parliamentary representatives. MICHAEL J. HENRY, Rector, Mission of Our Lady of the Rosary for the Protection of Immigrant Girls, New York."

The following is a telegram from Leeds :—

"CHAIRMAN, IRISH RACE CONVENTION, Leinster Hall. Hunslet Irishmen send greetings to brethren from all parts. Trust result of deliberations will restore party unity."

And the following has been received from Brisbane :—

Brisbane, July 21st, 1896.
THE CHAIRMAN, DUBLIN CONVENTION.

Sir,—At a public meeting of sympathisers with Home Rule for Ireland, held in this city on the 17th inst., the following resolution and address to the forthcoming Convention were unanimously adopted :—

Resolution.—Proposed by J. Leahy, Esq., M.L.A., seconded by J. T. Bell, Esq., M.L.A., and supported by A. Dawson, Esq., M.L.A., and J. Hoolan, Esq., M.L.A. :—

"That this meeting approves of the holding of the forthcoming Convention at Dublin for the purpose of uniting the ranks of the Irish Home Rule Party, and expresses the hope that, since disunion in its ranks must retard the realisation of self-government for Ireland, every effort will be made by all members of the Party to promote united action in support of the great principle."

Address.—Adoption moved by C. B. Fitzgerald, Esq., M.L.A., seconded by E. J. Sydes, Esq., M.A., LL.B. :—

We have the honour to acknowledge the receipt of an invitation to send a delegate from the Queensland supporters of Home Rule for Ireland to the Convention assembled for the purpose of restoring unity amongst its supporters in Ireland, and beg to thank you for the high privilege thus conferred on us. We tender our congratulations on the occasion of the meeting of such an important assemblage of the supporters of Home Rule from the different portions of the Empire, and sincerely hope that its deliberations will ensue in the achievement of the great purpose for which it has been called. It appears to us that under the most favourable conditions Home Rule will not be granted by the Imperial Parliament while disunion exists amongst Home Rulers themselves, and we are strongly of opinion that such disunion is disastrous to the cause. Such opinion being substantially sound, it follows that the necessity of union amongst its supporters in Parliament is a question of paramount importance. It follows also that every interest and difference of opinion, no matter by what party it may be entertained, should be subordinated to the primary necessity of restoring union amongst its supporters in Ireland, and in Parliamentary action as an undivided body. On behalf of the Queensland supporters of Home Rule we pledge again our assistance to the cause, and to the Irish Parliamentary Party to whom its conduct has been entrusted by the voice of the Irish people.

THOMAS J. BYRNE, Chairman,
Attorney-General for Queensland.

The CHAIRMAN—Gentlemen, a notice appeared on the agenda paper of a resolution dealing with the custody and trusteeship of funds. That resolution has been withdrawn. But I have been told by leading members of the party that they looked forward to the discussion of that resolution as an opportunity of explaining to the Convention their views and principles in regard to these funds. Hence, later on in the course of the debate, a leading member of the party will state to the Convention why it is the view of the party that the party should be the trustees, that the party itself should have the custody of the party funds. Dean Harris has a few words to say to you.

Very Rev. Dean HARRIS, St. Catherine's, Ottawa—My lord bishop and gentlemen, it is exceedingly courteous and kind of the distinguished and most rev. chairman to permit me to address you for a moment on behalf of a member of our delegation, who has been, not by insinuation but by interrogation, foully aspersed, I am sorry to say for the honour of the Press of Dublin, in one of the newspapers. This gentleman has brought his charming wife with him from Ottawa over here to attend this Convention, and the first reception he met with was that he was the companion and consort of Le Caron, the British spy. Gentlemen, this is not fair. This is not generous, this is not honourable, and, ladies, this is not Irish. Let me add that, as to the gentleman whom I will call upon this platform, there does not walk on the acreage of the Dominion of Canada a man more respected, a man who for the unparalleled series of thirty-three years sat on the Aldermanic Board of the Corporation of Ottawa. More than that, which will appeal more strongly to your manhood, a man who, when the cholera ravaged the streets and houses of Ottawa among the Irish emigrants, took off his coat and carried the coffins on his back at night and laid them in consecrated ground—a man who nursed the patients, stood by them, soothed them, bending over the sick, when, mad with the instinct of self-preservation, the friend deserted the friend and the brother turned away from the sister in the agony of self-preservation. This is the good man who, for his good deeds, his charitable deeds, has built up for himself a monument in the hearts of the people of Canada, that in Dublin, by one newspaper, was stigmatised as a spy of the English Government and a friend of Le Caron. A man who was honoured and decorated and knighted by his Holiness the Pope, not as a reward for military renown or prowess, not for distinguished literary achievement, but for the great and permanent qualification that he was an honest man. John Heney, stand up.

Chevalier HENEY (Ottawa) came forward, and was greeted with prolonged cheers.

Very Rev. Dean HARRIS—This is a man who has the proud boast that he has in his employment 150 Irishmen, and to minimise the importance of this venerable patriarch this newspaper, by interrogation —for it had not the manliness to say it straight, or Mr. Heney would proceed against it at the cost of a hundred thousand dollars—but by interrogation it suggested that this man was a friend of Le Caron, the British spy.*

---

* On Friday, August 28th, Mr. John Redmond's organ, the *Irish Daily Independent*, wound up a long article of attack on the American delegates to the Irish Race Convention by the expression of

"The hope that if the delegate described as 'Chevalier' Heney is the same who in company with the infamous Major Le Caron attended a certain meeting of Irish extremists as far back as 1866, that the fact will be duly notified. We have no desire to pry too closely into the antecedents of anyone who comes a long distance to attend the forthcoming funeral of Mr. John Dillon's reputation ; but in the interests of the public it may be well to know who exactly some of the delegates at large are when they are at home and abroad."

The paper in which this vile and utterly false insinuation was made against this veteran Irish patriot of stainless character was for some days kept from his knowledge, and the knowledge of his wife who accompanied him to Ireland. But at last a marked copy reached him through the post, and the insinuation is here repelled by Rev. Dean Harris and Chevalier Heney himself.

Next day, 4th September, the following reports of Very Rev. Dean Harris' and Chevalier Heney's speeches appeared in the *Independent ;* but, so far as can be found no apology whatever has been given :—

"Dean Harris, Toronto, complained of a statement made in one of the papers that Mr. John Heney, one of the most honest Irishmen in Canada, who had spent the greater part of seventy-four years of life in serving Ireland, had been the companion and consort of Le Caron the British spy. This was not fair, honourable, or Irish.

"Mr. Heney, the gentleman referred to, said that he always helped the Irish movement in Canada. If it were for nothing else but the Chairman's address he would go home satisfied. The paper that had made the statement complained of had not the manhood to come out next day and state they believed it was not true. Continuing, Mr. Heney mentioned that he was born, not in Cork, but in Killeshandra, Co. Cavan. His wife was born at Lisnaskea. Her father was a M'Manus, and her mother an O'Connor, and that was not bad breeding stuff."

The fact of the charge was cabled to Canada, and naturally caused the greatest excitement especially in Ottawa, where Chevalier Heney is universally respected. There was a constant interchange of cablegrams on the 3rd September between Ottawa and the American delegation.

The Hon. John Costigan received the following cablegram :—

"Costigan, Shelbourne, Dublin.—Papers report Heney charged associate Le Caron, Harris defending him. If true, intense indignation here.—ADAMS, WALSH."

The signatures affixed to this cablegram were those of Hon. Michael Adams, Senator, and another equally respected resident of Ottawa. A reply was forwarded calculated as far as possible to allay public indignation. But other cablegrams were received, amongst them two from the Rev. Father Whelan, of St. Patrick's, Ottawa, than whom no priest is better known or more loved—

"Ottawa, Ontario, 5.14 p.m.

"To Costigan, Delegate, Dublin.—Inquire attack Heney, suspicions.—Rev. FATHER WHELAN."

And later :—

"Ottawa, 9.35 p.m.

"To Heney, Dublin.—Unearth author.—WHELAN."

Chevalier Heney has since, we are informed, been unable to obtain audience, retractation, or apology.

Chevalier HENEY, Ottawa—Gentlemen, I am only just going to say one word. I am a workingman, and not a speaker. I came here with the one word—to try if possible to throw oil over the disturbed waters. That is my mission here to-day. I did take an active part in the affairs in Canada, and was an alderman of the city, and the city grew up with me. I believe I am the oldest delegate who came across the sea. I am seventy-six years of age, and still an active man. My lord, I am pleased with my visit, if it were only to have heard your lordship's splendid opening address. You, gentlemen, whom I see before me on these chairs, are the men who rule Ireland. It is for you to send your representatives into Parliament. They will do your honest work. It is you who can make your members tremble. When you go back to your districts, club together, and never forget this meeting. Let your members be honest and true to you, and we will be true to you. I left these shores fifty-three years ago a poor, naked lad, without a dollar in my pocket, and since then I put thousands and thousands of dollars through my hands, and I never closed my hand to the emigrant, and never will. I came not from Cork, but from county Cavan, half-a-mile from Killeshandra, where I was born seventy-six years ago. As an humble man amongst you here, I hope that good will come from our mission amongst you, and the message I have received to convey to you is: "For God's sake, do something to reconcile our people, and we will be delighted." Since I have landed I have done all in my power to do this. I am accompanied by my wife, and I may tell you that her father was a M'Manus and her mother an O'Connor, and that was not bad breeding. I do not wish to keep up this any longer. I have been, I think, intruding on this meeting, and I will resume my seat.

Very Rev. Canon M'CARTAN, Donaghmore—My lord and rev. fathers and ladies and gentlemen, my first impulse in addressing you is to express my own and, I am sure, your great pleasure at seeing a dignitary of the Church occupying the position in which Dr. O'Donnell now is. I think it is a happy omen that we are assembled here under the blessing of Leo XIII., and had our proceedings conducted orderly, wisely, and with dignity by a venerable Bishop of the Irish Church. I think, moreover, that he is exactly in the right place, because, ladies and gentlemen, our poor country has been very much lately distracted. Differences have arisen, giving rise to uncharitableness. Priests and people have been divided, and it is now high time that the episcopal body should take charge of a rather disorganised flock But it has come to this ; and the time is now when I believe action such as this must be taken in the interest of good order and in the interest of religion. Having said so much, I wish to say a word with regard to the honourable and right hon. gentlemen that I see around me from foreign parts. I hope and trust in God that they will not consider these aspersions which have been cast upon them by a miserable Press—that they will not take them as an expression of the opinion of ninety-nine per cent. of the people of Ireland. It is a sad commentary on the exigencies of faction and parties that men can so far forget themselves as to speak of men who to-day appear in Ireland as nobodies—I did not read their paper to-day—and to describe them as spies and informers. There are two gentlemen connected with that paper, and I think it is due from them, if they have any self-respect, if they have any gratitude, if they ever expect to look an honest man in the face, it is their duty to repudiate these charges. There are some of those men who went abroad to collect money, and only for such gentlemen as we have here from foreign parts, they would have to pawn their watches in order to get back to Ireland. I speak, however, now as a Catholic priest, and I say it is sad to think of it. I remember in '79 and '80 the late lamented Archbishop, Dr. M'Gettigan, came to the Conference, his pockets lined with money sent from America, to do what he liked with for the people of Ireland who were poor. He was enabled to give cheques for £50 and £100 to distribute amongst the poor people.

Here to-day we have men from all quarters—from America, Canada, and other places—all branded as "nobodies" or traitors. Gentlemen from foreign parts, I beg to assure you that it is an honour conferred upon you to-day, because the man is not worth his salt to-day in Ireland who does not receive attention from the same quarters that you have received it. Well, now, gentlemen, having said so much—and being the first priest that spoke after Dean Harris, I could not say less—I now turn to the third resolution. I will not read it. The pith of it is that as England has wrongfully, by coercion and against the people's will, governed Ireland, it is the bounden duty of the Irish Party to continue and maintain their independence of English political parties, and thus preserve its freedom to give an independent opposition or independent support to any party as may seem best to the interests of the National cause. Now, gentlemen, the success of this Convention will depend upon the practical results ; and I say the first resolution—I was sorry I was absent from the statement the chairman made upon some little points in connection with the resolution, but it is left to the Irish Party, in their solicitude for the welfare of the National cause, to take such measures as are possible to our cause in the promotion of unity. I pass that by, and pass to the subject of unity. It is a waste of time discussing it. It has been thrashed out. Without unity there is disorganisation. In the Church to which I belong we have infallibility. It is the power that keeps us right in the ecclesiastical and spiritual order. If you go outside of that, and treat of human affairs, there is no way devised by the ingenuity of man by which order or unity will be preserved except by majority rule. by majorities, Poor Law Guardians, Town Councillors, Parliament itself—even the bishops, when they meet, decide on questions by majority. If you don't admit the principle of abiding by the decision of the majority, you have nothing but political heresy.

Now, gentlemen, I am delighted that we have got this resolution, and I am particularly delighted that I have got it myself. I believe, by establishing the principle of independent opposition and no English alliance, we have made a platform broad enough for every honest Nationalist to take his stand upon. The policy of the future, as of the past, the successful policy now, as in days gone by, is the policy of no English alliance and independent opposition. That is the policy, gentlemen, that secured any rights that Ireland ever gained. Lately, perhaps, we may have trusted too much in English alliances. It is upon our own strength and upon our own selves we must rely. Grattan was not with the Whigs in 1782 when he got an Irish Nationalist Parliament. John Keogh and Wolfe Tone were not with the Tories when we got the Franchise Act. There was no alliance in 1829 when Daniel O'Connell wrung from an unwilling Government, an unwilling House of Lords, and an unwilling King, Catholic Emancipation. There was no English alliance in 1869, when the Church was disestablished, or when the Land Bill of 1870 was passed; there was no alliance when Parnell, leading a united people, placed the Land Act of 1881 on the Statute Book; and, above all, there was no alliance in 1885, when Gladstone was converted to Home Rule. England, ladies and gentlemen, will only yield to pressure, and that pressure must be applied at a long range; it is dangerous to get into close quarters with it, for if they stroke down your back "your integrity will be sapped." Our men must keep away from them; they must adopt Parnell's rule. A great English statesman having been asked in what he considered Parnell's strength principally lay, said it was in aloofness—it was in keeping away from them all. When he came down to the House they didn't know how, or when, or where he might strike them, and they were always watching what he was going to do. The Irish people want no union with any English party, but they want the union of the entire Irish nation against every English party. We want a clear, definite policy, as declared here to-day, and that policy shall be independent opposition and no English alliance. Will Mr. Healy refuse to join a party pledged to independent opposition and no English alliance? Will Mr. Redmond refuse to join a party pledged to independent opposition and no English alliance? What excuse have they now when the mandate of this Convention to the Irish Party is that they are to have independent opposition and no English alliance except on well defined lines which I will state afterwards? The time will come again when some English party will take up the question of Home Rule. We will force them to do it, and when that time comes we will give them every support. But we won't give them support of such a nature as to give over ourselves soul and body to them. We are not going to aid them in passing English measures to which we might conscientiously object. They must consult us about the measures they are going to bring in as well as we must consult them. We must not, in order to please the Non-conformist conscience or those Welsh reformers, bind ouselves now and say, "If you give us a vote for Home Rule, in which you believe, we therefore, will vote for you for measures in which we do not believe." There must be an honourable alliance. It must not be a thick-and-thin alliance, but it must be an alliance of self-respecting men for a defined purpose, and that we are prepared to make. The Irish members want to be the friends of England, but will never be their slaves. We can never get anything by truckling to England. We got a Home Rule Bill passed through the House of Commons because we compelled it, and we will only succeed by putting them in a tight place and keeping them in it. Home Rule was taken up by the Liberal Party. Why? Because Ireland was ungovernable. It was a policy of defiance, and not a policy of alliance, that obliged them to take up the Home Rule question, and obliged Gladstone to take it up, and drag the majority of the Liberals after him. There is need of a little caution, and there is need of great circumspection on the part of our members, because I can tell you this, that the English Liberals—the vast majority of the English Liberals—would drop Home Rule to-morrow if they would dare. They would rather drag out before you the abolition of the House of Lords, which is, perhaps, a question of half a century hence. They would rather dangle that before you, and at the same time not honestly agitate for it themselves. You got such measures as Catholic Emancipation, although the House of Lords existed. If the English people want the House of Lords abolished, and if they consider that is the only means by which you may win Home Rule, then let them make England, Scotland and Wales too hot for the House of Lords. But whether they do that or not we will get Home Rule, because we will force it from one or the other party. I say, then, that as a rule those English Liberals are not our friends (Hear, hear, and cries of " No, no,"). It may be that there is a brother of Harcourt here. I am going to ask you was Harcourt an enthusiastic Home Ruler? Is Henry Fowler a enthusiastic Home Ruler? (Cries of "Yes" and "No.")

The CHAIRMAN—I would suggest that interrogation and answer do not suit the deliberations of this assembly.

Canon M'CARTAN—Is Asquith a Home Ruler?

The CHAIRMAN—I must persist in the ruling that interrogation and answer do not suit our deliberations.

Canon M'CARTAN—That gentleman when he was Home Secretary left our poor prisoners in jail against the wishes of Ireland until a Tory Government had to release them, and then they were ready for the grave or the lunatic asylum. I give Mr. Morley credit for being an honest Home Ruler, but Mr. Morley, unfortunately for us, has been looking rather to the Nonconformist conscience of England than to the wants of Catholic Ireland. Gentlemen, I need go over no more names. I see it would only give rise to discussion. We must have a great many Englishmen in this assembly. I do not want to offend the admirers of those Englishmen. I wish in conclusion to say to you all here, and to the members of Parliament, that it is with a view to strengthen their hands, to assist them to keep a stiff upper lip and a stout under jaw, to meet those fellows that we wish to give them a mandate from this Convention, and that mandate would be that it is our wish except for a well defined purpose and upon honourable terms that they are to make no alliance with any English Party.

Mr. HUGH MURPHY, Home Government Branch, Glasgow—My lord and fellow-delegates, before supporting the resolution, you may allow me briefly to refer to a paragraph which appeared in the London Letter of yesterday's *Independent*. Gentlemen, I wish to point out what the *Independent* is foisting upon its readers at the present time. Yesterday it stated that the Home Government Branch, Glasgow, sent fourteen delegates to this Convention, and that there were only eight of its members left in Glasgow. I may state that we have sent fourteen delegates, and that in addition to that we have supplied other branches with ten delegates, and that we have fifteen members sitting in the gallery as visitors, making in all thirty-nine. As a matter of fact that thirty-nine would not be missed from the meeting on Sunday. We would still have as many left as there are Parnellites in Great Britain. I may further remind the *Independent* that one of our delegates is a Parnellite, but I would be more correct perhaps by saying he was a Parnellite before he came to this Convention, and in the whole of Glasgow they could not find a correspondent to supply them with information, and they had to have recourse to the Home Government Branch to get its secretary to be their Glasgow correspondent. Now, in supporting this resolution, I think we should make it abundantly clear before leaving this Convention what our intentions are for the future. We agree that there should be unity, and we also agree that there should be discipline. Some of our friends remarked before this Convention that Mr. John Dillon was simply the chairman of the majority of the Irish Parliamentary Party. I think, however, after the speech which Mr. Dillon delivered yesterday, when the Convention is over Mr. John Dillon will be leader of the Irish race at home and abroad. For six or seven years we have been supporting the majority of the Irish Parliamentary Party. We do not desire this to continue. From this time forward we say to Mr. John Dillon "We are not going to support the majority any longer; we are going to support the entire Parliamentary Party;" and we tell Mr. John Dillon that he must insist on that party on the minority abiding by the decision of the majority. In connection with the alliance spoken of by Canon M'Cartan—the alliance with the English Liberals—we are told that Mr. Redmond represented independent opposition. I have simply to point out that the alliance with British Liberals was formed not when Mr. Dillon was leader of the Irish Parliamentary Party but when Mr. Parnell was. I will simply say that from this time forward it will be our bounden duty to unite as one man in Great Britain, in America, and Australia, and we will send money and support to the Irish Parliamentary Party, and in return we ask Mr. Dillon to see that the members agree among themselves, or else clear out of the Party.

Mr. THOMAS LOUGHLIN, Bradford—Most rev. president, I heard some remarks of the Very Rev. Canon M'Cartan with the deepest pain. If I believed that we could win Home Rule for Ireland without converting some English party to the desirability of Home Rule, I, with some fellow-workers in Great Britain, would not look for their assistance for one moment. But the late Charles Stewart Parnell, after leading his party through splendid fights against both Whig and Tory, had to enter into an alliance with the Democratic Party in Great Britain, and that Democratic Party shed their aristocrats and became a democratic workingman's party. They lost the Devonshires and the other great titled men, and they brought in a splendid Home Rule Bill in the words of Mr. Parnell, spoken, too, on many of the platforms in Great Britain. They fought in the House of Commons, and when the fight was over there they went to the country, and for a time after Home Rule was defeated we, the Irish in England, worked in the fight, canvassing Englishmen and Scotchmen and Welshmen, and made friends, who are still true friends to us and Home Rule to-day. At that time the Tory policy was perpetual coercion for Ireland, and we supported the Home Rule party against the policy of coercion of the government that followed. When the Liberals returned to power, with a small majority indeed, they had some parties in their country to conciliate, and had to show to the workingmen that they intended to do some good for them, and in the midst of that they passed a Home Rule Bill through the House of Commons, and it was against the House of Lords that rejected it that we fought at the last general election in Great Britain. The result of that election was, that, owing to our divisions, a Tory majority was returned. Now, I don't say that every man in the present Liberal Party is sound, but I am profoundly and firmly convinced that the vast majority of the Liberal Party are sound to the core, and that Home Rule is still a plank in the Liberal programme, and so long as it so remains you are bound to support the Liberal Party.

The CHAIRMAN—Canon M'Cartan wishes to say a word in explanation of his views on the Home Rule alliance.

Canon M'CARTAN—I am sorry the last speaker has entirely misunderstood me. My contention was that until you convert some of the great English parties to take up the Home Rule question that you will fight them to death until you force that upon them. Once they take it up, then, you are at liberty to form an honourable alliance, not as I said before, an alliance of slaves, but an honourable alliance.

Mr. DAVITT—There never has been any alliance of slaves.

Canon M'CARTAN—Mr. Davitt says there never was an alliance of slaves, but if Mr. Sexton and other members of the House of Commons had yielded occasionally to the threats of John Morley, that he would resign if they did not do so and so, that would have been an alliance of slaves. All I want is that we shall get a *quid pro quo* that will be honourable on all sides, and as long as they are loyal to us we will be loyal to them, and if we want them to be loyal we must make them so.*

Rev. P. J. O'DONNELL, St. Mary's, Montreal—It is not for me to say much at this moment. I came with my fellow-delegates from Canada with a message, and, the message being identical, it was delivered in the beginning of this august assembly. It was a message of good-will, a message of peace, and a request that unity should exist for the purpose of carrying out and obtaining the grand result—the success of the sacred cause for which we have all struggled so long. The desire of the Irishmen of Montreal is this—that the cause should be pursued and the goal reached as soon as possible. But, as in other parts of the world, a spirit of despondency has for the last couple of years entered into their hearts. I am delighted to be here on this memorable occasion. A great many of my fellow-countrymen in honour of the cause I represented saw me on board my train, and one enthusiastic and patriotic gentleman wished moreover that the carriage should carry the Irish flag. This sentiment did not prevail. But this was decided—" No," they said, "wait until he returns." Now, gentlemen, having sat at the deliberations of this assembly, having witnessed the spirit which has animated the thousands present, I desire to say that I can bring back a message of

---

* Canon M'Cartan, in a letter to the Press, makes a correction which has been embodied in above. He says further :—" My whole argument was that on the Home Rule Bill, as on the English Education Bill, the Liberals were trying to coerce or bully our Irish members, who went straight and maintained their independence ; and I wanted to strengthen their hands by showing those English leaders, and the Price Hugheses and the English and Welsh Nonconformists, that our Convention was at their back in their present line of policy of independence, and of setting at defiance the threats of any English party."

hope, and can say that you are determined to stand together shoulder to shoulder at any sacrifice. I can say to the people of Montreal, to the Irishmen of the Dominion of Canada, that they may not now be ashamed to unfurl the green banner of Erin. We have heard a noble utterance from the great and distinguished prelate who presides so ably, and in the spirit of that address I think we may hope, by this Convention, to lay down the foundation deep and broad and solid enough to carry an edifice that will be a monument not only to ourselves, but for generations yet to come, that from this platform we may secure the desire of the Irish race throughout the world—Home Rule for Ireland. I think this will be the result of the deliberations of this assembly, and when we go home to the different parts of the world from whence we came I think we can encourage our people. I think I can ask them to unfurl the green flag, and not only to do that, but to put their hands deep into their pockets, and, each according to his means, give something that will not only stimulate the cause but help it along until victory is won. I have not the honour of having been born in Ireland, but my sentiments are the same. My love for Ireland is the same. Little over forty years ago my parents left their home in the land that has given to this assemblage the distinguished prelate whose name I bear. In conclusion, I thank you for your reception, and I feel assured and convinced that the results of the Convention will be all that you desire, and what all the people we represent desire to obtain.

The CHAIRMAN—I have been asked from many quarters to put on a time limit, but as an amendment is to be proposed to this resolution by Mr. Fitzgerald, of London, and as it deals with a matter of great public moment, I think it is well you should hear at some length Irish speakers who live in Ireland in reference to the resolution. I call on Mr. Joseph Devlin, Belfast.

Mr. JOSEPH DEVLIN, Belfast—My lord bishop, rev. fathers, and fellow-countrymen, my only claim to address this magnificent assembly of the Irish race at home and abroad is the fact that I am, perhaps, the humblest of the delegation that has come from a city in this country which, during the past five years, has thrown no chip upon the fires of faction. We learned from Mr. Parnell (applause), when the Party existed in all its power and strength, the power and potency of a disciplined Irish Party and a united Irish people, and when the unfortunate divisions arising out of the Parnellite split took place, we learned from Mr. Healy the doctrine of majority rule. But we are faithful to-day, as this Convention proves to be, to the doctrines laid down by Parnell and Healy before the unfortunate divisions that exist at present commenced. Our position in the capital of Ulster is this. There is an Irish Parliamentary Party. That Irish Parliamentary Party in a constitutional fashion meets in conclave; it arrives at a deliberate decision. Whether that decision is right or wrong, it is the duty of every man to obey it. And we not only declare our belief in the principle of majority rule, but once a legitimate majority expresses its view, our position is this—that we will back up the majority by substantial public support. I say to this Convention to-day that the support of the majority should not be a laggard support; it is not the way to stamp out faction by standing aside and leaving your leaders to fight an unequal battle. If you believe in the spirit and the letter of the pledge, you must stamp out faction, and you can do it best by supporting the majority. The best way in which you can support the majority—the best way in which you can stamp out the minority of mutineers—is by being generous and just in your help and in your spontaneous assistance to that party. We have heard that the divisions in the Irish ranks are merely internal divisions upon questions of party government; but if you look back to the time when these divisions arose in the ranks, they did arise out of the question of party government. But a few days ago, in consequence of the stretch of this question, you had certain men—pledged to sit, act, and vote with the Party—going into a different lobby in the House of Commons before the enemies of our race. You had the leader, duly elected—the leader of the people—publicly insulted in the House of Commons. You had the cause of Ireland degraded and lowered in the minds of her enemies, and had torture brought to the heart of every friend of Ireland. If so, the position is this:—If the people of Ireland declare to-day, as they have, and as they did in the past, that majority rule must prevail, the constitutional government of our movement must succeed. The way to do it is not by passing resolutions, but by spreading the branches of the organisation—the only legitimate organisation of the country—and by every man of means giving his help when he can to aid the Party in their difficult work. When the cry went out, "Starve out the Irish Party," Belfast commenced by trebling its subscriptions. That is the spirit which should actuate every man in this Convention. Our Convention has been a glorious success. It has been presided over, I am proud to say, by an illustrious Ulsterman. It it a great credit to our Church and the position we have taken up, and it is a great glory to the National cause, that we have a man like him at our head. We will go forward again with gladdened hearts, longing for the time when we can make another strong appeal together, and hopeful for the day when, marching as one man, we place ourselves behind our leaders in their march to victory.

The Hon. JOHN COSTIGAN, Ottawa—My lord, ladies and gentlemen, I feel it a great honour indeed, that is conferred upon me, and upon the Irishmen of the city of Ottawa especially, and that was endorsed by the Irishmen of Canada, that I was selected to come with a message of peace, a message of sympathy, a message of hope and confidence in the future in the attainment of the object which is dear to every Irishman at home and abroad. I feel that honour and realise it more since I came here. I feel proud, not as an Irishman, because unfortunately I cannot claim that I am an Irishman, but you would never make me say that I am not an Irishman. I am the descendant of Irish parents. They were always identified with the cause with which my deepest sympathies are enlisted now, and though I have not the honour of being an Irishman born in Ireland, I belong to a class all over the world that are the strongest friends of Ireland in the movement that you advocate to-day. Yes, I feel proud of being here to-day, proud of having the honour of addressing this vast audience through you, my lord, who have opened the business of this Convention in an address that has challenged the admiration of every intelligent man. We who come from abroad had some difficulties when we reached here. We do unfortunately see dissension and disunion in the Irish ranks and among the Irish people. We had the privilege of educating ourselves through the Press of the country, through the leading Press of this great city; but the education was unsafe and unreliable. And though it is supposed and charged against us who came from abroad that though delegate after delegate has on this platform and in the interviews which have taken place with representatives of the Press of the country, declare that the delegates came free and independent and unpledged to any particular party, and came as bearers of a message of confidence—they still publish all sorts of slanders against the delegates; and, gentlemen, if to be an Irishman instead of the descendant of an Irishman—if the qualification to make me an Irishman was the adoption of a policy like that, then I would say, "Thank God, I am the descendant of an Irishman." Sir, as a matter of courtesy, as a matter of cold policy, the reception given to the delegates from abroad was coarse and brutal to men who came across the ocean, not as tourists, but who left their business and came here as intelligent men to stand with you, and to express sympathy, and to give you the assurance that in a grand patriotic movement you may count upon the strong sympathy of your fellow-countrymen and their descendants. I have another complaint to make against the gentlemen who inspire, or are supposed to inspire, these articles.

We are told the delegation from abroad will be here, and will be misled; we will be fooled by the speeches of Mr. Dillon, by Mr. O'Connor, or Mr. Blake, and other prominent gentlemen I am proud to see on this platform to-day. Well, sir, I followed the history of this Convention as closely as I have been able to follow it, and I find that those gentlemen who make that statement seem to have done all in their power to make this grand Convention a failure, though I am glad to see, and every Irishman is glad to see, they have utterly failed in their efforts. Why are not these gentlemen, professing to be Irishmen, why are they not here to-day? Why are they not here to-day to save us from being misled by seeing that the question was fairly put and fairly discussed? We are told, and you know that, through the Press, we are told that this Convention represents nobody, that it does not represent the Irish people, that it does not represent the friends of Home Rule in Canada or in the United States. Well, to my mind, my lord and gentlemen, I believe honestly and sincerely that it would be difficult to gather in the city of Dublin a more representative and intelligent representation of the Irish cause than I see before me here to-day.

I know that time is passing, and I know how valuable that time is. I will not trespass much longer upon the patience of the Convention. I have delivered my message, and I expect to take back a message. You need not instruct me; I will draw my own conclusions. I will go back to my people in Canada, and I will tell them how proud I was to stand upon this platform. If they ask me if the breach is healed and union complete I will say I regret that I cannot go that far; but I will say this, that standing upon this platform and looking at that vast audience of representative men from England, Ireland, and Scotland, the United States, and our own delegates from Canada and from the distant colonies already named, I had no doubt that practically speaking union is established in Ireland to-day. And if they ask me for my reasons for coming to that conclusion I have many to give. But the only answer necessary in Canada, and the one that will tell in the United States and the other colonies, will be that when I found as the result of the call for this Convention the success which attended it, notwithstanding every effort, fair and unfair, that was made to make it a failure, the response to that call gave evidence to my mind that the call emanated from the proper quarter When speaking to my fellow-citizens in Canada I shall say that the movement has the approbation of my old friend, though my political opponent, the Hon. Edward Blake. No further guarantee would be required in Canada, and if it were I would say that I saw around the platform in front of this movement members of the Irish Parliamentary Party whose names on the Continent of America will inspire more confidence than the name of any man who is throwing his influence against this Convention. If I mention on any platform on the other side of the Atlantic the name of that Home Ruler, Michael Davitt, William O'Brien, John Dillon, and that of my old friend whom I am proud to say I met in Canada, Mr. Justin M'Carthy, these names will be the best endorsement of the action of this Convention here to-day, and the best justification for the calling of such a Convention.

The Convention has been a tremendous success. We who have come from abroad will return, having delivered an humble message to the Irish people; we will go back and deliver a message in return to our own people. We will say it may be impossible to bring within the folds of the great patriotic party all that we would desire to see within it. I am not going to talk about their motives—it is sufficient for me to know that as they are not with this movement they must be against it. They may not come in. I am glad the motion to negotiate with those gentlemen who would not recognise this Convention was not carried. The mover and seconder of that motion seemed to overlook the fact that those gentlemen, having protested from the beginning against the authority of the Convention, there was no guarantee whatever that they would submit to any action that would be taken by this Convention. I will go back and tell our friends in Canada that the Irish Parliamentary Party are surrounded by representative Irishmen who had the endorsation of the people of Ireland, and of the Irish people of the United States and other countries. I would like to repeat the words of that brilliant young Irishman who spoke before me, and in doing so I would be doing myself credit, and I believe I would be expressing the free sentiments of my colleagues. It has been said that if the people of Ireland will not agree to sink their differences and unite that they ought not expect any assistance to be given them by their friends abroad. That is true generally speaking, but if it were to be carried out too rigidly and too strictly it would mean that a few individuals would be able to carry on a policy of wreck. We will give the matter a more generous interpretation in Canada. When we see that the Irish people are standing by their leaders and by the Irish Parliamentary Party, and standing by the policy laid down years ago—that the majority must rule, we in Canada, I think I can say that much, will see that you are deserving of support, and it would be impossible for us to come to any other decision. I hear reference made to political parties. We have political parties in our own country. A descendant of Irishmen as I am in Canada, I may be allowed to say that when Home Rule came up I did not hesitate to join the Home Rule ranks. You may easily understand that that was not at all a popular or fashionable step to take. I am a staunch Conservative in Canada, and on the question of Home Rule, when I came to make up my mind, I said I did not see why the people of Ireland should not enjoy those same blessings of self-government as we enjoyed in Canada. I have no party when I speak of Home Rule. Give us Home Rule and freedom. Let Ireland rule itself, and I care not from whom it comes, whether you call them Tories or Whigs, or anything else. My lord, I thank you most sincerely for the permission to trespass so long upon the patience of the Convention. I look here to-day at this audience and see intelligent faces that I never expect to see again, and I am afraid that I am right in this opinion, that it will be many a year and many a day until such a representative gathering of the world over shall appear in Ireland again. Let determination and union, and further and greater effort in the cause of the attainment of Ireland's rights, go on, and if I can reciprocate, unworthily it may be, the words of a reverend clergyman yesterday in reference to the foreign delegates when he said—"God bless them," and say as an humble sinner, who may appeal to God also, " God bless the people of Ireland and those who fight her battles."

The CHAIRMAN—Mr. Fitzgerald, of Bermondsey Branch, has a resolution to move. I ask him to come to the platform.

Mr. FITZGERALD, Bermondsey—I was asked when I came here not to be long, and I won't be long, because I am not much of a speaker. I am about to propose an amendment, and it is for this meeting to say whether it will adopt it or not as a representative meeting, which I believe it to be, anything to the contrary notwithstanding, of the Irish race. I won't say a single word about unity, because I conceive that question was settled yesterday. I don't mind what newspapers say, because newspapers write for their readers, and we should not bother about them except in so far as they would create public opinion. Consequently our policy should be not to make speeches and round periods, but if we are in earnest and agree that Mr. John Dillon should lead the Irish Party—if they are going to stand by John Dillon and the Irish Party as represented by him, they will expect that party to give something in return for the support they gave to them. Therefore, if you will turn to your agenda paper, resolution 3, I want to add after the words "Irish soil" these words :—

"We declare that this Convention is of opinion that the time has arrived when the Irish Party should cease to treat with any English party for the granting of Home Rule, and should make English government of Ireland impossible in the English Parliament until the English nation is prepared to recognise Ireland's claim to be a nation by creating a Parliament in Dublin for the government of Ireland."

My lord, you truly said that it was a matter of some public moment. It is of great public moment for Ireland, because we have to consider when will England grant Ireland Home Rule? No man can say when, and I say—Why should Ireland wait? Is Ireland to wait for four years more? The Irish race has waited four years for England to grant Ireland Home Rule, and the demand for Home Rule has come to be a kind of glorified

County Council in the ideas of a great number of those Englishmen who voted for it at the last election; and I want to know why did not the Liberal Party go to the country on the question of Home Rule after its rejection, instead of on the Local Veto question? We are looking to you, Mr. Dillon, for statesmanship, guidance, and leadership, and the rev. gentleman who, I think, seconded the resolution covered most of the ground when he said that it is no use dealing with a section of the English nation. The Liberal Party is not the English nation, and the English people have condoned the action of the House of Lords, and they will condone it again and again and again. I tell you that, as a man who has worked in London for many of the Liberal Party—and men in this room know that I have the confidence of the Liberal Party in my constituency—but at the same time I say that the policy for Irishmen to take up is not to belong to any Liberal organisation. We want the party in the House of Commons to take up a policy of action, and I say that the country will justify you, sir, and I want to know the name of the Irish representative who will dare to depart from the policy of action worked by you in the House of Commons in that way. That is the way you will get unity. Englishmen stood as an example in that respect. Their policy is—England first, and politics after. I am prepared to do my share, to sink my prejudices, if you call them prejudices, for you, and to stand by Dillon and the party, and then they must do something in the House of Commons instead of discussing details of this and that English Bill. I have been in the House of Commons many times, and have heard impassioned speeches from Sexton, but does that eloquence take any effect in the English House of Commons? Not the slightest bit, but if you will do something, and if you will do something ugly and something uncomfortable, the Englishman will listen to you. Now for the representation. I say that these men know how to do that work, and they ought to do it.

A Voice—What work?

Mr. FITZGERALD—The men we have in the House of Commons ought to do something for Ireland.

At this point a delegate on the platform rose to order, and someone at the back of the hall also interrupted.

The CHAIRMAN—A point of order has been raised. I have been asked to rule that Mr. Fitzgerald's remarks are not pertinent. Mr. Fitzgerald intends to say very little more, and I think it better for me not to enter into the question as to whether his remarks are exactly to the resolution or in support of his addition to the resolution or not.

Mr. FITZGERALD—I am endeavouring to show the meeting why I want this addition made, and I will try and keep to the point, and I don't think I have deviated from it, gentlemen. I want this meeting and I want all Ireland to support Mr. John Dillon in the decision this Convention came to, and I want to convey to your minds, and through your minds to the men you represent as delegates, that the policy that will command success and approval, that the policy that will fetch the dollars across the Atlantic, that the policy that will make the men in Ireland work, that the policy that will command the respect of every man in Ireland who wants to see Ireland free, is not a policy of walking through the corridors of the House of Commons, but a policy of action there, that until the English nation recognises Ireland's claim to be a nation by giving her a Parliament in Dublin, and you will make it impossible for her to govern Ireland from Westminster. If you don't agree with that, don't accept my addition to the resolution.

A Voice—In what way?

Mr. FITZGERALD—The old way that made a united Irish Party, and the only way; if the work is too hard for our present representatives, Ireland has plenty of men who will do it.

The CHAIRMAN—The addition or amendment, however it is to be called, has been proposed to the resolution; is there anyone to second it? (Cries of "No, no.") The addition then falls to the ground. Father Clancy will now address you.

Rev. M. J. CLANCY, Tipperary—Although nobody has been found to second the addition to the third resolution, still it may not be out of place, in consequence of the manner in which the remarks of the speaker were received, to say a few words upon the question he has raised.

Rev. PATRICK LYNCH, M.R. (Manchester)—My lord, is this in order? It is not before the Convention.

The CHAIRMAN—I consider Father Clancy is in order, owing to the fact that some of the remarks made by Mr. Fitzgerald might have been made in discussing the resolution itself.

Rev. M. J. CLANCY—Mr. Fitzgerald, animated no doubt by the very best motives, has proposed a policy and a method of carrying on Parliamentary agitation which would make Parliamentary agitation in the present state of the Irish Party merely a scorn and a byeword. That might have been very well in the old days, when you had seven or eight men standing up in the House of Commons, every man's hand against them and their hands against every man; but these times have changed, and with the increase of numbers, and the increase of funds, has come increased responsibility, and what might have been very much in place in the old days would be very much out of place at the present time. With regard to this question I have decided opinions. I must say that one of the things that most grate upon me is that we should have to look to any English Party for the attainment of our freedom. But we must take things as they are, and having entered on the path of Parliamentary agitation, we must work it out according to the rules of the game. It is all very well to discuss what ought to be done by Dillon, Davitt, or Blake. We, here at home, do not know the difficulties under which they labour If consideration for them does not decide the course we ought to adopt—a little ordinary modesty ought to do so. We have elected these men because they are tried men, clever men, because they have spent their lives battling for Home Rule according to the rules of Parliamentary action. Are we in our petty wisdom at home here to be laying down strict rules for them as to how they are to conduct themselves when troubles and emergencies arise? Their main object must be Home Rule without any alliance except what would most conduce towards Home Rule. But once that indispensable principle is laid down you must leave them a great latitude of action. We are all very wise after the event, very clever politicians indeed when the march of events shows us that things would have been better if something else were done. I have no sympathy with men whose only policy is a policy of criticism, and who when things go wrong which they made no effort to set right, adopt the policy of "I told you so." As to supporting Liberal measures or standing by them in return for the action of the Liberals in passing a Home Rule Bill—whether a policy of give and take between the Irish and Liberal Party— all these things must be left to the decision of the trained politicians who are chosen, because they are trained and skilled parliamentarians It occurs to me that a very useful parallel might be drawn from the history of a portion of Napoleon's campaign. The Austrians were always brave soldiers, they had magnificent generals, but still they were always beaten; and why? Because there was a council at home which was always hampering the action of the men upon the field. It is the same with us. We have our men upon the field, too. We have chosen them freely and in open Convention, and no man will dare to tell me before this assembly that Conventions were rigged in '95. I would like to see the man who would come down to Tipperary to rig a convention. We have chosen them in open Convention because they were brave men, because they were clever men, and because they were self-sacrificing men. We are sending them into the heart of the enemy's country, and instead of twarting and criticising them we should leave them a free hand as long as they keep the principle before their minds that their only object is Home Rule for Ireland.

Now I may be permitted to make a few remarks upon that beautiful speech delivered by the Hon. John Costigan, from Canada. As soon as I heard that speech I remarked to those who were about me that the Convention was not without fruit. If there was no other fruit except the delivery of that speech our time was not lost here. He struck the keynote when he said that if you have not absolute unity you have practical unity. And further, when he said that in the maintaining of the Irish Party, in the working out of absolute unity if we can, there should be a generous and whole-hearted support from our friends at home and abroad. And some of the speakers will pardon me if I say that speaking about unity and speaking about majority rule in the same breath was somewhat illogical. If unity exists in the way in which they appear to speak about it no question of majority rule can arise at all. When does majority rule arise, or the necessity for it? When dissension exists, and when there is diversity of opinion, we require unity of action. There has been a good deal of balmy talk about unity and conciliation. Well I am for conciliation. I am for quiet measures as long as quiet measures or conciliation are of any use whatsoever. But there is a point, and I think it has been reached—there is a point beyond which conciliation, or forbearance, or toleration of the mutineers would be treason to the country. Let anybody passing through the streets read merely the placards of some of our Dublin papers, and I think they will convey that lesson just as well as I can. My last word would be—Here we are, laymen and ecclesiastics from every part of Ireland. Looking on this platform I see men present who bore, in the old times of the National League and against Balfour's Coercion Act, the burthen of the day and the heat when many men, who are brave critics now and bold Nationalists, were far more ready to attack the friends of Ireland than they were then to face her enemies. I can see them here—the men on whom we could depend—the men on whom we could depend to go to Woodford, and in the midst of the brave people of that district tear up to pieces and burn Balfour's proclamation. We have them here, and—

> " True men, like you men,
> Are plenty here to-day."

We claim to be the majority, and if we are not the majority why are not the men here who say we are not, and put us into the minority? Charges have been made, and I put it plainly and squarely to the foreign delegates whether it is not a fact that the reason why they were apathetic was, that they believed there was something behind the charges which were being levelled at the majority of the Irish Party. Well, there are the representatives of the majority. Where are their traducers? There are men amongst them who are not very reticent. I won't mention places, but if I liked I could mention places where they made charges against their colleagues, when the making of such charges was calculated to do almost fatal injury to the Irish cause. Why are they not here to substantiate these charges? Because they dare not. We have had grave discussion, we demand discussion, we challenge discussion, and if there is no response to our challenge, I ask the foreign delegates to disbelieve these charges, to believe that the men who form the majority of the Irish Party are not corrupted with English gold, that no bossism exists in the Irish Party, and really when you come to talk of bossism, it seems strange for people to imagine that John Dillon is able to boss Michael Davitt. We cannot, of course, expect absolute unity, but we pin our faith to majority rule. What does that lead us to? The resolution is there which calls upon us to support the Irish Party in carrying out discipline in its own ranks. How can that be done? Father O'Leary, Castlelyons, told you yesterday that it can be done if the funds come in to enable these men to insist upon discipline. You cannot expect absolute unity; it is impossible; and, as remarked by a previous speaker, this talk about absolute unity only enables a few mutineers to deplete the coffers of the Irish Party. That is their object. We must defeat that object. I have never asked anybody to do anything for Ireland that I am not prepared to do myself, and I pledge you, and I think I can pledge you, the people amongst whom I labour, and I think I can give a pledge on behalf of the people of Tipperary, where I now reside, and if the foreign delegates do their duty amongst their people we will do our duty amongst the Irish people at home, and, as far as I am concerned, my voice, my pen, and my pocket will always be at the service of the Irish Party and the Irish people.

The CHAIRMAN—I hear calls for William O'Brien.

Mr. WILLIAM O'BRIEN—My lord bishop, ladies, and gentlemen, I am wholly in the hands of the Convention, even in the matter of saying a few words, very much against my will, because so long as things were going on so triumphantly for Ireland as they have been going on yesterday and to-day I have no ambition in this hall but to hold my tongue, and sit and listen with joy and gratitude for the glorious work that is going on for Ireland. There is not a man here who has the least desire to exploit himself to the smallest degree except for the benefit of Ireland, and the triumphant success of this great Convention. Our good friend,

Father Flynn, of Waterford, may rest perfectly assured that if any section of our fellow-countrymen who differ from us, whether they be Parnellites, or whether they call themselves by any other name, if they will only imitate the spirit of Father Flynn, displayed here at this Convention yesterday, I can promise them they will find that, as far as some of us are concerned, we are willing now as we were willing always to go any length to meet them, to conciliate them. Anything to induce these men to conduct themselves, and work as loyal comrades as they did before. My lord bishop, one thing, at all events, is certain, whatever they do, or whatever any man does, the full effect of this Convention will not perhaps be felt all at once, but I say the decrees of this Convention if they are sustained by the Irish race in the spirit of the Hon. Mr. Costigan's glorious speeches, these decrees will, beyond all doubt, settle the course of events in Ireland for this generation, and will efface sooner or later any man, or any set of men, that dare to stand up against them. Gentlemen, if there has been possibly any weakness in the action of the Irish Party in the past in dealing with these troubles, as a gentleman, I think it was Dr. O'Meara, suggested yesterday—well it was perhaps through an excess of patience and of good nature, of conciliation towards brother Irishmen, and of a very natural shrinking and disgust for those scenes of discord as long as it was humanly possible to avoid them. I am bound to say, also, it was largely because members of the Irish Party, certain members at all events of that Irish Party, of whom I was not one, were discouraged at the apparent apathy of the country, and thought that the people of Ireland had not spoken out their will with sufficient determination to justify them in enforcing the discipline of the Party, even against men who were doing all that men could do to break the solidity of that Party.

Well, my friends, after this Convention no Irish member can ever make that complaint. The accusers of the Irish Party—their accusers in the English House of Commons, amidst the jeers of the grinning enemies of Ireland—have failed to face the music at this Convention. They have allowed judgment to go against them by default. This Convention is, and everybody who has spoken has admitted that it is, perhaps, the very greatest, the most harmonious, and the most representative assemblage of the Irish race that ever came together. You, my lord bishop and gentlemen, have now given that Irish party your unstinted confidence. A gentleman spoke here a while ago, and re-echoed statements that possibly might have been better left unexpressed, as to our relations with English parties. I venture to say that there is not a man listening to me in this hall, aye, and among the supporters of the Parnellites throughout the country, there is not a man who in his heart and soul does not know that we care more for the little finger of one Irish peasant than for the whole bodies of the two British parties together. There are men in that Irish Party who for every hour they have ever spent under an Englishman's roof have spent as many months in her Majesty's prisons; and even that record is child's play compared with the record of a man sitting on this platform who has spent nine years of independent opposition in the penal hells of England. No. That English party, whether Liberal or Tory, who are friends of Ireland are our friends. We know how to be true friends as well as to be pretty thoroughgoing enemies, and the English party, Whig or Tory, who are Ireland's enemies will have our undying hostility, a hostility that will be only all the keener if—as I for one don't anticipate—the English Liberal Party should ever abjure their solemn pledge to make Home Rule, and keep Home Rule, their very first business the moment they get into power. I am not able to go very much further. The excitement and my enthusiasm over all that we have been going through during the last few days are almost too great to allow me to say anything more than this. As I have said before, the Irish Party may have had some doubt until now what is the will of the Irish nation. You have spoken out your will. You have armed them with sovereign authority to enforce that will, and to stand no further nonsense (Great cheering, the audience rising and waving their hats), and—it may not come about in a week nor in a month—but you have to-day laid the foundations once more for a real Irish Party under a real leader, a man for whom no Irish Nationalist will ever have reason to blush, a party that will be generous enough and broad-minded enough to welcome every honest Irish Nationalist into its ranks, but that will be strong enough to put down any man, or any section of men, who from this hour forth dare to throw their own petty personal interests across the march of our exiled countrymen and our great old Gaelic race at home.

At the conclusion of Mr. O'Brien's speech there were loud and prolonged cries of "Davitt."

The CHAIRMAN—I must explain that Mr. O'Brien had sent me a message that he would not speak, and while noticing your cries, I was going to tell you—but was prevented by having to call on Mr. O'Brien—that you would have a speech from another distinguished delegate. That delegate will address you now. He represents the National Federation of America. He is the secretary of an organisation from which thousands and thousands of pounds have flowed into the national coffers.

Mr. JOSEPH P. RYAN, New York—I am sorry that the exigencies of business prevented the presence here of the President of the Organisation, Dr. Addis Emmet, and other capable officers. I am sorry they are not here to represent the Irish National Federation of America, and to voice its sentiments. The duty is imposed on me to bear to you a brief message. We demand that unity shall be established in this country, and that obedience to majority rule must be enforced by every legitimate means. Some question has been raised in some of the local journals as to whether we had a right to speak at this Convention. Now, gentlemen, I am well aware that no one knows better than the men who inspired a question of that sort the fact of our entire right to be present. We are the same men, or the representatives of the same men, who have given unceasing service and generous aid to every appeal from Ireland, and whose generous hospitality has been shared by every ambassador that visited our shores, until the breath of discord had chilled the hearts and palsied the hands of our generous people. We are some of the men who have poured help into the coffers of the National League and the National Federation to enable a fight to be made against the common enemy. We are the same men who, at the last meeting held under the auspices of the ambassadors of a united party, raised at the meeting 27,000 dollars to aid Ireland. We are the same men, or the representatives of the same men, who in two years, under the auspices of what is known as the Hoffman House Committee of New York, sent to Ireland 200,000 dollars. We are the same men, or the representatives of the same men, who even since division came to the National forces of Ireland have raised, in spite of the disaffection and of the despair that hung over our people, a sum of 150,000 dollars. I might go on enumerating reasons from a material point of view, if I chose to do so, to show our right to be here. But there are other reasons. We deny the right of any authority in Ireland to deny our connection with the glorious history, traditions, and sufferings of Ireland. They are ours. We have shared them; we have tried to remedy some of them. We may be the sea-divided Gael, but we are not divided in interest, so far as Ireland is concerned.

I would not for a moment occupy your time to answer the question that has been put to us as to who we are, except that it is used for the purpose of confusing Irishmen, to impose upon them the belief that we who come here are not representative of the sentiment of Irishmen in the States. Perhaps, therefore, you will allow me to refer to the *personnel* of delegates, and mention the names of the persons who are here as delegates from the United States. At the moment in which the division occurred in the Irish Party, we were engaged, as some gentlemen on this platform can avow, and some others also on the other side of the house, we were engaged in the commencement in New York of a movement which promised to raise half-a-million of dollars for the Irish cause. That movement was cut short by division. At the meeting in New York the gentlemen who are here were the accredited messengers from the surrounding cities, and became the instrument of those particular cities to bear the money that was contributed in their different places. For instance, we have here Mr. James Duggan, of Norwich, Conn, who brought to the treasury, on behalf of the National Federation of Norwich, the money collected there. I think that is a fair title to be a representative here. We have Mr. Anthony Kelly, Minneapolis, whose service in the West, and whose social attention and money contribution when Mr. Parnell was there, gained the gratitude and favour of Mr. Parnell and those who accompanied him. We have here Mr. P. W. Wrenn, of Bridgeport, Conn, who at the meeting in the Metropolitan Opera House brought 3,000 or 3,500 dollars to the treasury. We have Mr. Denis O'Reilly, of Boston, and Mr. Edward Tracey, of Boston, who have been in the organisation in Massachusetts, and have been constant friends, and unceasing workers, and generous contributors, according to their means, in the National service. We have here Dr. P. J. Timmins, of Boston, and I couple with him the Reverend Denis O'Callaghan, whose names are a synonym for good work for Ireland; and, as for Father O'Callaghan, he has been the leader in Boston of every public movement organised to aid Ireland. We have here Mr. John Cashman, of Manchester, New Hampshire, who is the treasurer of the organisation in that city, and through whom, from time to time, I got the money collected in the city for your service. We have Mr. Patrick Dunleavy, Vice-President of the National Council of Philadelphia, and need I say that Philadelphia was always foremost in the Irish cause?

We have here Mr. John B. Devlin, of Wilkesbarre, who, to my knowledge, has been a constant, unselfish, and ever energetic worker in the National cause. We have here a gentleman who is a curiosity in his way, and it shows how long he has been in the service. We have Mr. Patrick Cox, of Rochester, who was the treasurer of the first branch of the Irish National League, and through which branch alone 30,000 dollars were raised for the service of Ireland. We have Mr. Patrick Martin, and need I say to Irish Nationalists, whether strictly within the physical force ranks or outside them, who Mr. Patrick Martin is? He has been in both sections of the service, and I honour him for it. Now, I think I need not say any more to show that we are not all nobodies. For myself, I represent the certificate of the City Council of the New York Irish National Federation of America, and that title represents something. I do this, Mr. Chairman, not for the purpose of winning your applause or recognition, but to satisfy the minds of those who might possibly give some credence to the statement that we here are tramps or tourists.

We came here without instructions, except the general one, that we demand unity, obedience to majority rule, and that discipline which is necessary to the existence of the Party, and we will do our best to enforce it. Before leaving the United States we studied very carefully the call for this Convention, both individually and collectively, and it was the general verdict of those most interested and competent in the United States to pass upon it an opinion that it was bound to be a success in its scope and extent. We in the United States have had twenty years' experience of conventions. In the great Race Convention of Philadelphia, held in 1881 or 1882, we had no such great and wide provisions for admission to that assembly. For instance, the clergy had no privileges other than the laymen had. We did not consider them any better as politicians, or that they were entitled to more recognition than the laymen, and when they came they came as delegates. We did not throw it open to all the organisations and literary societies; in fact, not to occupy your time, we demanded that there should be some service to the political movement before the society or organisation should have a right to representation. We had not the great breadth and scope of this Convention. We, therefore, said that there could be no man found who would have the hardihood to assert that this Convention had been rigged. How could it be possible when the sources of this Convention were so varied and so wide? We claim that every Irishman who is honest and singleminded will adhere to the decrees of this Convention, and we think that the constituencies of Ireland should demand obedience from their representatives. It is enough to know that the power is placed in the hands of the people, who are bound by discipline to obey the decrees of this Convention, to make every member of Parliament be very careful in his work. Now, Mr. Chairman, and fellow-delegates, I think that so much has been said on every point to which I could possibly address myself, that I would be only doing a superfluous work, and occupying your time unnecessarily by further speech. I think I have established their right to speak, and I think I have established the character of the delegation.

I desire to say one word more on obedience to majority rule. In

America the question is raised amongst us; it is taken as a law that is unchangeable, and must be accepted. If a man, or men, decide that they cannot obey and be in affiliation with the party of the majority, they quietly go out of that party, and either remain silent or become active opponents on the other side. That is what we expect to find, and do find, in the United States. On coming over here, from the nature of my position in the organisation as secretary, of course I am liable to a very large correspondence—I think I could have brought with me letters enough to have occupied your attention this whole session—every one ending with a prayer for unity and "God bless your mission; give us unity, and demand obedience to majority rule as the very essence of the government of the people." While on this platform to-day, a telegram to me arrived from a gentleman whom we know in New York to be one of the most faithful servants of the movement, and one of its most generous contributors:—"Sacrifice everything, save honour, for unity; bring about union in Ireland, and America will respond.—Peter M'Donald." Now, Mr. Chairman, the impression created on us has been that this Convention has been called on such a breadth and scope, that it has such a diversity of sources from which the delegates came, that we must naturally conclude that it is the expression of the popular will; and if the gentlemen who tell us it is not will only come here and present their grievances, nobody is more anxious to redress them. If those gentlemen will abandon the whispered mouthings of calumny, and come like stalwart men to the Convention of their fellow-countrymen at home and abroad, present their protests and grievances, how readily we will redress them, if possible. But they are silent! Silent except the whispers of calumny; and to those men we say: "You have refused to come before the only court that was entitled to redress your grievances; you have refused to come before the only court that is entitled to make reforms and changes in the basic condition of the party." No other power in Ireland has a right to change any single article under which the Federation exists in Ireland to-day. Here alone can it be done. In God's name, are these men not intelligent enough to know that. Is not this the place to do it? And failing to do it, let these men be silent. And I say to one class of these gentlemen—and if I did not say it I would be certainly betraying my own convictions and the opinions that I know will be held when I state the facts in America—I say to reverend gentlemen who may have grievances to remedy or protests to make, that this is their place, as well as the place of laymen. No station among the hierarchy is too great or too grand to come before this Convention and say to the people of Ireland represented here: "Such and such are the changes that we believe are necessary for the Irish people." And I tell you, gentlemen, who have watched the experiences of the past, who have learned the misery that followed some of the actions of this class of gentlemen in the past—I tell you that they will make more infidels than all the Agnostics in the world.

Now, Mr. Dillon, you have received a mandate in the first two resolutions adopted at this Convention. It is, by every means in your power, to see to it that the grievances are redressed and reunion restored. That mandate is given to you by the public will of Ireland. We in

America will look to it that that effort is being made, and that, while yielding nothing to the criticism or calumny of persons who won't come here and declare their grievances, we demand that every effort of yours, and that everything but honour, be sacrificed to restore the unity of the Irish people. It has been my experience just before I left to have had put into my hand a series of letters. Some were from cloistered nuns; some were from the humble miner; some were from gentlemen in possession of great wealth ; some came from archbishops, who, as you saw in the first day's publication of the proceedings of this Convention, promised at the holy altar of God that daily would they offer the sacrifice of the Mass for the success of the Convention. And, Mr. Dillon, if the prayers and protests of the Irish people at home and abroad fail to conciliate, then, in the name of the God who stamps upon mankind the distinctions of race, I charge you, as leader of the Irish race, to spare no man who stands in the way. If conciliation fails, if reason fails, if reason and logic are defied, I charge you to mercilessly crush the man or men who stand in the way. In that I pledge you the assistance of every true Nationalist in America, no matter who the man is. The result of all our labours for the past twenty years in the present movement, and for centuries in the past, shall not be nullified by any man or set of men. We will not consent that our labours and sacrifices, and sufferings of famine and persecution in the past and present and future, should be sacrificed and made nothing of. I swear it is the duty, in my belief, of every Irishman to crush dissension and to crush out the man or men who stand in the way of union. To you, the men of Ireland outside the Irish Party, we charge you, and honestly, to act in this matter with unanimity. If you criticise, let it not be a carping, nagging criticism. Remember the position of your members is a very curious one in the House of Commons; they stand there in your cause, awaiting to meet emergencies that may occur. Individual members may err, but consideration should be extended to them as men, and you must exact discipline—discipline.

The CHAIRMAN put the third resolution as already read. It was carried unanimously.

The CHAIRMAN—Gentlemen, you will consider, I think, I am following the proper course in confining the debate in very narrow limits on the resolutions that follow. There are some notices here sent up by gentlemen who wish to address the Convention. Those notices shall be carefully attended to, but, before we proceed to them or the next resolution, I have to say that the gentleman in whose name the notice of motion stands in reference to the Paris Funds has explained to me that he did not withdraw that part of his resolution; consequently he shall have an opportunity of moving his resolution. And as I stated to this Convention that the leading members of the party were anxious to explain the party's position with reference to the Party funds, I now ask the Hon. Edward Blake to make the promised statement.

Hon. EDWARD BLAKE, M.P.—My lord, ladies and gentlemen, the Irish Parliamentary Party, owing to the unhappy circumstances which have for so long a time so unnaturally divorced from the National funds the greater proportion of the wealth and of the opportunities for getting wealth to be found within this island, the National Party is labouring under the disadvantage, if it be a disadvantage, of being and of acknowledging that it is relatively to English political parties a poor party in worldly wealth. There are amongst us those whose circumstances and exertions have enabled or enable them to offer gratuitous services to the country which they love. And there are amongst us also those who submit to a still greater sacrifice in the interest of that country because they have foregone the opportunities and chances of their lives—the opportunities which their own exertions directed to their own advancement would have produced to them—in order to execute the somewhat thankless office of serving their country at Westminster. I say that the sacrifices of those men, from the worldly point of view, are not comparable in point of lightness with the sacrifices of those who are able to afford gratuitous services, and that their position has to be considered with a generosity, a chivalry, a respect greater than that which is due to those who may happen to be better in the accidence of the possession of worldly dross. The Irish political party in Parliament though a poor party is an independent and self-respecting party. It has held its head high—as high and deservedly high as the parties with whom are associated wealth and rank. And those of us who entertain, as my colleagues with whom I generally act, do entertain, very strong views upon the subject of the management of the Party funds entertain them largely and mainly with reference to that respectable and independent position which the Irish Party ought to have in Parliament, in order that it may do its duty to the country which it represents. The Irish Party provides for the distribution or allotment amongst its own members of the funds entrusted to the Party itself for distribution, and is its own paymaster. But I do not believe it to be consistent with the independence and respect of that party as a whole, or of individual members of that party, who may be in the position to which I have alluded, that any other body or set of men—chosen by I care not whom, and holding their power I care not from what source—should be the paymaster of one or more or any number of my colleagues in Parliament. We do not want to degenerate into a kept party. We do not want to degenerate into a party to any one of whose members it may be said in this island, or still more outside this island, at Westminster, " You owe your stipend to some committee sitting in Ireland—selected and chosen I know not how, and holding office by I know not what tenure. Unless you follow the orders of that committee and obey their voice, your stipend will be cut off for your independence." You tell me that it has been said that the independence of Irish members is threatened by the system of these arrangements for the payment of those who require to be maintained in Westminster is worked. If that be, so I want to know how much less the independence of that Party will be threatened by the members owing the determination of that question to a party outside Ireland or elsewhere. They are men, and being men of like dispositions to our own, they are animated by the same prejudices and feelings, and would find themselves under the same difficulties, and you would only transfer the arena of unworthy contention and suspicion to some other quarter. You would by no means eliminate it by the change you suggest, and as I think, improvidently suggest.

I have known very little, though I have known, I dare say, quite as much as anybody else, of how this matter was managed during the last four years in detail, because the old customs and practices which had been established before the split commenced, were observed as rigorously as possible. Treasurers were appointed, to whom sums were handed in the gross, and they alone knew how much was paid to the Party. To the Party at large, to the committee of the Party, that knowledge was not communicated. It may be thought the system requires reconsideration within the councils of the Party. I am inclined to believe that the system which answered admirably so long when unworthy suggestions were not made, so long as the honour of the Irish Party was not assailed within its own ranks, so long as suspicions were not flung broadcast—these suspicions which never ought to be flung abroad—unworthy suspicions, suspicions for which if there were any foundation would render my friends opposite me, and every man who takes a part in this struggle, unworthy of any place in the councils of the nation, or the Party, or its ranks, so long as these suspicions were not in the old days past thrown out, the old plan might have been as it has been, left alone. Some change in detail may be required under the new rule of casting aspersion wholesale upon every man charged with the responsibility, but that any rule or change can be made which shall divert the Irish Parliamentary Party from the control and responsibility of the management of its own funds, and which shall yet be consistent with its retaining its self-respect and independence, I, for my part, utterly deny. If you trust the Irish Party in Parliament with the most sacred interests of your country, if you trust them, as you do by electing them to Parliament, with the business and the affairs of Ireland, if you say to them, "We trust you to decide which—in the stress and strain of Parliamentary conflict, and in the difficulties—the lines it is best to take for Ireland, we trust you and we follow you," is it not absurd and foolish to say you cannot trust the men whom you trust with these enormous interests to observe the commonest dictates of honest fair play and decency in the distribution of the funds which you give for the support of these men.

I did not think when I joined the Irish Parliamentary Party, in whatever rough work it might be my duty to engage, that I should ever personally have anything to do with the collection of funds for their maintenance. It has been, however, my duty during the last four years —in that constant, unceasing dissension, and the suspicions engendered by the aspersions, and the unworthy statements promoted through the country—it has been in some small part my duty to help, as far as I could amongst my friends and the supporters of the cause abroad, to get the Parliamentary Party supplied with the necessary funds. I tell you, then, that after the unexpected duty devolved upon me, my friends —and you see what sort of friends Home Rule has in Canada—my friends, making some collections in that country for the purpose, remitted them to me personally, telling me to dispose of them as I myself thought best in the furtherance of the Irish cause. So convinced was I that there was but one appropriate method of disposing of the contributions of the friends of Ireland that I declined to take the slightest responsibility as to their disposition. I said, "I will hand them over to the Party itself, to be dealt with by the Party itself according to its rules and regulations. I shall never be a party to the degradation and loss of self-respect and independence of the Irish Parliamentary Party involved in the confession of its incapacity to be fair and just and honest and decent in the administration of its moneys," and I say, if we can't do that we are not fit to serve you in those infinitely greater concerns.

Now, I have known something of these most painful and degrading controversies, and I have watched as carefully as man could watch what the true course of events has been, and I declare to you upon my honour that I am as satisfied as that I am standing here that there has never been the slightest foundation in fact for the suggestion—the base suggestion—that any man has been mean enough to consider for one moment the complexion and opinions upon subjects of Party differences of any member in his relation to the Party funds. I don't believe that even my bitterest opponent will charge me, dissociated as I was necessarily with many of the rancours of the past, with any ill-feeling, and I know that every man with whom I have been connected is as absolutely free and entirely above any sordid and unworthy action as I feel myself that I am. My lord, this Convention has evidenced its determination to give a renewed mandate of confidence to its faithful servants who have endeavoured to hold aloft the flag of Ireland in the stress and strain of the conflict, torn and tattered in that conflict, and besmeared by mud cast on it by those who should be the last to soil it. They have determined to hold up and strengthen their hands, and I am well assured that after this short explanation of the reasons why we felt bound to invite confidence in this as in other respects, there will be no dissenting voice here to the proposition that the Irish Parliamentary Party ought to be in this, as in other respects, trusted to do its duty subject to that account, in case malversation is charged and proved against it, which every representative of the people ought to be subject to, and which we are fully willing to submit to.

Mr. MICHAEL DAVITT, M.P.—My lord bishop, ladies and gentlemen, the fourth resolution which I have the honour to submit for your adoption reads as follows :—

"That, while hailing with satisfaction the release of some of the Irish political prisoners, we are indignant that relief has come so late, after their health had been broken by long years of suffering. We condemn the brutal treatment which England, while boasting herself to be the advance guard of freedom amongst the nations, inflicts on political prisoners sentenced for offences arising out of Irish grievances. We mark the contrast in feeling and in action exhibited by England towards the Irish prisoners, and towards other political offenders, as, for instance, the Johannesburg Committee and the Jameson Raiders. We call for the immediate liberation of all the remaining Irish political prisoners still enduring the horrors of penal servitude, and we request the Irish Parliamentary representatives to press with insistent urgency for their liberation."

I say, ladies and gentlemen, that it is not altogether inappropriate that I should have been asked to submit this resolution to this great Convention. We demand a response to the prayer of this resolution on grounds and for reasons which would not be denied to-day by any other civilised nation throughout the world. The sentences in themselves were monstrous in the first instance, while the punishment inflicted upon these men could not be equalled in cruelty by even the Russian despot who sends his foes to Siberian mines. There is an instinct of humanity common to every created being which prompts a man to give food even to a hungry dog. But it is left for England, enlightened England, to include semi-starvation in the system of punishment she metes out to her Irish political foes. I have undergone over nine years' imprisonment, because I have been a rebel against misgovernment from the moment I was first taught that, next to my duty to God was my duty to Irish liberty, and I say here to-day that during seven long years of that imprisonment, under England's system of punishment, I never for one hour ceased to feel the pangs of hunger. God has made man a talking being, but England insists that silence, perpetual silence, shall be enforced on her Irish political foes, no matter how long their brutal sentences may have been, and the men—the few men—who were turned out the other day to die by England's magnanimous Tory Government —aye, but I hope not before they will help us to settle accounts with Ireland's brutal rulers—believe it, fellow-delegates, or not, I assert here to-day that during the thirteen long years that John Daly and Dr. Gallagher and others have been kept in England's prison pens it was a crime against England's rulers to say "good morning" or "good evening" to a fellow-being undergoing the same brutal punishment. England has had to beg for clemency and justice for incriminated Englishmen from President Kruger. Ireland demands through this Convention of the Irish race that the remaining Irish political prisoners shall be liberated.

Mr. WILLIAM LUNDON, Kilteely, Co. Limerick—My lord bishop and brother delegates from all parts of the world as far as the Irish race has extended, I feel highly privileged in being called upon to address you on this question of amnesty, so dear to all your hearts. No question spoken of at this great assembly catches a greater hold of your hearts, or the hearts of the Irish race throughout the world, than the question of amnesty. Some people might say there was a vast difference in the various phases of the National movement, as evidenced by moral force and physical force. I say the cause has been the same for the last seven hundred years, though it may have presented itself in different shapes. It has been like a kaleidoscope, at one time moral force, at another time physical force, and so on, but in whatever way it presented itself it was Ireland first, Ireland centre, and Ireland last. We all know that only for the Crowleys, the Davitts, the O'Briens, and the others, we would not have been able to carry on the moral agitation of the last fifteen years. I also feel proud to speak on this question of amnesty, because I was the companion of dear John Daly. We stood side by side on platforms in the old amnesty movement of '69. He and I often differed, but no matter what our differences may have been in detail, I tell you, if you had one hundred thousand men of John Daly's calibre with arms in their hands, it would be easy for you to obtain Home Rule. I was present at the first meeting in the city of Limerick when this present movement was organised, and I was present at meetings in Tipperary, including the great amnesty demonstration held in that town. I don't want to say anything contentious. However, there is one matter I would like to put before you. I refer to the men in whose very nostrils the word amnesty stinks since the fall of Mr. Parnell. Two years before the split I was the very man who proposed that Mr. Parnell should be invited to the great demonstration we were going to hold with reference to amnesty. He may have been a great man as a leader, but I tell you his heart was not bent on amnesty. In addition to him, other gentlemen were invited to attend, and I may tell you that not from one of them did we receive even a single reply, except a negative one that was not worth reading. Mr. Davitt has told you that his own experience of prison life was a hard one. I wish to tell you also that my experience of prison life was hard enough. I was imprisoned, under Eager, in Limerick. I was afterward taken to Mountjoy, and subsequently I graduated under the Old Gorilla at Kilmainham. I say that in whatever agitation you have before you, you will always have the amnesty question to the front, and I believe we will all leave it as a legacy to those who come after us. As regards our representation at Westminster there is no use in specious arguments there. If the Irish Party is united, and has the Irish people solid at its back, it will be able to get anything it wants, but otherwise you will get nothing, and they will look upon you as slaves. Dr. Gallagher and Mr. Whitehead and those other men are now nearly oblivious of what they went through. They have been simply driven into madness. There is not on God's earth a more efficacious way of driving a man to madness than the mode described by Mr. Davitt—the silent system. Man is a gregarious animal, and he must herd with his neighbours, and if he has to live in solitary confinement the ordinary man sinks to the level of the beast. Englishmen have gone down on their knees to implore President Kruger to release the men who invaded a free country to deprive a people of their rights. They went in, if not for that purpose, they went in simply to rob. The English have robbed the whole of the world, and nobody felt the truth of that more than the Irish people. Look at how France treated her political prisoners. They did acts revolting to humanity during the Commune. They killed fifty priests and the sainted Archbishop D'Arboy, and all these men were now released. It was said the Liberal Government did not release the political prisoners. Well, the Tories would not release them until they saw that they could not disregard the condition they were in. I knew a case in Mountjoy Prison when I was there, and when the doctor at Mountjoy Prison said the man should be released they had three military doctors in to know whether they could keep the man in jail another month. We are here to ask for the release of the remaining political prisoners, the Land League prisoners, the Invincibles and others, and I hope you will never forget in this matter the names that adorn your walls, of Allen, Larkin, and O'Brien.

Very Rev. D. O'HARA, P.P., Kiltimagh—My lord and fellow delegates, I have only to say as a delegate, and for my fellow-delegates, that we longed to see this day. We have seen it, and we are glad. We began the Convention well; we began it with an Irish prayer; we had the blessing of the Pope; and we have an Irish Bishop in the chair. We are bound to succeed on these conditions, and, from the honest faces I see before me, I think it won't be your fault if we don't. I have been asked to say a few words in favour of amnesty, and I will say this much, that I think we ought to be prepared to set the example, and to give a general amnesty all round to every man, to every Irishman, no matter what he may have done in the past, provided that he comes into the fold and says that he will fight once more for the sacred cause of our country. We are here assembled, on a most solemn occasion, to help on the good old cause. In the name of the delegates that are here, priests and laymen, I venture to make bold and to proclaim a general amnesty to every man. Let them come, and we have

"A hand for the grasp of friendship,"

and it may be well to know that we have

"A hand to make them quake,
And they're welcome to whichsover
It pleases them best to take."

The Irish nation is met here in council. It is the most historic and the most representative meeting of Irishmen that was ever held on Irish soil, and there is not a delegate here, no matter from what part of the world he came, who is not proud, and will for ever feel proud, that he is one of those who came to settle the affairs of Ireland. We came to discharge a solemn duty, the most solemn that man could discharge. We are able to tell the delegates who have come here from distant lands that the Old Guard are true to the old cause of Ireland, and that Ireland stands to the front as ever she did before. Though it is too much to expect that we could be all absolutely united, we can assure them that the country is practically united. I only wish to endorse the observations of Mr. Davitt on the sufferings of the political prisoners. I cannot, I am sorry to say, claim that I have experience of the sufferings of prison life, but this I can boast of—that I was the first priest in Ireland marked out for imprisonment. It was not my fault then, for I never yielded one inch. I would say to our delegates in this assembly that our proceedings here show that Ireland is a country worth fighting for, for we are no ites, but Irishmen, and whatever little mites might stand in our way, all we need is a long pull, a strong pull, and a pull altogether to achieve our rights. We mean to do our duty. We will do our best at home; we are bound to do it, and we ask the American and other delegates to back us up. We will help ourselves, no matter who helps us; we will fight, no matter how few are left; and as a priest from America eloquently put it, no matter how few they are, as long as there are three Irishmen left we will fight for the good old cause. There are not three, but three thousand in this hall, priests and laymen, united as ever in the old cause, and, please God, when we go home we will tell the other priests, and his lordship, perhaps, may tell the bishops. All may agree in this, that at all events the Irish Party must get fair play—nobody must stand in the march of the nation. It wants the help of every man, and, please God, from the highest bishop in the land to the humblest curate, from the highest layman to the poorest living on the mountain side, we will all unite once more, we will dress our ranks, and we will march on to victory.

The CHAIRMAN—Gentlemen, I shall soon propose a more rapid way of getting through the other resolutions, and I would put this resolution to you now were it not that a very distinguished American priest, Father Phillips, of Pennsylvania, has a word to say.

Rev. E. S. PHILLIPS, Luzerne Co., Pennsylvania—I did not intend to add one word to the few remarks that I made on the opening day of the Convention, but I was so much pleased by the sentiment conveyed by the last speaker in regard to general amnesty, when he said that the Irish delegates, priests, and people, were sending to America a feeling of unity, not only towards the men who belong to their regular party in Ireland, but to those who differ, a general amnesty. I wish to say on behalf of the American delegates that our principal is in America that " more flies are caught by molasses than by vinegar." A few days before I left my home I had the pleasure of spending a delightful hour with a priest of the diocese of Raphoe, which is represented in so magnificent a manner by his lordship, our chairman, and he said to me, which I now see verified, " that if Bishop O'Donnell of Raphoe would consent to be present at the Convention, his spirit of true Irish Nationality will dominate the Convention, and a good result must come." Now, gentlemen, one of the speakers from America, representing the Irish National Federation, has given practical proof of the Irish-American loyalty to Ireland by the statement he has made of the contributions of Americans, as well as of Irish-Americans, and of Irishmen who have adopted America as their home, to the Irish cause. But he made a remark with which I must in part disagree, that is, that America expects the honourable chairman if he cannot rule, to crush. Fourteen years ago I sat and worked with Mr. Dillon in America, when he visited that country with the late Mr. Parnell, whose soul, I am glad to say, is still marching on. But I think that it is well for parties to remember that men have opinions, and that these opinions are sometimes honestly expressed ; therefore, that the sense of this Convention is, I believe, that we extend the olive branch to these men still, and I do not think that it is beneath the dignity of the regular Irish National Party, through its chairman, or in a body to make an appeal.

Mr. Dillon was understood to make some remark.

I wish, therefore, as the honourable chairman says " Yes," I wish to state on behalf of America, on behalf of the greater Ireland here represented, that we are all united in believing that the Irish Party now represented by the present chairman, is the party of Ireland. Let me recall a sentiment which I remember being uttered by the honourable chairman at a banquet somewhere in London last March, which electrified me and thrilled me. He said, and with this I will close my remarks, as the sense of this Convention, as the sense of the people who are not here, but who should be, the sense which I hope they will experience after the thoughtful words that have been uttered on this platform, and which now comes from my heart—this language of Mr. Dillon's was this, " If I can but add a sentiment to ' Ireland a Nation ' it is, the ' Nationalists of Ireland all over the world united.'"

The CHAIRMAN—I consider resolution G is pertinent to the next resolution, 5. I consider the second part of the resolution O is pertinent to the sixth resolution in this series. I consider that the fourth part of the resolution O is germane to the tenth resolution of the series, and now the procedure I intend to follow it this : Mr. Kilbride will propose these resolutions *in globo* and they will be seconded and supported.*

---

* For text of all these resolutions see conclusion of proceedings.

THIRD DAY—MR. DENIS KILBRIDE, M.P.

Mr. DENIS KILBRIDE, M.P.—I have been requested to move this resolution dealing with the land :—

> "That the Irish landlord system and methods have tended to impoverish, exterminate, and expel the Irish race, and have thus been the fruitful source of misery, discontent, violence, and disturbance in Ireland. That the last Land Act, whilst bettering the condition of certain classes, fails to give the vast majority of the Irish tenantry that security against excessive rents and confiscation of improvements which is essential to their well-being, and to the success of any scheme of land purchase ; fails to give necessary powers for the enlargement of too small holdings by the compulsory purchase of grass lands from which the people have been driven ; and fails to make adequate provision for the restoration to their homes of the evicted tenants, to whose courage and endurance such benefits as the farmers of Ireland have obtained are largely due, and whose case must ever appeal to the sense of honour and gratitude of their fellow-countrymen. We condemn the lateness of the period and the shortness of the time allowed for discussion, and the indecent threats of withdrawal, by which legitimate debate was curtailed ; and we declare that the Act cannot be accepted even as a temporary settlement, and that the only hope of the tenantry rests in a united and determined Parliamentary Party, backed by a great agrarian combination, watching the operation of the Land Laws, exposing cases of injustice, and demanding a full measure of reform."

Unfortunately we as Irishman know that this question of the land is a very vital one. The first portion of that resolution is that the land system in Ireland has impoverished our people, and is a system of confiscation. At the door of that system in Ireland may be laid the fact that the foreign delegates amongst us are the sons of men that the accursed land laws drove from their country. The resolution deals with the last Land Bill—it deals with the Bill passed this session by the Tory Government—and the resolution asks the people of Ireland, and especially the tenant farmers of Ireland, to boldly declare in the face of the world that they do not, and will not, and cannot accept this Land Bill as a settlement of the Irish Land Question. I want your delegates to tell the authors of this Bill, to tell the Solicitor-General for Ireland and the Chief Secretary for Ireland, that you repudiate the Bill and repudiate the men. We never went so far as to say the Bill was an utter fraud or a sham. We admitted all the time that there were provisions in it which brought relief to a certain class of tenants ; but we said, and we say again, that this Bill brings no relief to the vast body of the Irish tenant farmers. But this Bill to my mind should be refused and rejected by any body of Irish farmers or by any body of justice-loving men. What does this Bill do? The clause of this Bill which deals with improvements enacts that the labourer—the man who has expended the money, the man who has reclaimed the land, is not entitled to the full value of his labour. I say that when a tenant-farmer improves his holding, the value of that labour has increased the letting value, and adds to the value of the holding. But this Bill says that the whole of the increased value—the whole of the value of your labour—is not to be your property, that you are to have in the first instance a certain recognition for it—a certain percentage which this Bill does not define, but leaves it to the idiosyncrasies, the whims, and the fancies of a body of the Land Commissioners. After it gives you a certain percentage on the value of your improvements this Bill then says that any further increased value should be divided between the landlord and the tenant. Our main objection to this Bill is that it does not give full recognition to the improvements of the tenants, and the only final settlement of the Land question can be the purchase system, under which you will not be obliged to buy your own property, and will be obliged to pay for nothing but what is the property of others.

Rev. Mr. LYTTLE, Moneyrea—My lord and gentlemen, I am proud to stand on this platform and to take my side with my fellow-countrymen in the advocacy of Home Rule, and second the resolution. I am inclined to speak on this land question, but I am sure you don't wish any technical details, so I shall only say a word or two as to how the land question affects in the province of Ulster the great cause which has brought us all here—the cause of self-government for Ireland. I believe, gentlemen, that already there are economic forces at work which will make the Unionists of Ulster shift their present political moorings. We remember that during the last century economic tyranny and pressure paved the way for the work of the reformers who marshalled the Volunteers and United Irishmen among the planters of Ulster. Commercial restrictions which ruined the Protestant planters of Ulster during the last century helped Henry Grattan and his co-workers in influencing the minds of the Ulstermen. The seeds of patriotism sown in the minds of the people of the North in due time brought forth splendid fruit in the Volunteer movement and the '98 party. Well, at the present time I have no hesitation in saying that the majority of the Ulster farmers are on the verge of bankruptcy. Wages have risen, and are still rising, and God forbid that any of us should do anything to deprive the labourer of his hire. Prices are falling, and will continue to fall. Now, we know that the Irish farmers must keep a grip of their holdings. Ulster farmers, Unionists though they be at the present moment, will be forced, in order to save themselves, to help to save their country. So, for this reason, I have no hesitation in saying that the time will yet come when Ulster will take her place at last, her proper place, in the very vanguard of the struggle for self-government and prosperity for Ireland. I have the honour, my lord, to speak on behalf of the Liberal and National Union of Ulster. May I be permitted to inform this great Convention of our race that this is a comparatively new organisation—an organisation that already is nearly 2,000 in number, made up in its vast majority of those belonging to the various Protestant denominations? But you will be glad to hear that the old narrowness has left us entirely, and that Roman Catholics are numbered among our most honoured members, and that Catholic and Protestant representatives from our body are here at this Convention to-day. Well, we know of at least 10,000 Protestants of the province of Ulster who are already in sympathy with the cause of self-government, and we aim at making this merely the nucleus of a great Protestant army—a great Protestant auxiliary in the army of Irish patriotism. But our efforts have been neutralised by the dissensions which disgrace our cause. We came here to this great Convention of our race because the doors have been opened to us, and because of a hope that this Convention might show the Irish people which way victory lies, and I, for one, feel that much has been done already. It now remains for the constituencies to accomplish the great end which we all have in view. I am not going into particulars, but I will say this, that we in the North, who have taken this stand, hope that the movement will be kept pure and noble. We hope that those at the head of it will set the noble example of magnanimity, of toleration, and let the world see that there is a great moral force in this movement. We cannot win by numbers, but we hope we shall win by the moral force of our cause. What would be the good of victory if we had not this great moral force? Ours is not a dream of a small kingdom. I trust that our National ideal is not merely a great material thing—not merely that our people shall be fixed as rocks in their native soil, not merely that they shall enjoy material prosperity and the blessings of freedom—but also that they shall be illustrious in purity and nobility of public life, and glorious in the culture of literature, science, and art. This ought to be our ideal, and I hope it is. My lord, in conclusion, allow me to say, as an Irishman in whose veins runs a mingled tide of Celtic and Teutonic blood, that I am proud to stand here on this platform as an Irishman. I have devoted some of the energies of my life in recent years to the effort to make men sink distinctions of creed and party in the common designation of Irishmen. Allow me further to say, as a Protestant, and also, my lord, as an Ulsterman, born and reared in all the traditions of our province, that I am proud to speak on this platform under your distinguished presidency. He is a poor, misled man, indeed, whatever may be his race or creed, who is not proud to associate with a man bearing the honoured name of a clan which in Ireland's past history rushed to glorious battle so often and so well in the service of Irish freedom. Once again Ireland has gone into battle with the glorious war-cry, "O'Donnell Aboo."

Mr. THOMAS DUFFY, County Delegate for Longford—My lord bishop, rev. fathers, and ladies and gentlemen, I have heard a distinguished clergyman say a few minutes ago he would not pass the time limit, you may be quite sure I won't pass the time limit, but coming as a member of the Central Council of the Federation, I think I would not be doing my duty if I did not say a word on behalf of the county I represent, I come from a county represented by the distinguished Mr. Blake, I come from a county represented by the father of the Irish Parliamentary Party— Justin M'Carthy—and you will permit me on behalf of Ireland to return our sincere thanks to the foreign delegates who have come here to settle this petty dispute amongst Irishmen. We are here assembled in council, the greatest assembly of Irishmen, perhaps, that ever assembled in Dublin before. I always held it as a motto, and I hold it to-day, that majority rule must be obeyed. I am not at all surprised, If I am the oldest delegate in this great assembly, for I wore the badge of O'Connell on my breast when I was in the cradle, and what I say to the delegates is to go home and do their duty in organising their counties. Let us stand loyal and firm, shoulder to shoulder, determined to fight out to the bitter end, and Home Rule will be the glorious result.

Mr. DAVID DORAN, Vice-chairman of the Kenmare Board of Guardians—My lord and representatives of that old race that seven centuries of oppression and tyranny could not stamp out—I rejoice in this Parliament of our race, first since ninety years, to speak on behalf of the unfortunate evicted tenants who are mentioned in the resolution before you. When the unfortunate strife amongst Irishmen commenced, and when the Prisoner of Tullamore was laid aside and was prevented from fighting for the unfortunate evicted tenants together with the Chairman of the Parliamentary Party, the evicted tenants have been since suffering privation, want, and misery, owing to this miserable strife. A meeting was held within the past week in the city of Dublin by the exterminators of our race for the purpose of trying—now that the second time for fixing the rents in the Land Courts has come—to secure that the reductions will be so small that the unfortunate Irish farmer will be starved. The unfortunate Irish farmer will be forced to part with his little girl and his little boy, and let them go to foreign countries to seek the bread that they ought to be able to earn in the land of their birth. You know that the only industry we have in Ireland is the land. Since Strongbow came over the unfortunate tiller of the soil has been robbed of his right in the land, the proceeds of which have gone into the pockets of a wortless class to spend in Paris and in the dens of London. The unfortunate tenants appeal to you. The strife in the Irish Party robbed them of friends and of the means of getting back to their homes, and the evicted tenants throughout Ireland and the farmers of the South and West look for the glorious day when union is restored once more in the Irish ranks. Go back and organise. Stand together in your own districts and parishes, band yourselves into one great organisation that will conquer landlordism, and be the means of planting the old flag on the Old House in College Green.

Mr. G. J. LYNSKEY, Liverpool—I would not intervene at this hour but I think that the action of the Irish people in Liverpool deserves that their voice should be heard at this Convention. In every movement, whether constitutional or otherwise, the Irishmen of Liverpool have been in the forefront of it. We look upon it as the Capital of Ireland in England. We come here to-day to deliver one message, and speaking the unanimous voice of the Irish people of that city, I say that we come here for the purpose of supporting, maintaining, and helping majority rule and discipline in the Irish Party. I shall not dwell upon the questions that are coming before you, because I intend to be particularly brief. We feel that dissension has paralysed our action in England. We feel that dissension has deprived us of the support of men that ought to be in our ranks. We feel that dissension has disgusted Irish people who are always ready to support Ireland's demands, and we ask the Irish people at home that they should have union, and that they should have discipline. We care not whether they shall get it by toleration or by conciliation, but get it by any means is what we demand. We have the honour, the distinguished honour of returning an Irish representative to the Imperial Parliament. You, yesterday, heard his eloquent tongue and his fearless speech; but I say on behalf of our people, that if he was against the majority of the Irish Party, no matter how great his tongue, no matter how great his services, we would not stand him one hour. We would not tolerate him for one hour unless he was prepared to stand by union, to stand by discipline, and stand by majority rule. I don't suggest to you how you should deal with those who are against that rule, but I tell you how we should deal with them. I tell you how we should deal with our representative, proud as we are of his distinguished ability, and I say the

Irish people of Liverpool would not tolerate Mr. O'Connor to stand against union, to stand against discipline, or to stand against support to the chairman of his party constitutionally elected. We have a very difficult task in England. You in Ireland have not the same sacrifices to make. Even in America, in Australia, in Africa, and other places, to be an Irishman, to be a Nationalist Irishman, does not prevent one from being successful in the world. In England it means boycotting, notwithstanding that, we have as true, as earnest, and as patriotic a body of men as ever left Ireland's shores. What we come to say to you is this :—" For God's sake close up your ranks and be united once more." If you cannot heal up your differences by reconciliation, then, in the last resort make an appeal to the constituencies. No man has the right to stand between Ireland and her onward progress ; and I say to you, as you stand together united in Ireland, helping and assisting each other, that we, in Liverpool, will stand by you until we are driven to the last ditch in the cause of Home Rule.

Mr. ALPHONSUS QUINN, of Arboe, said—My lord and gentlemen, I wish to say a few words. I have been a Parnellite up to very lately, but seeing this tremendous struggle going on, this great battle going on amongst ourselves, I did not see any reason why I would not come to this Convention, and, by my presence, support the resolution which was carried yesterday. This great Convention has been called, and its doors have been thrown open to everybody, and I think it would be a great medium to ask the Parnellites to join. What do they want to stand outside for ? I cannot see. I admired Parnell. I can also admire the great ability of Mr. Redmond, but what does he want but Home Rule and the land for the people ? What more does he want ? I was glad to hear Mr. Dillon say that he was prepared to throw over his position for the sake of unity. I may say I am a farmer myself, but I do not agree with Mr. Kilbride that the Land Act may not be of some use to the farmers. The courts will be open, and the people cannot be prevented from going into them. What we want now, as soon as the fifteen years have expired, is to go into the courts and get our rents reduced fifty per cent. That would be a pretty fair reduction. I would ask the farmers what will they do when the courts are open. Fifteen years ago I heard the cry, "Don't go into the Land Courts." But how can you keep the people out when they are bent down by starvation ? If the tenants go into the courts and get their rents reduced, they will be better able to fight the landlords. It will give you a strong hand, and when you get Home Rule you will have plenty of money.

Rev. Dr. FLANNERY, St. Thomas, Canada—I am one of the last of the Canadian representatives, and I think you may easily see by my countenance that though I come here from Canada, I am not a Canadian. I had the distinguished honour of being born in the County Tipperary. For the last five years of my life I have been working on the prairies, and along the Canadian lakes, and on the borders of the great Niagara. During all that time I have had experience of Home Rule—Home Rule for Canadians—an absolute necessity for that country ; Home Rule for Australia—an absolute necessity for that country—yes, Home Rule for every country but Ireland. The British Government have allowed us Home Rule and self-government for every one of the seven provinces, which enables us to promote the prosperity and industries of the country. It is difficult to understand why Great Britain should grant self-government to almost every portion of her dominions and refuse it to the most intelligent people on the face of the earth. We have sent you from Canada, money, and, as Father Ryan said on the morning of the opening of the Convention, we sent you a man. We sent you that great, grand man, the Hon. Edward Blake. Men have been trying to asperse his character and to impugn his motives, but we have known Mr. Blake from his boyhood, because he grew in our midst. It was asked down in the County Tipperary, about four or five years ago when I came to visit my relatives : " Did not this man, Mr. Blake, come over to look for office, and to get office under Gladstone?" "What nonsense," I said, "that man is above anything that Gladstone could offer him," and so he is, for if he liked he would be to-day Prime Minister of Canada, instead of his friend Mr. Laurier. Mr. Blake is a man who has an immense practice as a lawyer, and he had a retaining fee of 20,000 dollars a year from the great Pacific Railway, which unites the two oceans, the Pacific and the Atlantic.

Mr. BLAKE—No, no.

Rev. Dr. FLANNERY—Mr. Blake left Canada because he wished to serve men like Davitt and Dillon in working for Ireland. He came here to stand in the gap and work for Ireland until you have succeeded in getting the restoration of the old Parliament in College Green.

Mr. J. B. DEVLIN, Pennsylvania—I esteem it a great honour to be called on to address this Convention. I have come from the land beyond the seas where we have Home Rule in all sincerity. We are the spokesmen of the prosperity and the progress of that country, which was the outcome of the principle that you demand to have adopted, Home Rule for Ireland, and we are the bearers of a message to Great Britain, that so long as she continues to rule Ireland as at present, not only does she act unwisely but tyrannically. The road of patriotism is a rough and rugged path, but it has a goal which is worth striving for. In America we have a sharp and swift way of dealing with a traitor to his political party. We ignore the man who becomes a renegade from his party. They are put aside, and are known as " Dead Ducks." Since I left the country there was no movement for the advantage of Ireland that I did not do my utmost to serve, and we on the other side of the Atlantic have been unselfish, and have made sacrifices in support of the cause of Ireland.

Mr. CHARLES HERRON, South Derry, said that he hailed from a constituency in the North of Ireland which had played an important part in the struggle of the last fifteen years. The people of South Derry were tolerant of no faction. They had shown that in two important and trying crises. At the time of the great fall of Mr. Parnell, Mr. Healy put into their hands the weapons with which they fought Parnell—the issue of the independence and the sacred interests of the country—and they chose the interests of the country, and with sorrow put aside Mr. Parnell. Little did they think then that a second crisis would arise when they would be obliged to use these same arguments against Mr. Healy. The speaker continuing, said—South Derry was indebted to Mr. Healy, but yet, when it came to the question of the country's interests or Mr. Healy's interests, we stood a second time by the country. If the rest of

Ireland imitated the example of South Derry there would be little occasion for this great meeting to-day. I tell you here that there is no dissension in South Derry; there is unity—strong enduring, and lasting. South Derry has never for one moment varied from the principles of unity and majority rule, and I have been asked, when coming here, to say that South Derry was again prepared to follow in the old footsteps and fight the old battles, but that this was surely a time when we should forget the past, meet others half way, and shake hands, and that in this great Convention, which has not unjustly been compared to the great Convention at Tara, we should be prepared to draw a veil over the past, and at least make a solemn and determined attempt to build up a new and bright future for our country. I trust that this great Convention will not separate without expressing its acknowledgment of the giant services Mr. John Dillon has rendered to his country. Mr. Dillon has in season and out of season advocated the principles of unity in that Party, and he has endeavoured to do his duty as a man to reunite the Party in future and for all time.

Mr. DAVITT —His lordship desires me to read the following telegram:

"Two thousand Irishmen join heart and soul wishing God-speed, unity, peace. TYNAN, Rector, Farnworth, Lancashire."

Mr. JOHN M'KEOWN, Q.C., St. Catherine's, Canada—It is with some diffidence that I rise so late in the day to address an audience so vast as this which has been for some time engaged in such serious deliberation. I come here with my fellow delegates from Canada, and I do not desire to take up the time of this meeting by going over the ground which they so clearly, so forcibly, and so eloquently put before you. I have simply to say that so far as the district from which I come, St. Catherine's, where Dean Harris is the parish priest, is concerned, we are united as one man in standing by the chairman of the Parliamentary Party, no matter who that man may be. I have only to tell you this, that from Halifax to Vancouver, from north to south of the great Dominion of Canada, the Irish Catholics and the Irish Liberals will follow and support by their voice and their purse any man that Edward Blake will follow and support. I have confidence in him; I know him from boyhood; we have been fellow students and life-long friends, and we feel that when Edward Blake can follow a leader chosen by the Parliamentary Party that the whole dominion of Canada, so far as the Liberals and Home Rulers are concerned, will follow him without asking who he is. I will promise that the district from which I come will stand true to the cause of Home Rule and for the benefit of Ireland. Mr. Blake, Mr. Justin M'Carthy, both of them know that we in that section of the country have shown our good-will by the contributions we collected, Dean Harris and myself, and transmitted to Mr. Blake. I have no desire to take up all the time allowed me. All I say is that it surprises me as an old campaigner, who has fought side by side with Mr. Blake in the past, following him as a leader, to hear the question of majority-rule called even into question. It is with us as an accepted maxim that every man in the party when he goes into caucus or counsel gives his opinion, and if the majority is against him he bows, and is loyal in the ranks.

Dr. TIMMONS, Broadway, South Boston—Ladies and gentlemen, a moment or two ago, at the solicitation of a few friends, I permitted my name to be handed in on condition that the water of your mill was running dry. Now, I do not see any evidence of that, and I think that Boston has been heard sufficiently of late. Consequently, I shall not trespass on your time at any length. From the other side of the ocean we are unanimous in our hope and belief that there should be unanimity on this side also. Perhaps, if we lived within the confines of your small isle, closeness to the objects you have to look at might also obscure our vision, and we might act wrongly, as many of the inhabitants of this country have acted. You know it is said that "distance lends enchantment to the view." We have determined that majority rule shall prevail. Why should it not be so? Why should not the majority govern in all well-constituted and legally-constituted bodies? In America we have a homely phrase that " the dog wags the tail—not the tail the dog," and therefore we take it that the majority should be more than the minority. "Two heads are better than one," and, *a fortiori*, many heads are better than a few. What is the difficulty in this question? A kindly invitation has been extended to all dissentient factions, and yet they had not put in an appearance. Did they need to have a gilt-edged card on a silver plate lined with gold presented to each of them? Gentlemen, these persons were suffering from what is known in America as " swelled head." Why should not the majority rule? We cannot understand it, and I am sure you will agree that the majority here should rule, especially as the head of your majority is the man these very traitors taught us to call " Honest John Dillon." Why, my friends, nothing has pleased them from the commencement of this Convention to the end. I took up a paper this morning—I know not what gentleman or what coterie it may represent—but nothing, from the prayer in Irish, from the Benediction of the Pope down to the very minutest act, was satisfactory to this party. I am not here to apply the knife nor to advise its application, because, as a physician and surgeon, the knife should be the last remedy. I merely would repeat which was so well said by the distinguished representative for Longford, the Hon. Edward Blake, who was regarded not only as an ornament to Canada, but an ornament to all America. He tendered the olive branch of peace to those who are at variance with you, and did it in a spirit that should force any Christian gentleman to examine his conscience and see if he could any longer remain apart. I will merely add, that while we are in this country a little while longer we will watch and pray that the peaceful remedies offered, and the peaceful means presented by Mr. Blake and others to this assembly, may be accepted before it is too late. I will tell the electors of the country—if they will take my advice, and I know some of them will take it—I will tell 'the electors of what has been, perhaps, from time immemorial called the Black North, from which I have come, to fall into line, as I am glad to see it is falling into line—I shall instruct them, if these members continue obstinate as they have continued, they are to work the guillotine, and they are to be the executioners. There is a gentleman from Massachusetts and Boston of greater reputation and size than myself, and as probably he will have a word to say from that section, I beg to be excused from saying any more. A word to the wise is sufficient. You have had many words, and many eloquent words. Let them be sufficient; take them home—meditate upon them—ponder upon them, and do not forget, that the members of Parliament are your servants, and not your masters.

The CHAIRMAN—Gentlemen, a number of other speakers would be willing to address the Convention, but at this hour of the day it is absolutely necessary to get through with the agenda paper. Is it your will that these resolutions do pass? (Loud cries of "Aye.")

The CHAIRMAN—I declare these resolutions carried unanimously.

(5) LAND.—" That the Irish landlord system and methods have tended to impoverish, exterminate, and expel the Irish race, and have thus been the fruitful source of misery, discontent, violence, and disturbance in Ireland. That the last Land Act, while bettering the condition of certain classes, fails to give the vast majority of the Irish tenantry that security against excessive rents and confiscation of improvements which is essential to their well-being and to the success of any scheme of land purchase; fails to give necessary powers for the enlargement of too small holdings by the compulsory purchase of grass lands from which the people have been driven, and fails to make adequate provision for the restoration to their homes of the evicted tenants, to whose courage and endurance such benefits as the farmers of Ireland have obtained are largely due, and whose case must ever appeal to the sense of honour and gratitude of their fellow-countrymen. We condemn the lateness of the period and the shortness of the time allowed for discussion, and the indecent threats of withdrawal, by which legitimate debate was curtailed; and we declare that the Act cannot be accepted even as a temporary settlement, and that the only hope of the tenantry rests in a united and determined Parliamentary party, backed by a great agrarian combination, watching the operation of the Land Laws, exposing cases of injustice, and demanding a full measure of reform."

(6) TAXATION.—" That we rejoice that the evidence taken before the Financial Commission has at length made too clear for argument the injustice under which Ireland has been so long and is still labouring in the matter of Imperial taxation, and we record our grateful thanks to Mr. Sexton for his arduous and most successful labours in this regard. We call upon the Irish Party at the earliest moment to press upon Parliament our demand for the redress of past wrongs and for the relief from present unequal burdens imposed by the representatives of rich and powerful Britain upon weakened and impoverished Ireland."

(7) LABOUR.—" That while we hail with satisfaction the improved condition of those labourers from whom homes have been provided under the Labourers Act, we regret that the great body are still without decent habitations and plots of land. Notwithstanding recent improvements, we claim that, whilst maintaining due supervision, the procedure should be further shortened, simplified, and cheapened, the appeal to the Privy Council abolished, and the Act made more widely useful; and that the Irish labourers shall be given the same franchise for the elections of guardians as is possessed by the English labourers; that we recognise the just claim of urban labour to an improvement in the laws as applicable to the housing of the working classes of the towns, and we sympathise with every effort for a reasonable reduction in the hours of daily toil."

(8.) LOCAL GOVERNMENT.—" That we condemn the non-representative and irresponsible system of Local Government in Irish Counties by Grand Juries, and the narrowness of the franchise in Irish boroughs; we demand the immediate application in Ireland to Local Government in all its branches of those principles of democratic control which have been so fully carried out in Great Britain."

(9.) EDUCATION.—"That for Catholics we demand perfect equality in the law and administration in the matter of education—primary, intermediate, and university —and the recognition therein not only of the national spirit but also of the highest educational right, namely, the religious training of youth in accordance with the priceless principles of religious liberty and freedom of conscience; we demand the establishment of a University which shall afford to the Catholic people of Ireland educational opportunities equal to those enjoyed by the favoured minority of her population in the University of Dublin; we ask for a practical extension of technical education in agriculture and other industrial arts on a system adapted to the special needs of Ireland, so that her children may be better fitted to develop the resources of their country.

(10.) GAELIC LANGUAGE.—"We hail with satisfaction the successful efforts that are being made at home and abroad to revive and extend interest in the preservation of the Gaelic tongue, and we urge upon all those who can further the interests of this movement to give every help and encouragement to the preservation and study of our ancient Irish tongue by the children of the Gael."

The CHAIRMAN—I find on the paper a number of notices handed in to me relative to particular Members. Now, considering the course of this debate, the mandate that you have given to the Parliamentary Party, and the desire of all to see that peaceful counsels should prevail, I would suggest to the gentlemen charged with these resolutions at this hour of the day to allow them to drop. There is another resolution thanking the two gentlemen—the leader of the National Party and Mr. Blake, for their unrivalled services to the National cause. I think I may be interpreting the views of both, when I also ask those in charge of those resolutions not to put them to the meeting. There is also a notice of motion expressing condemnation of a particular newspaper, and perhaps the same course is the best in regard to that motion. There is a resolution with regard to the form of the Parliamentary Pledge, and perhaps the gentleman in charge of that motion would allow me to say that it is a great subject to enter upon at this stage of our proceedings, and that possibly we have done enough to secure the object these gentlemen have in view. The last resolution of all, I would suggest might be treated in the same way, as it proposes somewhat of a new procedure. There remains two resolutions. With one of them I think you will have no difficulty. It might easily be added, I suggest, to the resolution about the Irish language. It is—

"That, in order to give employment to the poorer classes, and remedy the poverty and misery due to the oppression and legalized robbery under which our country has so long suffered and still suffers, we appeal to all Irishmen of means to assist in establishing manufactures in Ireland, and on all, to promote their success by using articles of Irish manufacture as far as they can be obtained."

The next division contains a suggestion in addition to what is contained in the resolution on the Irish language already passed. I shall read it for you—

"That the most strenuous efforts be made to create and foster a healthy National sentiment, by disseminating the knowledge of Irish history, and by the cultivation of the Irish language, Irish literature, music and games."

There remains a motion with reference to the Paris Funds, and it is different in character from those I have alluded to. Mr. Thomas M'Govern will move the resolution, and then I think we can bring the matter to a conclusion in a short time.

There being no response, after a pause,

The CHAIRMAN—I will ask Mr. Dillon to make a short statement on the matter.

Mr. JOHN DILLON, M.P.—My lord and fellow-delegates, I stated before that I came before this Convention prepared to deal with anything in the nature of a charge that might be made, and I have no fault to find with Mr. M'Govern for putting that notice on the paper. On the contrary, I thank him for taking that manly course of raising the question, and also for giving me notice that he proposed to raise it. Now, the answer is exceedingly brief and simple. The Paris Funds, as most of you are aware, were released under agreement between ourselves and the Parnellite Party, when we were informed by the London solicitors who had charge of the matter, on behalf of Mr. M'Carthy and our party, that it might be twenty years before they could be got out by means of litigation. The terms of that agreement were published to the world, and were approved by unanimous vote at a meeting of the Irish Party in the month of November, 1893, at which fifty-four members of the party were present. Under that agreement, in the month of November, 1894, the Paris Funds were released, and I may say, for the information of Mr. M'Govern, as he asks me to state how much was received by Mr. M'Carthy and myself, that since January, 1890, nothing was received until the month of November, 1894. The total net sum—after the payment of law costs paid under the agreement—the total net sum released was £38,471 14s. 11d. Under the agreement we were bound to set aside £14,000 of that sum to meet what were known as prior claims, and that £14,000 lies to-day, untouched as yet, in the Hibernian Bank, in O'Connell Street in this city, in the names of Messrs. Michael Davitt, T. Harrington, and John Dillon. Many claims have been lodged against it, and I fear it may be some little time yet before we can arrive at an agreement as to the apportionment of the money to the various claims, as they are largely in excess of that sum. That left a balance of £24,471 14s. 11d., which, under the terms of the agreement, was to be devoted to the relief of the evicted tenants, and I am here to-day to state that, when that sum is fully expended, a careful audit of the account will be published, which will show that not a single farthing has gone to a member of the Irish Party, or to any political purpose whatever. Up to the date of the commencement of this Convention, that fund of £24,471 4s. 11d. was disposed of as follows:—£23,084 7s. 4d. has been distributed amongst the evicted tenants of Ireland, £395 0s. 9d. has been the cost in office expenses and in the salary of a secretary for the distribution of that large sum, and £992 6s. 10d. still lies in bank for the use of the evicted tenants. And I have only further to say that Mr. M'Govern's motion asked me to state, on behalf of the party, the name and address of every individual who got a payment out of the Paris Funds. I have that actually prepared (cries of "It is not wanted"), but inasmuch as there are over twelve hundred names and over twelve hundred addresses, it would cover two sheets of the *Freeman*. But I can inform Mr. M'Govern, or anybody else interested, that by giving me notice, and calling at my house, No. 2 North Great George's Street, I shall hand the whole document over to him, and let him study it for himself.

Mr. T. P. O'Connor, M.P.—My lord, I have to propose the following resolution, which I am about to read. If the hour were earlier, and if the case required any speaking, I might address some observations to you upon it; but I think the case is so clear, and the motion expresses what you think so lucidly, that it will not be necessary for me to do more than read the motion. I hope my friends to whom the resolution is addressed will not misunderstand me in thus moving the resolution without any comment—

> "That this great National Convention of the Irish Race offers its profound gratitude to the distinguished gentlemen from the United States, Canada, Australasia, Newfoundland, and South Africa who have been self-sacrificing and patriotic enough to travel such vast distances to attend this Convention. That we recognise in them, holding as they do, great positions in politics, the Church, and commerce, not only the most influential representation of the scattered children of the Gael which has ever visited Ireland, but as living proofs of the genius, energy, and capacity of the Irish race when free institutions give Irishmen a fair chance. And finally that the presence of these men of our race from so many parts of the earth shows to the whole world that the struggle of Ireland can rely on the steady, generous, and energetic support of a great and powerful race in almost every part of the world, and can look thus confidently to complete and triumphant success."

Mr. DAVITT—It gives me the greatest pleasure—in fact I feel an honour in performing the duty—in seconding the resolution so well put by Mr. O'Connor.

The motion was carried amidst enthusiastic cheering and waving of hats.

Very Rev. Dean HARRIS—On behalf of the foreign delegates, I wish to thank you for this warm expression of your kindly feelings towards us. If have served no other purpose by our visit we have at least infused into the hearts of those present some of the warmth of feeling towards the old country that we have entertained ourselves. For coming these long distances we are more than repaid by the courtesy with which we have been received by you, and by the instructions we have received in listening to the magnificent speeches delivered from this platform. I thank you.

Mr. JOHN DILLON, M.P.—It is now my duty to move that his lordship the Bishop of Raphoe do leave the chair, and that Mr. Edward Blake do take the second chair.

Mr. BLAKE here took the place of the Bishop of Raphoe in the chair.

Mr. DILLON—I have to submit to you a resolution, which, indeed, will not require that I should approach the limit of time, and that is—

> "That the thanks of this great Convention and the thanks of the scattered children of the Gael should be accorded to that illustrious and eloquent prelate who has presided over our deliberations for the last three days, and who has shown that the blood of O'Donnell is still warm."

I shall say nothing more, for the reception you have given to the resolution shows that it is idle for me to recommend it to you.

Rev. J. SCANLON, P.P.—I have very great pleasure indeed in seconding this vote of thanks to his lordship, the Bishop of Raphoe, for the great services he has rendered to Ireland by presiding over this great Convention during the past three days. In accordance with the traditions of his honoured place he heard the call of Ireland, and he came to point out to the Irish people the road to duty, and I hope every man here will find in his heart a command to follow in that path of duty. At the opening of the Convention he made a speech that was at once eloquent and patriotic. During those three days he guided our deliberations with a wisdom that could not be surpassed, and for which Ireland owes him a debt of thanks. Under his lordship's auspices great good is bound to come from this Convention, for when you go home to your respective parishes you will be bound in honour as patriots and as men to give effect to the resolutions that were passed here during the last three days. The Convention was a noble sight to see, but except you put life into your branches when you go home the Convention will be robbed of half its fruit, and his lordship will be deprived of half the pleasure due to him for having presided on this remarkable occasion. I think the very best thanks we could give him would be to put new life into the different branches of the organisation in our respective parishes, to gather our friends around us, and thereby give pleasure to Ireland and put fear into the hearts of her foes. With these few remarks I beg formally to second the vote of thanks to his lordship, who, in accordance with the traditions of his ancient and royal race, has done us great honour by presiding over our Convention.

Mr. BLAKE then put the resolution to the meeting, and declared it carried amid a most extraordinary and unprecedented scene of enthusiasm.

The Most Rev. Dr. O'DONNELL, on rising to reply to the vote of thanks, was the recipient of an extraordinary ovation. The whole crowded audience rose to their feet and cheered loudly, and waved hats and handkerchiefs for several minutes. After several renewals of the demonstration, and when silence was restored, his lordship said—Mr. Chairman, ladies and gentlemen, it is beyond my power to return thanks as I ought for the far too kind words spoken of me by the proposer and seconder of this resolution, or to express my gratitude to the Convention at large for the generosity with which it has received those words, and the forbearance and kindliness that have been dealt out to me since the beginning of these memorable proceedings. When I took the chair I thought to myself it was likely to involve some strain, but I reflected that I should have the compensation of being in a good position to listen to a debate that promised to be fruitful with lasting blessings for the land we all love. I think this Convention has not been behind the expectation of anyone, and I say, whatever other convictions our friends from abroad bring back with them, they will bring this conviction—that when Ireland has a Parliament, that Parliament will be worthy of a nation. As regards the chair, my position was very largely a sinecure; and if ever a wave threatened to ripple the placid face of this great sea of Irish public life, a little bang by Mr. Davitt on the gong at once stilled the storm. I venture to express the opinion to Mr. M'Neill, who, I understand, is writing a history of Irish Conventions, the best theme he can find for any chapter will be the proceedings of this Convention. I confess, indeed, on a secondary matter I had for a while some anxiety. I had a fear, when that strain of eloquence from across the seas poured into my ears, that the ungrateful children of Ireland who had left her soil were going to bear away the palm of eloquence. Fortunately, the balance became pretty fairly and evenly dressed. As one who occupied that chair, I take great pleasure in saying that I am proud of our people and very proud of our clergy who did so much good work in this Convention. One thing gave us enormous power in this hall during the proceedings, and that was the presence and patient hearing and sympathy of those most representative friends who have come to us from every land in which Irishmen can be found; and I say to them, because at first sight it might appear somewhat strange that in the capital of the land they came to serve there were not more public demonstrations in their honour—I say to them that they have had a demonstration of respect and honour from the intellect and heart of Ireland in the vote that has been passed them this afternoon. And I tell them that if they go down to Tipperary or Connemara, or to a place called Donegal—if they send to rural Ireland, where the Irish population chiefly lives—if they send a large deputation, we will make our Irish hills blaze with welcome in their honour.

Gentlemen, can any man doubt that this Convention has been a magnificent success? You know there are two peace-making ways in which unity may be promoted—there is the way of aggregation and fusion, on the one hand, and there is the way, on the other hand, of growth and assimilation and attraction, and survival of the fittest. Now, none of our friends leaving their homes thought it at all likely that on this platform the aggregation would actually be effected, but they are convinced, and we are convinced, that the tone of this assembly, and the voice of this assembly, and the brotherly love and toleration exhibited by this assembly towards every man who is honestly a friend of Ireland, are eminently calculated to bring all true Irish Nationalists together. Then, as regards growth and attraction and assimilation, has not the principle of growth been strengthened and renewed with a new spirit from the deliberations and decisions of this Convention? And is it not a fact of which we feel well assured, that when the spirit of this Convention has its full influence on public opinion, when our delegates go back home and report, and when the whole country is vitalised anew by the sentiments poured forth so unanimously here, soon, and very soon, those who now linger outside the regular army will come in and obey the drill? Gentlemen, our friends from abroad, have you any doubt now as to where the Irish Party is? Well, the work of the Irish Party, my friends, would be very much easier if, besides being the Irish Party, they had every Nationalist Home Rule member working cordially with them. But, gentlemen, I want to put you this. We have no claim on you except the great claim which constrains you of your love for our cause. And I say this to you unhesitatingly—it is my belief that it is a logical conclusion for you—that as a united Irish Party would have dominant claims on your sympathy and support, the true Irish Party that has spread out its hands to all true Nationalists, and asked them to come to meet you, and is surrounded with so much trouble and danger and difficulty in doing its work, has a greater claim on you than any party could have in which every Nationalist member would stand with his brothers. It is well known at home and abroad that for years past our Party in Parliament, owing to a sort of paralysis with which it was afflicted on the right and on the left, did not receive from the public that amount of financial support which is absolutely essential for the conduct of any movement or for maintaining an army in Westminster to fight our battles there. Well, if I interpret the spirit of this Convention aright, the men who compose it will not let our army starve for the want of commissariat.

I will, therefore, read to you a resolution which I propose for the acceptance of friends from Ireland and from beyond her shores:—

"That this Convention, representing the Irish people, pledges its financial support to the Irish party, and calls upon them to make an appeal for such support to the people in the course of the present autumn."

You will give that resolution effect, I am sure, in the full confidence, as Rev. Mr. Lyttle suggested, that in our own day, with God's blessing, Ireland will be a nation once again, with the mission to maintain highest intellectual culture, supreme devotion to faith, and true liberty for all its people.

Mr. BLAKE put the resolution proposed by his lordship, and declared it passed with acclamation.

Mr. BLAKE, again rising—Gentlemen, in one moment this great Convention will be dissolved. Our collective power, our organised force, will be at an end. Our works will live after us. And with the moment that our collective power ends our individual responsibility commences, and as we separate and dissolve into individual entities, we carry away with us a solemn duty to spread the light and to cause every place wherever we live and every man and woman with whom we have influence, to know what has been learnt and what has been decided here these three days and to see that the seeds, the good seeds, sown here, shall blossom and bear fruit all over Ireland. Gentlemen, I declare this Convention dissolved.

The Resolutions of the Convention.

The following is the full text of the resolutions as finally adopted by the Convention of the Irish Race during its deliberations :—

(1) REUNION.—"Seeing that divisions amongst Irish Nationalist representatives paralyze to a great extent their power of serving Ireland, cast discredit on the country, and tend to alienate the support of the Irish race and to destroy their confidence in the efficacy of Parliamentary action, we record our firm conviction that it is of the first importance to Ireland that the Nationalist representatives in Parliament should be reunited into one party; and, in the spirit of the recent resolution of the Irish Party, we declare that, 'In our earnest desire to accomplish that result, we are prepared to meet on fair and equal terms all Nationalists who will join in the attempt to reconstitute a united Home Rule Party, in which every supporter of the movement shall be cordially received and justly considered, regardless of all past differences, and having regard only to his capacity to render service to the common cause.' We are glad to observe in the composition of this Convention, and in the spirit shown throughout the country, marked evidence of a growing tendency to reunion, and we invite the Irish Nationalist Party to take such further steps as may to them seem calculated to promote the cause of reunion."

(2) UNITY.—"That we recognise as the essential element of the existence of an effective Irish Party the hearty co-operation and cheerful subordination of each individual in carrying out the Party policy, as settled (after free discussion) by the judgment of the greater number. That while we are glad to observe that on grave questions there have been but few intelligible differences of opinion in the Irish Party, and none difficult of reconciliation by reasonable men willing to agree, we most strongly condemn those public disputes regarding minor questions of persons and tactics which have so gravely impaired the power of the Party. We solemnly call upon every man belonging to the Irish Party, in answer to the prayers of our people all the world over, to forget old differences, to sink personal feelings, and to act for the future as good comrades and fellow-soldiers in the spirit of this resolution and in the support of that party unity on which the fate of Ireland so largely depends. We ask the Irish Party to take such steps as may in their judgment be found necessary to the establishment of unity and discipline in their own ranks, in accordance with the resolutions of this Convention; and we assure them of our unfailing support in the execution of this essential task."

(3) HOME RULE.—"That this Irish Race Convention reasserts the immemorial claim of IRELAND A NATION. We declare that England is governing Ireland wrongfully, by coercion, and against the people's will; that each year proves afresh the futility of the attempt; that Irish evils mainly flow from alien, irresponsible, uninformed, and unsympathetic rule; and that no policy, whether of severe repression or of partial concession, can allay her rightful discontent, or will slacken her efforts to obtain a Legislature and an executive making and administering laws for Ireland by Irishmen on Irish soil. We declare it the prime duty of the Irish Parliamentary Party to continue to maintain its absolute independence of English Political Parties, and thus to preserve its freedom to give an independent opposition or an independent support to any Party, as may seem best in the interests of the National cause."

(4) AMNESTY.—"That, while hailing with satisfaction the release of some of the Irish Political Prisoners, we are indignant that relief has come so late, after their health had been broken by long years of suffering. We condemn the brutal treatment which England, while boasting herself to be the advance guard of freedom amongst the nations, inflicts on political prisoners sentenced for offences arising out of Irish grievances. We mark the contrast in feeling and in action exhibited by England towards the Irish prisoners and towards other political offenders, as, for instance, the Johannesburg Committee and the Jameson Raiders. We call for the immediate liberation of all the remaining Irish political prisoners still enduring the horrors of penal servitude, and we request the Irish Parliamentary representatives to press with insistent urgency for their release."

(5) LAND.—"That the Irish landlord system and methods have tended to impoverish, exterminate, and expel the Irish race, and have thus been the fruitful source of misery, discontent, violence and disturbance in Ireland. That the last Land Act, while bettering the condition of certain classes, fails to give the vast majority of the Irish tenantry that security against excessive rents and confiscation of improvement which is essential to their well-being and to the success of any scheme of land purchase; fails to give necessary powers for the enlargement of too small holdings by the compulsory purchase of grass lands from which the people have been driven, and fails to make adequate provision for the restoration to their homes of the evicted tenants, to whose courage and endurance such benefits as the farmers of Ireland have obtained are largely due, and whose case must ever appeal to the sense of honour and gratitude of their fellow-countrymen. We condemn the lateness of the period and the shortness of the time allowed for discussion, and the indecent threats of withdrawal, by which legitimate debate was curtailed; and we declare that the act cannot be accepted even as a temporary settlement, and that the only hope of the tenantry rests in a united and determined Parliamentary party, backed by a great agrarian combination, watching the operation of the land laws, exposing cases of injustice, and demanding a full measure of reform."

(6) TAXATION.—"That we rejoice that the evidence taken before the Financial Commission has at length made too clear for argument

the injustice under which Ireland has been so long and is still labouring in the matter of Imperial taxation, and we record our grateful thanks to Mr. Sexton for his arduous and most successful labours in this regard. We call upon the Irish Party at the earliest moment to press upon Parliament our demand for the redress of past wrongs and for the relief from present unequal burdens imposed by the representatives of rich and powerful Britain upon weakened and impoverished Ireland."

(7) LABOUR.—"That while we hail with satisfaction the improved condition of those labourers for whom homes have been provided under the Labourers Act, we regret that the great body are still without decent habitations and plots of land. Notwithstanding recent improvements, we claim that, whilst maintaining due supervision, the procedure should be further shortened, simplified, and cheapened, the appeal to the Privy Council abolished, and the Act made more widely useful; and that the Irish labourers shall be given the same franchise for the elections of guardians as is possessed by the English labourers; that we recognise the just claim of urban labour to an improvement in the laws as applicable to the housing of the working classes of the towns, and we sympathise with every effort for a reasonable reduction in the hours of daily toil."

(8) LOCAL GOVERNMENT.—"That we condemn the non-representative and irresponsible system of Local Government in Irish Counties by Grand Juries, and the narrowness of the franchise in Irish boroughs; we demand the immediate application in Ireland to Local Government in all its branches of those principles of democratic control which have been so fully carried out in Great Britain."

(9) EDUCATION.—"That for Catholics we demand perfect equality in the law and administration in the matter of education—primary, intermediate and university—and the recognition therein not only of the National spirit, but also of the highest educational right, namely, the religious training of youth in accordance with the priceless principles of religious liberty and freedom of conscience; we demand the establishment of a University which shall afford to the Catholic people of Ireland educational opportunities equal to those enjoyed by the favoured majority of her population in the University of Dublin; we ask for a practical extension of technical education in agriculture and other industrial arts on a system adapted to the special needs of Ireland, so that her children may be better fitted to develop the resources of their country."

(10) GAELIC LANGUAGES.—"We hail with satisfaction the successful efforts that are being made at home and abroad to revive and extend interest in the preservation of the Gaelic tongue, and we urge upon all those who can further the interests of this movement to give every help and encouragement to the preservation and study of our ancient Irish tongue by the children of the Gael. That the most strenuous efforts be made to create and foster a healthy National sentiment by disseminating the knowledge of Irish history, and by the cultivation of the Irish language, Irish literature, music and games."

(11) IRISH MANUFACTURE.—"That in order to give employment to the poorer classes, and remedy the poverty and misery due to the oppression and legalised robbery under which our country has so long

suffered and still suffers, we appeal to all Irishmen of means to assist in establishing manufactures in Ireland, and on all to promote their success by using articles of Irish manufacture as far as they can be obtained."

(12) THE DELEGATES FROM ABROAD.—" That the great National Convention of the Irish Race offers its profound gratitude to the distinguished gentlemen from the United States, Canada, Australasia, Newfoundland, and South Africa, who have been self-sacrificing and patriotic enough to travel such vast distances to attend this Convention. That we recognise in them, holding as they do great positions in politics, the Church and commerce, not only the most influential representation of the scattered children of the Gael which has ever visited Ireland but as living proofs of the genius, energy and capacity of the Irish race when free institutions gave Irishmen a fair chance. And finally, that the presence of these men of our race from so many parts of the earth shows to the whole world that the struggle of Ireland can rely on the steady, generous, and energetic support of a great and powerful race in almost every part of the world, and can look thus confidently to complete and triumphant success."

(13) THANKS TO THE MOST REV. CHAIRMAN.—" That the thanks of this great Convention, and the thanks of the scattered children of the Gael, should be accorded to that illustrious and eloquent prelate who has presided over our deliberations for the last three days, and who has shown that the blood of O'Donnell is still warm."

(14) FINANCIAL SUPPORT.—" That this Convention, representing the Irish people, pledges its financial support to the Irish Party, and calls upon them to make an appeal for such support to the people in the course of the present autumn."

Resolutions 1 to 10 appeared on the Agenda as Series A—with the exception of the last sentence of 10, which was added from Series O, Clause (4).
Resolution 11 was taken from Series O, Clause (3).
Resolutions 12, 13 and 14 were drawn up and added in the course of the proceedings.

Resolutions Dropped.

THE following, placed on the Agenda by the persons whose names are attached, were either not proposed when called, were taken as embodied in other resolutions, or were, on the suggestion of the Chairman, not pressed.

B.

" That, owing to the miserable squabbles which have disgraced the Irish Parliamentary Party during the past six years, the cause of Home Rule, in our opinion, has been seriously imperilled, the influence of the party considerably lessened, and the hopes and aspirations of the best and truest of our people chilled and thwarted. Believing that [the cardinal principle of unity should form the basis of the deliberations of this important gathering, we would respectfully urge when, after due consideration, its decisions have been arrived at, every effort should be made to impress on the various constituencies the absolute necessity of demanding the immediate resignation of any representative, no matter how marked his abilities, or how great his services, who neglects or refuses to abide by majority rule."

DANIEL SMITH and WILLIAM MORAN, Edinburgh (on behalf of the John Dillon and W. E. Gladstone Branches, I.N.L. of Great Britain).

C.

"That we view with deep concern the present unfortunate dissensions among the Leaders of the Irish Party; we hold strongly to the opinion that the interests of Ireland can never be advanced until a United Party reverts to the old system of absolute independence of all English Parties; and we hopefully look to this great Convention to enforce unity under the leadership of one who shall be acceptable to the whole Irish race."

M. FOX, Birkenhead (on behalf of the Wilfred Blunt Branch, I.N.L. of Great Britain).

D.

"That this Convention tenders to John Dillon its sincere gratitude for a life of service to Ireland, and for that crowning act of unselfish patriotism in responding to his country's call to the leadership at a period of unspeakable difficulty; and congratulates him on the success of this Session at the helm, and the admirable qualities of statesmanship he has displayed in the face of unparalleled opposition; we are proud to recognise his efforts to restore unity again in the Irish ranks. And this Convention calls on Mr. Thomas Sexton to return to the service of his country, and continue the magnificent work he has already done on its behalf."

COUNCILLOR D. M'CABE, Manchester, for the Michael Davitt Branch, I.N.L. of Great Britain.

E.

"That, in the opinion of this Convention, it is necessary for the good of the cause that a representative Committee be appointed for the purpose of carrying out the resolutions of the Convention, with power to visit and summon meetings in any constituency where, in their opinion, the sitting Member is not conducting himself in conformity with his pledges to his constituency and Party, and calling on them to demand from him strict discipline, failing which to duly convene a meeting of the electors in the place of his nomination for the consideration of his conduct, and to take what other steps may be considered advisable in the circumstances."

THE DELEGATES of the A. M. Sullivan Branch, I.N.L. of Great Britain, Dundee.

F.

"We strongly condemn the *Nation* Irish newspaper for continuing to sow dissension, and for misrepresenting and treating with ridicule this Convention, composed of patriotic men, many of whom have travelled thousands of miles in the hope of promoting unity amongst the people of Ireland."

DELEGATES, Bristol Branch, I.N.L. of Great Britain.

G.

"That as the occupation by graziers of large tracts of land, suitable for agricultural purposes, constitutes a land monopoly which is most detrimental to the best interests of our country, and is the chief cause of the continued emigration of the flower of our people, it is hereby resolved—'That no settlement of the land question shall be accepted as satisfactory or final that shall not provide for the expropriation of these large grass farms, for the purpose of relieving, as far as possible, the congestion of the overpopulated districts, and providing farms and homes for those agriculturists and labourers who must otherwise be compelled to emigrate, as under the present iniquitous system they are locked out from a great portion of the land of the country.'"

JAMES KILMARTIN, Ballinasloe Branch I.N.F.

H.

(1) "That as a vacancy occurs in any constituency, the Irish Party, or Committees if there be such, do immediately communicate with the constituency, and if they, in conjunction, decide upon contesting the constituency, a Convention be forthwith called in the most convenient part of the constituency, and at least one week's notice be given of the date and place of holding said Convention; said notice to be published in the Daily National Journal, also to be given to the Local Branch of I.N.F., or other duly representative association qualified to send Delegates. That said Convention be presided over by a representative of the Irish Party; that the Convention be constituted as heretofore; and that before the name of any candidate is submitted to the Convention he be compelled to sign the pledge hereinafter named; and that the vote of the majority of delegates in all cases be binding; and further, that it be the duty of all delegates and Nationalists to support the candidate as chosen."

(2) "That, at and after this Convention, all Nationalists Members of Parliament and any candidate seeking the representation of a National constituency, before his name be submitted to the Convention, shall be compelled to sign the following pledge :—I hereby pledge myself that if elected as Member of Parliament for the constituency of ——, that I will sit, act, and vote with the majority of the Irish Party; that I will abstain from criticising, in the Press or elsewhere, the actions or conduct of any of my colleagues until he or they have been tried and condemned by a majority of the Irish National Party; further, that after I have given my opinions within the councils of the Party, I will support the carrying out of the programme, and uphold its decisions to the utmost of my ability; also that I will respond upon all occasions to the summonses of the Whips or other duly-elected officers of the Party; and that I will not absent myself from any meeting of said Party, or from attending in the House of Commons without sufficient cause, and giving notice to the Chairman and Whips of the Party; and any time I feel unable to comply with the above I shall give notice to the Secretaries of the Party, and forthwith resign my seat."

(3) "That the Irish Parliamentary Party do elect at their next meeting a Committee of eight members to act as a consultative or advisory Committee in conjunction with the Chairman to determine the policy and programme of the Party, in the interval between general meetings of the whole Party, and to discharge such other duties as the Party may from time to time empower them with."

(4) "That a Committee be formed immediately after this Convention in every County or Electoral Division, such Committee to be called the County or Divisional Committee as the case may be, and to consist of five per cent. of the members on the books of each branch."

"The place of meeting and the interval between each to be regulated by the Committee at its first meeting, and that a Chairman and Secretary shall be elected on the same occasion, each to hold office, unless re-elected, for one year only. The principal duties of the Committee will be to make all the necessary arrangements relative to Parliamentary Elections in the County or Division which they represent, working up the Branches of the I. N. F., and attending to all the matters brought under their notice by same through their delegates."

J. MAGRATH, M. A. LAZENBY, and J. NUGENT,
Blackrock Branch, I.N.F.

I.

"That, as it is impossible for the Irish Nationalist Party to render much service to Ireland in the London House of Commons without unity and discipline being observed within the ranks of the Party, we, the members of this Convention of the Irish Race, demand that any member of the Irish Party who will in the future refuse to observe and submit to the ruling of the majority of his Party, shall be called upon by his constituents to resign his seat, and if his constituents fail to do so, that the Irish Party expel him from their body, and that the Executive of the Federation cut off that constituency from the organisation."

PATRICK REGAN, Delegate, Crossna, Co. Roscommon.

J.

"Whereas, dissension and disunion have done material damage to the National cause in the past, and whereas, the raking up of disputes would only open up old sores, be it therefore resolved—'That this Convention do not entertain contentious matters relating to past disputes amongst the Irish Party, but proceed to lay down a programme for the future guidance of the National cause.' Whereas, we believe that it is only by strictly adhering to majority rule that the efficiency of the Irish National Party can be maintained for effective Parliamentary action: Resolved—'That any member of that Party who, either in the Press or on the platform, publicly repudiates any decision arrived at by a majority of the Party, should be immediately called upon to resign his seat.'"

THE DELEGATES, Cloonloo (Co. Sligo) Branch I.N.F.

K.

"That as unity and discipline, so essential to the success of our cause, can only be established and maintained by the recognition of majority rule, this Convention is of opinion that any member of the Irish Party guilty of insubordination, and thereby violating his solemn pledge to his constituents, should be immediately called upon by his colleagues to resign his seat, and in the event of his failing to do so, should be expelled from the Party, at a meeting of which each member has received fourteen days' notice, held for that purpose."

NEAL HAUGHEY, Dillon Branch, I.N.L. of Great Britain, Greenock.

L.

"We ask the Delegates at this Convention of the Irish Race to throw faction and ill feeling to one side, and call upon the Irish Party to unite in one body, to be recognised by all Irishmen as the Irish National Party; and we strongly condemn the action of the Parnellite Party in issuing a manifesto denouncing this Convention as a snare to entrap Irishmen. We ask that all Nationalists would join hand-in-hand and work in peace and harmony, as this is the only way that they will be able to attain any good for their native land."

THE DELEGATES, Daniel O'Connell Branch, I.N.L. of Great Britain, Hamilton, Scotland.

M.

(1) "That a committee, consisting of the following gentlemen, be appointed to amend the Constitution of the Irish National Federation, viz:—John Ferguson, Glasgow; Michael Davitt, M.P.; J. P. Farrell, M.P.; Jeremiah Jordan, M.P.; a Delegate from the United States, America; a Delegate from Canada; a Delegate from Australia; and the Mover and Seconder of this resolution."

(2) "That Mr. Justin M'Carthy, M.P., and Mr. John Dillon, M.P., do furnish this Convention with a detailed statement showing the receipts and expenditure of the Paris Funds, giving amount received from said Funds since 1st January, 1890, the names and addresses of the persons to whom money out of this Fund has been paid with the amount paid to each, with the nature of the services rendered by such person."

THOMAS M'GOVERN, Gortmore, Bawnboy.

N.

"That we deplore the unfortunate dissensions that have arisen in the Irish Party, and we confidently hope that its members may recognise the fact that unity is the essential condition of its permanence and of its realising the hopes of Ireland."

Rev. W. FOLEY, D.D., Delegate, Halifax, Nova Scotia.

O.

(1) "That English rule in Ireland having its origin in conquest, and being upheld by force against the will of the people, is immoral and an outrage on the rights of men, and it is the duty of all honest and patriot Irishmen to strive by every legitimate means for its destruction."

(2) "That we protest against the over-taxation of our country, which has been made manifest by the researches of the Financial Relations Commission; and we call

on the English Government to make restitution for the hundreds of millions sterling of which Ireland has been robbed by England since the Union."

(3) [Passed as Resolution 11.]
(4) [Added to Resolution 10.]
(5) "This Convention recognises that only as people learn mutual toleration, forbearance, and consideration, are they fit for freedom and self-government, and that national and social progress is impossible apart from moral improvement. It earnestly entreats all Irish politicians to sink personal and party jealousies and animosities for the sake of their country, and to set an example of self-control and moderation of speech, realising that the people of Ireland ought to forgive as they need to be forgiven. It utterly repudiates every thought of retaliation for wrongs inflicted in the past. It is opposed to every kind of religious or class ascendancy, and aims at the securing of equality of opportunity for all the people, without distinction of class or creed, and it desires to link the movement for justice to Ireland with the movement for justice, freedom, and fraternity all the world over."

(6) "That for these objects it is essential that the whole country be organised as thoroughly as possible."

DELEGATES, Liberal and National Union of Ulster, Belfast.

P.

"That as the Irish people are fully convinced that without vigorous organisation it is utterly impossible for them to gain their rights or liberty, or even to retain the small concessions granted them of late years; and, whereas, there are at present many parishes in Ireland where no branch of the National Federation exists, and to remedy this great defect, and to give vigour, and vitality, and stability to patriotic sentiment, I, therefore, beg leave to move the following resolution: Resolved—'That, in the opinion of the members of this Convention, every member of the Irish Parliamentary Party should visit (or depute some of his colleagues) every parish within his Parliamentary Division, at least once a year, for the purpose of ascertaining how the National movement is progressing therein; and that he uses, to the utmost, his influence and power, with the view of having established and maintained an active branch of the National Federation in every parish within his Parliamentary Division.'"

CHARLES CLARKE, Lower Badony (County Tyrone) Branch, Irish National Federation.

Mr. Justin M'Carthy on the Convention.

(From the *Daily News*.)

PERHAPS it may be considered by some people that I am not an absolutely impartial or unprejudiced critic when I declare my opinion that the National Convention, which began in Dublin on Tuesday and closed on Thursday, was a complete and splendid success. But I have seen a good many political conventions and political movements in my time, and I think I have acquired observation enough and common sense enough not to confound my own personal wishes with the positive facts and the actual results. The Convention realised all my best desires and dearest hopes as an Irish Nationalist. The Convention was fortunate in its President. The Bishop of Raphoe is a very young-looking man for a prelate, and has a clearly-cut statuesque face, which must have won upon every spectator. The Bishop of Raphoe has a fine voice, and is richly endowed with power of argument and with thrilling eloquence.

Let me say, that throughout the whole of the three days' proceedings there was hardly any display of that kind of Irish oratory which Mr. Davitt once described as "sunburstery." The meeting did not want sunburstery; it wanted reason and argument. It might have been an English meeting, or a Scottish meeting, so far as quiet, practical intelligence, and a desire to get at substantial results, could constitute its principal characteristics.

Was it a representative assembly? Well, I can only say that the vast majority of those who attended it were regularly elected delegates, openly appointed by the various local branches of the Irish National Federations over all parts of the world. There were delegates from the cities of the United States, from Canada, from the Australasian Colonies, from South America, from South Africa, from England, from Scotland, and from Ireland. The great Leinster Hall was literally crowded with delegates. It was a somewhat curious fact that on the same platform sat Mr. John Costigan, long Conservative Minister of the Dominion of Canada, and Mr. Edward Blake, for many years the leader of the Liberal Party in the Dominion Parliament—both alike, devoted to the cause of Home Rule in Ireland. As somebody asked, how could an American, or a Canadian, or an Australasian, fail to be a believer in Home Rule? Is it not certain that one of the most distinguished Irishmen living, Lord Rosmead, lately known as Sir Hercules Robinson, became from an extreme opponent of Home Rule a convert to Home Rule because of his colonial experiences?

The object of the Convention was, as most people know, to bring about, if possible, a re-uniting of ranks among the Irish Nationalists, on the principle that in a political party the majority must rule. I remember well—I am not likely ever to forget—how things went at the time when Mr. Parnell was in the zenith of his power. Before any decision on some important question in Parliament was taken the Irish Party met in one of the Committee Rooms. The whole subject was debated and discussed; everybody was free to express his opinion. Some of Mr. Parnell's lieutenants occasionally differed from the opinion of their leader. In the end a division was taken, and the will of the majority became the rule of the Party. Often and often it happened that the decision was only arrived at just in time to enable the members of the Irish Parliamentary Party to go into the division lobby and give practical expression there to the will of the majority. Of course, it is perfectly obvious that under no other conditions could a small party of men do any substantial and practical service to their cause in the House of Commons. The main object of the Convention then was to bring back that recognition of the right of the majority to dictate, which was recognised so absolutely through the greater part of Mr. Parnell's career.

I have heard people argue that unless you have Mr. Parnell's power you cannot enforce Mr. Parnell's policy. But surely the very fact that we have lost Mr. Parnell is only another reason why we should resolutely set ourselves to maintain his policy. It is pure fantasy to suppose that Mr. Parnell was a mere dictator and despot in his party. I have known him more than once to refuse to express any opinion of his own on some pressing question, simply because, as he put it, he was anxious to get the unbiassed judgment of the majority, and was, therefore, unwilling to influence it by any argument of his own. Anyhow, the main object of the Convention this week was to re-affirm, and, if possible, re-establish the right of the majority to declare the policy of the Irish Parliamentary Party. Of course, an Irish Nationalist Member of Parliament is not compelled to act against the judgment of his own conscience. The pledge he has taken secures him his freedom of action in any extreme case where his conscience will not allow him to act with the majority of his colleagues. In such a case he can resign his seat. There is no eternal necessity for his remaining a Member of Parliament. Let me say, however, that in my opinion the occasions must be rare indeed when such a conflict could arise. We are all pledged to Home Rule—if we were not so pledged our constituencies would never have elected us to the House of Commons. The questions which arise are questions as to whether this course of policy or that is the more likely to advance the cause of Home Rule. It is a question of policy altogether, and not of principle—a question of what we are to do—which way we are to vote—now, this moment, or at all events when the division bell rings, and what solution can the wit of man devise better than, or, indeed, other than, the rule that the judgment of the majority shall decide? Mr. Parnell never believed himself to be an infallible dictator ruling by sheer force of inspired wisdom an obedient band of followers. He would not have been the really great leader that he was if he had any such nonsense in his mind. I have known him again and again to admit that he was mistaken upon this point or that. But we all recognised the fact that he was magnificently endowed with the insinct and the genius of the commander-in-chief, and that where a decision had to be taken at a moment's notice he was the one man whose judgment was best qualified to lead him and us to the right action.

Assume the fact that we have not now a captain with the genius of Mr. Parnell. That is assuredly no reason for breaking up the camp. But if we are to hold the camp, we must keep up the discipline, which alone can keep the camp together. This was really in substance the principle which the decisions of the Convention endeavoured to enforce. We have yet to see how far the effort will be successful. For myself, I anticipate with confidence the best results from the meetings of these three days. The Convention was practically unanimous. In one instance an amendment was proposed which called on the Irish Nationalist members to return to the policy of unconditional obstruction. The amendment did not find one single supporter. The common sense of the Convention saw at once that if the country has elected a Parliamentary party to fight its battle, it would be absurd to attempt to chalk out some particular and unique course of strategy for them. But how is the rule of the majority to be enforced? Of course, the Convention cannot enforce. It can only recommend—it cannot compel. But if any members of the Party should, after the deliberations and the warning of this week, persist in ignoring the authority of the majority, the constituents of such men will have to take action at the next General Election. I sincerely hope that long before that time we may have come to a complete understanding among ourselves. Odd as it may seem to the outer way, there is absolutely no question of principle—none whatever—in dispute between us. It would, to my mind, be a very serious calamity, a national, an imperial calamity indeed, if the present constitutional movement were to be brought to nothing. For I think there can be little doubt that the failure of the constitutional movement would only stimulate and inspire the wish of many men at home and abroad to have a try at other means. Nothing on earth can get out of the hearts and spirits of the Irish race all over the world the desire and the determination to obtain national self-government for Ireland. It would be a misfortune indeed if the Irish Parliamentary movement were to be compelled, even for a week—for a day—to give way to the different and the wilder enterprises. If I were an Englishman, and were only possessed of any reasonable amount of liberal thought and purpose, I should wish with all my heart that the endeavours of the Dublin Convention should set up again the constitutional movement in Ireland, and enable a great, and, ultimately, a certain reform in our system of domestic legislation to be accomplished in peace and with goodwill.

Impressions of the Convention.

(By a "Spectator," in the *Freeman's Journal*.)

THE great Convention of the Irish race has come and gone, and before its characteristic lines be lost it may be well to jot down a few impressions made upon a spectator to whom the proceedings suggested a comparison with similar assemblies in recent times. Such a comparison gives the measure and standard of its importance, and enables a forecast of its effect to be made with something approaching to accuracy. And first, as regards its size. The Convention greatly exceeded in numbers any of the Conventions called by the Irish Party since 1890, and was considerably larger than any Convention assembled since the beginning of the Home Rule agitation. The Convention that founded the National Federation in March, 1891, when the National League had been converted into a sectional and particularist organisation, met in the Antient Concert Rooms, and was easily accommodated there. The same hall, though less conveniently, gave space to the assembly in the autumn of 1892, after the general election, to frame a constitution for the National Federation. Neither of these gatherings at all approached in magnitude the Irish Race Convention. Not half those assembled in the Leinster Hall during the week could have crushed themselves into the rooms in Brunswick Street. In the March of 1893 a third Convention was held to consider, and, as far as approved, rectify the Home Rule Bill just introduced by Mr. Gladstone. The subject, it is not necessary to say, excited intense interest in the country, and the delegates outnumbered those that attended the Convention of the preceding autumn. But the Rotunda gave ample room for the seating of the delegates, and left a good deal of floor space to spare. The Leinster Hall was uncomfortably full on Tuesday, Wednesday, and Thursday, and the delegates present could not possibly have been seated in the Rotunda. Even excluding the delegates who came from abroad, there was a larger representation of Nationalist Ireland present than on any of the other occasions mentioned. If the opposition to the Convention is to be accurately measured by the effects produced on the attendance, then it would seem to have power merely to stimulate the National forces. The home delegation present at the Race Convention was far larger than that which founded the National Federation, far larger than that which framed the constitution of the organisation, and much larger even than that which, in the name of the Irish Nation, accepted substantially the Home Rule Bill of 1893 as a settlement of the Government of Ireland question.

Not alone was the attendance larger, it was more variously representative. The delegation from abroad gave the assembly a character that no other Irish Convention ever possessed. Not since the Irish dispersion began has there been such a representation of the scattered provinces of the Irish world called to the capital of Ireland. But, apart from that impressive and distinctive feature, the composition of the Convention was most significant. There were more chairmen of Irish municipalities and chairmen and vice-chairmen of Irish poor law boards present than ever attended an Irish Convention previously. This extensive participation in the proceedings by the men elected to public positions by the votes of their fellow-citizens is especially encouraging to the Irish Party as indicative of the influences working for the promotion of unity throughout the country.

The Convention was not only larger and more representative than any of recent years, it was also a freer Council of the nation. In none of the Conventions mentioned was there such full and frank discussion of the political position, none was so deliberative, none elicited such a display of the mind of the assembled delegates, and of the various phases of political thought and sentiment to be found in the ranks. The resolutions passed unamended, but there was a candid debate of them all, and a clear indication of the spirit and manner in which the resolutions were to be interpreted ; and the final temper of the assembly was evolved after a process of debate and intercommunication which undoubtedly influenced many of the composing elements. The charge of political "bossism" so often levied against the National leaders in times present and past was never more ludicrously inapplicable than to the conduct of this Convention.

The discussions discovered a wealth of political capacity among the delegates There were speeches from priests and laymen that reached an extremely high level of ability. Good speaking may always be expected in an Irish assembly. But the speeches referred to were not merely good talk, good oratory, they were most striking as specimens of reasoned politics, as expressions of sound statesmanship and political tact. The Bishop of Raphoe was more than justified in his boast that the Convention had proved that when Ireland has a Parliament of her own it will be one worthy of a nation.

There never was a more tolerant assembly. It was intolerant of nothing but disorder. There was a fair hearing readily given to every speaker, no matter whether his opinions were out of harmony with the prevailing conviction or not ; and the warmest appreciation was shown of any concession that made for the cause of unity. The Convention was evidently one that would have welcomed any Nationalist to a place in its councils, provided that he came loyally resolved to assist in securing to the National forces unity of strength and direction.

But combined with this spirit of toleration there was a predominant resolve to have an end of indiscipline and disunion in the Parliamentary representation. The Convention was all of one mind as to the necessity of unity and majority rule, though there was some slight difference as to how best to secure the desired ends. One large section of the Convention was evidently against further truce or negotiation with dissentients; a small section was for peace at any price ; but the spirit of the body of the delegates was expressed in Father O'Hara's speech : amnesty and oblivion if the opponents of unity will; if not, a resolute struggle to end the disastrous indiscipline that has imperilled the Irish Party and the

National movement. That was not only the predominant mandate at the close, it was the unanimous mandate ; for the course of the discussion, frank, free, and open, had moulded the feelings of the delegates into one.

The proceedings were tonic. There was a perceptible rise in the spirit and hardening in the resolve as the Convention wore to a close. It was always in earnest from beginning to end ; but doubt, and something of despondency, gave way to confidence as the discussions progressed. Before the end came it was manifest that the Convention would be fruitful, that promise would be followed by performance, and the profession of the National faith by a revived activity of patriotic effort.

One other remarkable impression was made by the Convention—it was from beginning to end a Home Rule Convention. There were resolutions referring to many pressing Irish questions proposed and passed. But again and again through the discussions the speeches reverted to the topic—how to secure unity in the ranks in order to win Home Rule? And the attitude to all minor questions was expressed in the Most Reverend Chairman's opening speech, when he said that in pursuing minor reforms they should not lose sight of the main question. The Convention was very largely composed of men of the farming class, yet the interest exhibited by them in the resolution on the Land question was quite subordinate to that which they displayed on the National question. There was never a more complete answer to the argument that the Irish question is purely a social question than that furnished by the course of the discussions in this Convention. It was inspired by the National idea ; and in tone, temper, and capacity was worthy of the inspiration.

Address of Delegates from Abroad to the Irish People at Home and Abroad.

BEFORE leaving for our respective homes we deem it our duty to place on record our grateful appreciation of the courtesy and kindness with which we have been received and treated by the home delegates to the Irish Race Convention.

We came absolutely unbiassed in our views towards any party or section of party in the Irish Parliamentary representation, determined to form an independent opinion based on our own observations. We are bound to add that the gentlemen who are responsible for the arrangements of the Convention scrupulously abstained from any attempt whatever to influence our judgments. We have kept separate and independent our own organisation, and have asked no one who was associated with the movement at home to attend our conferences. We are satisfied that the great Convention which we have attended was, in its composition, character, and numbers, representative of the Nationalists of Ireland, and that it voiced the Irish National spirit.

We have watched the proceedings of the Convention from beginning to end, and we have heard the fullest and freest possible discussion of every point brought under its deliberations, and we have seen that its decisions have been unanimously taken.

We have been particularly impressed by the earnest unanimity with which the Convention declared for genuine party unity necessarily involving discipline and respect for majority rule.

We record our own entire belief in party unity based on the only foundation possible—submission to the majority.

We believe in a real unity, and we exhort all who have the welfare of Ireland at heart to support the majority of their representatives, who have acted up to their pledge.

We believe in Party discipline as the means by which unity is maintained; and we declare that the preservation of discipline can be entrusted only to the men who keep the Party pledge.

As delegates from the Irish Race in the United States, the Dominion of Canada, Newfoundland, South Africa, and the Australasian colonies, we earnestly call upon the people of Ireland to stand together for unity in the cause of Home Rule and discipline in the Home Rule Party in Parliament.

As citizens of countries enjoying the blessings of free government we affirm there is no other line of effective action known to us than submission to the rule of the majority in political organisations.

We undertake, on our return to our various homes, to convey to our people our sense of the magnitude, authority, and order of the Convention; and, as delegates, we pledge ourselves to give our loyal and unfailing support to the Parliamentary Party until the blessings of self-government have been won for Ireland.

(Signed),

UNITED STATES.

Martin F. M'Mahon,	Rev. Denis O'Callaghan,
Anthony Kelly,	John Cashman,
P. W. Wren,	Patrick Dunlevy,
William L. Brown,	Rev. George F. Marshall,
Patrick Gallagher,	John B. Devlin,
James Duggan,	Patrick Cox,
Denis O'Reilly,	Patrick Martin,
Edward Treacy	James O'Sullivan,
Patrick Kinney,	Martin Fitzgerald,
John W. Corcoran	Joseph P. Ryan,

P. J. Timmons, M.D.

DOMINION OF CANADA.

Rev. T. Ryan, representing Archbishop of Toronto.
John Costigan, Ottawa.
John Heney, Ottawa.
Very Rev. Dean W. R. Harris, Ontario, Canada.
Rev. William Flannery, D.D., St. Thomas, Ontario.

ADDRESS OF DELEGATES.

Rev. FRANK O'REILLY, Priest, Hamilton, Ontario, Canada.
Rev. P. F. O'DONNELL, Priest, Montreal, Canada.
JOHN M'KEOWN, St. Catherine's, Ontario.
HUGH RYAN, Toronto.
J. J. FOY, Toronto.
Rev. M. A. CLANCY, Priest, Placentia, Newfoundland.
JAMES D. RYAN, St. John's, Newfoundland.
EDWARD HALLEY, Montreal.
WILLIAM FOLEY, D.D., Halifax, Nova Scotia.
Lieut.-Col. M'SHANE, Halifax, Nova Scotia.
GERALD B. TIERNAN, Halifax, Nova Scotia.
P. F. CRONIN, Secretary, Canadian Delegation.
JAMES J O'BRIEN.

AUSTRALIA.

CHARLES HAMILTON BROMBY, Northern Tasmania.
THOMAS HUNT, Victoria.
Mr. KENNEDY, Wellington.

SOUTH AFRICA.

H. G. HASKINS, Johannesburg.
MOSES CORNWALL. J.P., Kimberley, representing Griqualand West.

Dublin, September 4th, 1896.

Speech by Very Rev. Dr. Ryan, of Toronto,

DELIVERED AT A RECEPTION GIVEN TO THE DELEGATES BY THE CITY OF CLONMEL, 22ND SEPTEMBER, 1896.

HE said he felt it difficult to respond to and answer the addresses and the magnificent reception which they had received at the hands of the people of the city of Clonmel and of gallant Tipperary. He knew very well the people had not assembled there to do them the pleasure of personal gratification. They had come there to honour them as the representatives of their kith and kin of the Irish race beyond the seas, to join in the grand struggle that has been going on so long, and which would go on until they had achieved the victory of their just rights—the struggle for the Legislative Independence of Ireland. As this was the last occasion on which probably he would address them in Ireland, he would desire to put before them, in a summarised form, his own views, first, as a representative from without and then as a witness from within, how he and his fellow-delegates considered the Irish movement in its present surroundings, their view of the Irish Parliamentary Party and the present Irish representatives, their view of what had passed at the late Convention, and what were their hopes for Ireland in the future. He might be considered as an outsider, but he felt to-day that for the first time he stood upon his native heath, for his forefathers for generations had been cradled in the lap of the Golden Vale, and had triumphs and trials in the city of Clonmel.

Now, the first point on which he was going to speak was on their attitude in coming to Ireland. What was that attitude? Some people called them foreigners when they came. He did not care, but there were gentlemen who did not like it. He thought they would agree that they were not foreigners in the real sense of the word. They were men of Irish birth or Irish blood, all true Irishmen, sympathising with Ireland heart and soul. He came to Ireland as the representative of an Irish bishop, a Kilkenny man, who was a combination of all that was magnificent in Irishmen. The delegates were asked what right had they to interfere in the domestic affairs of Ireland, and his answer was they did not come to interfere in Irish domestic affairs; they came to Ireland, and they contended they had a right to come to Ireland on several grounds. First, they had the right of friendship; secondly, they had the right of kinship; and thirdly, they had the right of invitation—a sacred right. Next, to put the matter on the lowest ground, they had a business right, for the Irish people asked them to help in the National movement at home, and they had a right as a mere matter of business to come and see whether they should invest in the work or not. They did not come to Ireland to dictate or to coerce or to interfere, but they came merely as friends, and the Archbishop of Toronto expressly emphasised the fact that he as his representative was merely coming as a friend, not to interfere with the magnificent hierarchy of Ireland, so learned, so prudent, so wise, and so patriotic, not to interfere with the splendid, the historic priesthood of Ireland or with the great Irish people, for they knew they were well capable of managing their own affairs; but they came as outside friends to ask permission to tender their advice and give them the honour of continuing their moral and material support to the old struggle of the people at home. That was the position they took up, and he wished it to be perfectly understood. They came to Ireland not to any man or to any party, but they came emphatically to the Irish nation and the Irish people.

They had come to the great people of Ireland, and having come he would tell them what they had found. They had found the Irish Party and the Chairman of that Party, and they had found representatives of the Irish people assembled in a great Convention in the city of Dublin, and having fully considered everything bearing on the call of that Convention and the constitution of it, they had come to the conclusion that that Convention was a representative Convention. They knew the men from abroad. These represented the Irish race abroad, for they knew how these men were selected and elected. They saw at that Convention the great majority of the Irish Parliamentary Party with their Chairman. They saw nearly five hundred priests, and that splendid representative of the Irish hierarchy, the brave Bishop of Raphoe, presiding at it. They saw duly elected representatives from public boards and political organisations in Ireland, and, having taken part in that Convention, they said—"We cannot expect unanimity in Ireland any more than in any other land; we must expect differences of opinion amongst intelligent men; but still we can see that here in this Convention we have Ireland at home really and truly, and honestly represented." After that Convention the representatives from abroad held a caucus, and they came to the conclusion as men of business—many of them men of great experience in the political affairs of Canada, the United States, and Australia—they came to the solemn conclusion to support the resolutions passed at the Convention as the resolutions of an honest and truly representative Convention.

He had heard difficulties raised, and there was one resolution proposed at the Convention with which he certainly sympathised, and that was the resolution proposed by that patriotic priest, Father Flynn of Waterford. Well, he might tell them a secret. The delegates from abroad had already considered a similar resolution, and they had come to the conclusion that though it was a very good thing to wait as proposed on various gentlemen, still that was impracticable. They came to the conclusion that it would be a good thing to wait on Mr. Healy and Mr. Redmond as proposed, but now that the Convention was sitting, and as Mr. Healy and Mr. Redmond did not put in an appearance, it was practically impossible. Why, in God's name, did not these gentlemen come to the Convention? They were free to come; they were invited to come. He called on these gentlemen—he called on Mr. Healy, and he also called on Mr. Redmond—but he did not find them at home; and he had interviews with the ablest and most representative men on all sides. There was, in his opinion, an answer to all that was alleged, and let it go to the public. It was alleged, first, that the difficulty was the incapacity of the chairman and the incapacity of the Party; and then that the Party was led by money.

Well, he knew the chairman of the Irish Parliamentary Party personally, and he had also inquired of persons he could trust, and he would say this, that though the chairman might not be a heaven-born genius, he was a worthy leader of an intelligent and honest Parliamentary Party. The question really was whether the chairman was rightly elected or not, and if he was then obey him. As for the party, it was elected by the people, and why should they not stand by the men that the people elect? It was a party elected by the people of Ireland, and so far as the delegates from abroad were concerned, they were determined to stand by the present Irish Parliamentary Party. There was no other course open to them that was either constitutional or sensible.

Now, as to funds, what he would say he would state on his personal responsibility and personal knowledge. There were two funds. There was the Parliamentary Party Fund and there was a parish fund. It had been said that the Parliamentary Fund was administered for the purpose of personal coercion, and the leader used it for the purpose of gathering men around himself, and that no account was given as to the manner in which they were used. Now, just take this view of the matter. The Irish Party were elected to stand up for the interests of Ireland. In God's name, could not such men be trusted to manage a few paltry thousand dollars a year? They who were outsiders gave the money freely and generously to the Party, for they said to themselves, "These are the men our fellow-countrymen elect, and we feel sure they will deal justly, honourably, and honestly with the money." But what did he find was the fact? The books were there audited, and any committee appointed by any party could go there and see them. Of course, no political party would print such accounts and publish them to the world. He knew the accounts were there, and he was satisfied with them.

Then it was said, the leader having coerced the party, the party coerced the country. Now, in his opinion, the Irish people were an intelligent and a noble, free people, and they would never allow themselves to be coerced by any persons.

Then he was told that, in the case of the Castlebar Convention, the people were coerced by the leader, in order to force a candidate of his own on the constituency. Well, he went down to Castlebar, and he interviewed the priests, and he interviewed the leading electors, and it was proved to his absolute satisfaction that the people were not coerced by the leader, but that if the leader did anything, what he did was to preserve the liberty of the constituency to elect its own representative. Now, of those who criticised the party, he had asked, what was their alternative programme?

Up to the present he had only heard suggestions as to difficulties, and accordingly he asked the critics for their own programme. One person suggested to destroy all the parties. Well, a great American statesman had impressed upon the people the proverb as to the danger of changing horses crossing a stream, but that was all the more true when there was not a second horse to change with. There was a party in Ireland who wanted quiescence, who wanted no representation at all. Oh! God forbid that Ireland should ever adopt this policy. Then it was said that the priests were not with the people. That was not so. The priests of Ireland were always with the people of Ireland. They were with the people still, and with the help of God they would always be with the people. They, from abroad, did not expect political perfection in Ireland.

They did not expect perfect unanimity. There were no men who felt and thought more on the question of the rights of minorities than the Irish in Canada. Minorities had the right to be heard, the right to argue, to influence by argument, and, if possible, to convert a minority to a majority; but minorities had no right to dictate any more than the majorities had. Minorities had not the right to calumniate, as majorities had not. Minorities had not the right to use opprobrious epithets, as majorities had not. And if a majority had not the right to coerce, then certainly a minority had not the right to coerce. They had a bitter experience in Ireland of minority rule.

The people had men to guide them in the wise pronouncement of their able parish priest, a splendid representative of the priesthood of Ireland. He said, if the party proceed with wisdom, prudence, and discretion, and exercise a spirit of conciliation, he was convinced, and on going home he would tell his people, that though things were disturbed at present, still, by the time the General Election came round, they would find all parties in Ireland united—the bishops, the priests, and the people. Thus united they would have the moral and material support of every Irishman the world over, and the Irish race, united at home and abroad, would march on in one solid phalanx until that victory was secured, by which they would have a native Parliament, a free people, and a glorious future for Ireland.

Irish Race Convention 1896.

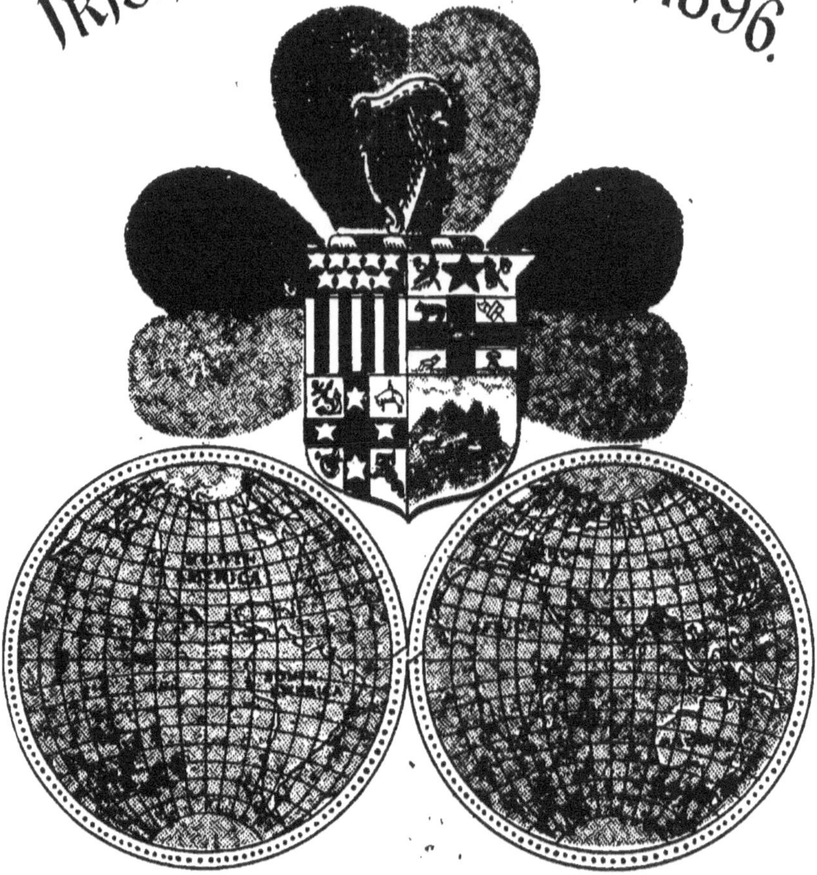

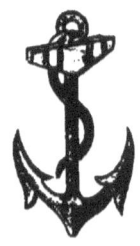

www.ingramcontent.com/pod-product-compliance
Lightning Source LLC
Chambersburg PA
CBHW030434190426
43202CB00036B/131